PASSING THE TORCH

An Apology for Classical Christian Education

LOUIS MARKOS

An imprint of InterVarsity Press
Downers Grove, Illinois

InterVarsity Press
P.O. Box 1400 | Downers Grove, IL 60515-1426
ivpress.com | email@ivpress.com

©2025 by Louis A. Markos

All rights reserved. No part of this book may be reproduced in any form without written permission from InterVarsity Press.

InterVarsity Press® is the publishing division of InterVarsity Christian Fellowship/USA®. For more information, visit intervarsity.org.

Scriptures marked KJV are from the King James Version, public domain.

The publisher cannot verify the accuracy or functionality of website URLs used in this book beyond the date of publication.

Cover design: Faceout Studio, Molly von Borstel
Interior design: Daniel van Loon
Image credits: © Nenov / Moment via Getty Images
　　　　　　© CSA Images via Getty Images

ISBN 978-1-5140-1130-0 (print) | ISBN 978-1-5140-1131-7 (digital)

Printed in the United States of America ∞

Library of Congress Cataloging-in-Publication Data
Names: Markos, Louis, author.
Title: Passing the torch : an apology for classical Christian education / Louis Markos.
Description: Downers Grove, IL : IVP Academic, [2025] | Includes bibliographical references and index. | Summary: "In this highly energetic volume, Louis Markos makes his case that education must recover its power to form persons. Drawing from both Christian and the classics of the literary and intellectual tradition of the West, Markos takes a stand in today's debates around the purpose and means of education. Education, Markos thinks, is ultimately about the formation of whole persons to be responsible citizens in our shared public life. To make this case, he brings together theologians like Augustine, philosophers like Plato and John Dewey, and novelists such as Dorothy Sayers to model the essential value of Christian classical education"– Provided by publisher.
Identifiers: LCCN 2024043435 (print) | LCCN 2024043436 (ebook) | ISBN 9781514011300 (print) | ISBN 9781514011317 (digital)
Subjects: LCSH: Christian education. | Spiritual formation. | Classical education.
Classification: LCC BV1465 .M295 2025 (print) | LCC BV1465 (ebook) | DDC 268–dc23/eng/20241206
LC record available at https://lccn.loc.gov/2024043435
LC ebook record available at https://lccn.loc.gov/2024043436

32　31　30　29　28　27　26　25　|　13　12　11　10　9　8　7　6　5　4　3　2　1

"Dr. Markos' ability to refine complex ideas into coherent and actionable expressions astonishes me. In this treatise, he shows some of the main differences between a Christian classical education and a progressive-pragmatic education. The people he discusses are representative figures for the various views and practices. The issues he addresses lie at the heart of the debate—and the answers we apply to those issues will determine our future. This book provides a valuable contribution to one of the most important deliberations our non-deliberative age needs to discuss."

Andrew Kern, president of the CiRCE Institute and author of *Unless the Lord Builds the House: Shared Foundations for Christian Education*

"This book is a staggering achievement. Written by the foremost contemporary authority on the intersection of classicism and Christianity, this triumph of scholarship encompasses the best that has been thought and said about education and virtue in the entire Western tradition from Aristotle through C. S. Lewis. This book is a complete sourcebook for thinking Christianly about education today."

Leland Ryken, emeritus professor of English at Wheaton College and author of sixty-five books

"Modern education is in crisis, and Louis Markos shows us why. More to the point and more importantly, he shows us how to overcome the crisis facing modern education through the rediscovery of ancient wisdom and the rejection of the bad ideas which have had such bad consequences. The crisis in education is a challenge, and Louis Markos rises to the challenge and shows us how to do the same."

Joseph Pearce, author of *The Quest for Shakespeare*

"In *Passing the Torch*, Louis Markos brings to the issue of classical education what he brings to everything else: scholarly wisdom, a broad knowledge of the subject, and just plain common sense. Classical Christian education has grown into a national movement despite the fact that many of those involved in growing it were not entirely certain of what it was they were trying to rediscover. Fortunately, a new generation of Christian classicists have arisen to tell them, and Markos may be the best of them. He has retrieved from the sands of time the ancient scrolls of learning, blown off the dust of neglect from the scholarly relics, and returned them to the light of our attention. *Passing the Torch* is one of the best articulations yet of the importance of passing on the culture of the Christian West to a new generation."

Martin Cothran, provost at Memoria College in Louisville, Kentucky, and editor of *The Classical Teacher Magazine*

THIS BOOK IS DEDICATED TO

JODEY HINZE, *DEAN OF HUMANITIES,*

EMILY STELZER, *ASSOCIATE DEAN,*

AND MARYBETH BAGGETT, *CHAIR OF ENGLISH,*

for their continued support of me and my work,
and for fighting hard to preserve and provide
a true classical Christian liberal arts education that fosters

WISDOM, VIRTUE, AND ELOQUENCE

CONTENTS

Preface   *ix*

Introduction: The Nature of Man   *1*

Part 1—The Nature of Education

1   Liberal Arts Versus Vocational   *33*

2   Canonical Versus Ideological   *47*

3   Books Versus Textbooks   *67*

4   History Versus Social Studies   *75*

5   Humanities Versus Social Sciences   *90*

6   Goodness, Truth, and Beauty Versus Relativism   *101*

7   Virtues Versus Values   *112*

Part 2—The Nature of the Debate

8   Plato's *Republic*: The Educational Journey of the Philosopher-King   *125*

9   Augustine's *De Doctrina Christiana*: Learning to Think Rightly   *137*

10   Jean-Jacques Rousseau's *Emile*: The Pedagogical Implications of Denying Original Sin   *146*

11   John Dewey's *Democracy and Education*: The Birth of Progressive-Pragmatic Education   *156*

12   C. S. Lewis's *The Abolition of Man*: Building Students' Chests   *168*

13   Dorothy Sayers and Charlotte Mason: How Best to Train the Young *178*

14   Mortimer Adler, E. D. Hirsch, and Neil Postman: How to Educate Americans   *189*

Conclusion: From a Philosophy of Life to a Theory of Education   *205*

Bibliographical Essay   *207*

Appendix | *215*   Scripture Index | *221*

PREFACE

FEW AMERICANS TODAY WILL DISPUTE that our system of education is broken, ineffective, and in crisis. Students progress from grade level to grade level and then graduate high school with little knowledge, fewer skills, and even fewer virtues. They are as unprepared for the academic rigors of college as they are for the practical demands of the workforce or the physical and emotional sacrifices necessary for marriage and the raising of children.

Remedies for this crisis tend to come in one of two forms. Either utilitarian methods of pedagogy and classroom management are instituted that promise to order and regiment schools as if they were factories, or sociopolitical agendas are imposed that promise to unite students under a common progressive cause. Unfortunately, most of those conservative-marketplace methods and liberal-ideological agendas are cut off from the wise and stable traditions of the past, unmoored from the very things that have made and will continue to make us human. While the methods more often than not prevent real engagement with goodness, truth, and beauty, the agendas have the effect, whether intended or not, of setting students in opposition to the tradition rather than encouraging them to preserve that which is good, true, and beautiful in the legacy passed down to them by their forefathers.

What is needed is not more methods and agendas but a refocusing on what education is and what it should do. I could be, technically speaking, the finest surgeon in the world, but if I do not know the proper function of the heart or the brain or the lungs, my attempts at operating on those organs will likely result in great harm to my patient. All things, Aristotle argued, have a telos, a purposeful end, which defines their essence and guides their growth. Both education itself and the children who are educated possess a telos that must be understood and heeded if one generation is to properly pass down its knowledge and its culture to the next.

In chapter one of *The Abolition of Man*, C. S. Lewis, writing during World War II, sums up succinctly the difference between an educational system that knows the proper telos of education and one that does not:

> Where the old [traditional form of education] initiated, the new merely "conditions." The old dealt with its pupils as grown birds deal with young birds when they teach them to fly: the new deals with them more as the poultry-keeper deals with young birds—making them thus or thus for purposes of which the birds know nothing. In a word, the old was a kind of propagation—men transmitting manhood to men: the new is merely propaganda.

All the methods and agendas in the world will not restore education to its proper function until we are willing to ask again what that function is; but we will not be able to determine what that function is until we reclaim a proper understanding of whom that education is for. If we begin from a purely Darwinian view of man as a product of undirected time and chance with no essential nature or transcendent purpose, then we will treat the children in our schools as animals on a farm or cogs in a machine to be herded, manipulated, and reengineered.[1] If we begin from a purely Rousseauian view of man as innately good but corrupted by society, then we will do all we can to protect students from feeling shame while removing from them all moral (and instructional) accountability and inflating their self-esteem in an individually and societally destructive manner.

---

[1] True to the legacy of the classical vision I will be defending in this book, I will be using traditional English grammar throughout: that is to say, I will use *he* and *his* as gender-inclusive pronouns and *man*, *men*, and *mankind* to refer collectively to the human race.

Preface xi

The situation is a grave one, and I propose to address it in a three-step fashion. In my introduction, I will define and celebrate man as a human person endowed with innate dignity and worth but fallen and in need of limits, rules, and discipline. I shall treat him as a rational, emotional, and volitional creature whose choices shape his feelings and determine his habits, and who must have his virtues cultivated, his affections trained, and his desires ordered. I will treat him further as a dramatic, passionate, creative being impelled to bring order, harmony, and beauty out of the chaos around him.

Only after defining our essential human nature in its adult and adolescent phases will I be ready to move on to part one and address directly the subject of education. Given who we are as people, what kind of pedagogical methods will best allow us to pass down the wisdom of our culture to our children? How shall we best train their minds to live as full human beings who should and must wrestle with the eternal questions? What books should they read and activities should they engage in if they are to grow to become virtuous, morally self-regulating citizens?

Rather than create this needed educational vision out of whole cloth, I will look back to a traditional form of pedagogy that flourished during the Middle Ages and Renaissance and that provided the foundation for the university. That traditional form, which has seen a resurgence over the last three decades, goes by the name of classical Christian education. Though many prefer the phrase "Christian classical" because it (seemingly) puts the emphasis on the first word, I would contend that the second word is the more important one. If I were asked to identify my pedagogical orientation, I would respond that I am a *Christian* educator. If I were then asked what *kind* of Christian educator I am, I would respond that I am a *classical* Christian educator.

Having laid out a classical Christian vision for education, I will then develop that vision in part two by putting myself in direct dialogue with such influential educators as Plato, Augustine, Jean-Jacques

Rousseau, John Dewey, Mortimer Adler, and C. S. Lewis. Rather than praise some and demonize others, I will seek to sift out the wheat from the chaff, the perennial from the merely fashionable.

Although Lewis was a Christian apologist who defended the faith boldly and well in such books as *Mere Christianity*, *The Problem of Pain*, and *Miracles*, when he wrote *The Abolition of Man*, he chose to confine himself to the kind of general revelation that is available to all people at all times and in all cultures. Like Lewis, I am a Christian apologist who has written defenses of the faith. In this book, however, I will follow the model of *The Abolition of Man* and draw on the wisdom of a wide range of Christian, non-Christian, and pre-Christian thinkers.

Everything I say below about the nature of man and of education will be, so I trust, compatible with the Scriptures and with the creedal, orthodox theology of the church catholic, but it will also be grounded in the great tradition that began with the Jews in the East and the Greeks and Romans in the West, and united in the writings of Augustine to create the European Middle Ages and the Renaissance and to guide our Founding Fathers in the establishment of our nation. Because of that, I am confident that many readers who do not share my belief in the Trinity, incarnation, atonement, and resurrection will yet agree, as Plato and Aristotle did, that there are such things as objective standards of goodness, truth, and beauty and that those standards have or at least should have a direct bearing on the way we live our lives and educate our children.

Rather than bog down this book with notes and statistics or engage directly with social and political infighting, I will step back and take a broader look at our shared humanity and our collective desire to train up our children in wisdom and virtue. What is needed today is not another scheme dreamed up by reductive-minded social scientists or utilitarian-minded businessmen but a reclaiming and reimagining of who we are as human beings and what our duties are to the generations that came before us and to those that will carry on after us.

INTRODUCTION

THE NATURE OF MAN

BEFORE WE CAN DETERMINE how children should be educated, we must determine who those children are as human beings. Here are ten aspects of our common humanity that have implications for the way we educate the next generation.

WE ARE NOBLE

In act 2, scene 2 of *Hamlet*, the prince of Denmark, freshly returned from his studies at the University of Wittenberg, gives voice to a gloriously high view of man that reverberated throughout the Renaissance: "What a piece of work is a man, how noble in reason, how infinite in faculties, in form and moving how express and admirable; in action how like an angel, in apprehension how like a god: the beauty of the world, the paragon of animals."[1]

It is true that the melancholy prince follows his paean to man's greatness by quipping, "And yet, to me, what is this quintessence of dust," but I will defer his pessimistic coda to focus on what can be learned about the unique status of man in nature by parsing Hamlet's speech phrase by phrase:

---

[1] In order to allow readers to look up my quotes and allusions online or in their own personal libraries, I will identify them throughout by where they appear in the original text: act and scene, book and line number, part and section, etc. When I quote a work written in English, I will not provide a footnote, since such passages can be found easily and for free online or, in the case of twentieth century–writers such as C. S. Lewis and G. K. Chesterton, in numerous editions. I will only provide a footnote to a specific text if the passage has been translated into English from another language or if it is from a recent secondary source.

- "What a piece of work is a man": Man is a work of art, a creation that has been carefully crafted and lovingly fashioned. There is nothing in him that is random or haphazard. He is God's workmanship (see Ephesians 2:10), and anyone who does not see that lacks eyes to see man's inherent design.
- "How noble in reason": Unlike the animals, man has been endowed with reason, and that reason is the chief source of his nobility. There is a part of him that stands outside nature, that can in fact analyze, assess, and even alter it.
- "How infinite in faculties": Though there are individual animals that exceed him in their powers of sight, smell, hearing, taste, and touch, man possesses a wondrous combination of faculties that allows him to explore his world through a multitude of lenses.
- "In form and moving how express and admirable": Though, again, there are beasts that can run and swim, jump and swing with a dexterity that surpasses his abilities, there is a meaning and a beauty in his movements that speak of a greater harmony and proportion.
- "In action how like an angel": Though he shares qualities with the animal kingdom, there is a part of him that reaches upward to the angelic, that soars past the limits of his heavy physical body.
- "In apprehension how like a god": Not just angelic, there is a part of him that is truly divine, a kind of overarching vision that takes in all the world, from the lowest depths to the highest heavens.
- "The beauty of the world": Man is the crown of creation, so much so that all the wonders of nature find their completion in him.
- "The paragon of animals": He is the standard against which all other living creatures are measured.

Despite the ongoing efforts of modern thinkers such as Peter Singer to break down the dividing wall between humans and animals, the fact remains that man's reason lifts him above the narrow confines of the

Introduction 3

natural world.[2] Our reason is at once supernatural and metaphysical. It renders us unique in the animal kingdom, as does our ability to use our reason in coordination with our bodily senses and mental faculties.

We do not merely react to stimuli, as the behaviorist would have it, nor do we confine ourselves, as the empiricist would have it, to the evidence presented to our senses. Like animals, we move up, inductively, from causes to effects; unlike animals, we can also reason downward (deductively) from first principles that are engraved in our psyche rather than observed in the ever-shifting ephemera of nature. There are many animals that perform intricate bodily movements, but they do so for purely practical reasons: to evade predators or attract mates. Only man moves his body in accordance with an external standard that he perceives by his rational and aesthetic judgment and that he calls beauty.

Only man believes propositions because they are true, performs actions because they are good, and creates works of art because they are beautiful. Indeed, only man has the rational capacity to determine that some things are true and others false, some good and others evil, some beautiful and others ugly. In his philosophical, ethical, and aesthetic judgments, he so soars above the animals that he touches on the precincts of the angelic and even of the divine.

Truly, man is a marvel and a paragon; his connections to the natural world only highlight the many ways in which he transcends the clay out of which he was formed. Rightly does David exclaim with joy and wonder at how each individual human being is fearfully and wonderfully knit together in the womb of his mother (Psalm 139:13-14).

Such is man, and as such should he be treated: not merely as a product of unconscious material forces but as a creature endowed with purpose and design; not merely as a slave to natural instincts and primordial desires but as a rational and volitional agent whose choices affect his

---

[2]See Peter Singer, *Animal Liberation Now: The Definitive Classic Renewed* (New York: Harper Perennial, 2023).

own destiny and that of the world; not merely as a means to some political or social or economic end but as an end in himself. There is no doubt that we are strongly shaped and influenced by our surroundings, but there is that within us which transcends those influences.

No pedagogical scheme, no theory of education, no initiative for training up the next generation can hope to succeed if it does not take into account the nobility of man: his reason, his freedom, his giftedness, his high status in nature. I do not mean to suggest there are nefarious American educators out there, whether utilitarian or progressive, who consciously deny man's dignity, freedom, or rationality. I maintain, rather, that when educational institutions, whether public or private, secular or Christian, do not hold that vision at the center of their pedagogical goals, they risk reducing students to an army to be regimented, a workforce to be trained, a faction to be indoctrinated, a commodity to be molded, or a consumer to be conditioned.

Hear again the distinction Lewis makes in chapter one of *The Abolition of Man*:

> Where the old [traditional form of education] initiated, the new merely "conditions." The old dealt with its pupils as grown birds deal with young birds when they teach them to fly: the new deals with them more as the poultry-keeper deals with young birds—making them thus or thus for purposes of which the birds know nothing. In a word, the old was a kind of propagation—men transmitting manhood to men: the new is merely propaganda.

When educators forget or downplay the dignity of each student, they will be tempted to do things *to* them rather than *for* them. Rather than form them in a manner consistent with their unique and essential nobility, they will be tempted to form them in accordance with principles of utility or ideology that are foreign to that nobility.

We Are Depraved

Educational schemes that do not take into account man's nobility can be easily manipulated by corporate agendas or progressive ideologies

Introduction 5

to shape students for ends that violate their inherent worth and value. Pedagogical theories and initiatives, however, can be equally compromised if they deny that man, though noble, is fallen, broken, rebellious, and depraved. There is that within us that strives upward to the angelic, but there is also that within us that sinks downward to the beast—or the devil.

G. K. Chesterton hits the nail squarely on the head when he argues, in chapter two of *Orthodoxy*, that original sin, the belief that we have inherited a sinful nature from fallen, disobedient Adam, is the only doctrine of the Christian faith that can be proven. Just look around you; if you have the requisite courage and honesty, look at yourself. The greatest mystery of man is not that the same human race produced an Adolf Hitler and a Mother Theresa but that every one of us has a little Hitler and a little Mother Theresa wrestling within us.

It is not just that we think and say and do bad things; it is that there is a corruption at the core of our being. Like the apostle Paul, we do not do the good we know we should do, and we do the bad we know we should not (see Romans 7:18-23). We know that we do bad things, that we have violated a universal law that transcends time, place, and culture. We may claim that such a law does not exist, but we prove every day that we know it does, for we expect other people to treat us in accordance with that law.

The ancient Greco-Roman writers lacked a theological understanding of sin because they lacked the biblical revelation of a just and holy God against which to measure human sinfulness. Yet, that is not the whole story. The pagans knew full well that there were certain heinous acts that violated the divine order of the universe. Such taboo crimes brought bloodguilt on both the perpetrator and his community and called out for expiation.

In the *Oedipus* of Sophocles, those crimes are patricide and incest; in his *Antigone*, judgment falls on King Creon for leaving a dead body unburied (his nephew Polyneices) and burying a live one (his niece

Antigone). Taboos abound in the *Oresteia* of Aeschylus: cannibalism, human sacrifice, matricide, and the treacherous murder of a husband by his wife. In the *Bacchae, Medea,* and *Hippolytus* of Euripides, a young man's aunts and mother tear him to pieces, a mother murders her children to punish her unfaithful husband, and a woman unsuccessfully seduces and then bears false witness against a stepson before committing suicide. All of these taboo acts establish a situation that demands retribution and sacrifice.

James Frazer in the nineteenth century (*The Golden Bough*) and René Girard in the twentieth (*Violence and the Sacred*) document the ubiquity of scapegoat figures across human culture and their link to our deep-set notions of personal and communal guilt and impiety. We would not transfer our feelings of pride, lust, and envy to other individuals or groups if we did not recognize them in ourselves.

For the last two centuries, modern man has convinced himself of an evolutionary delusion: that we humans are somehow improving morally and will, at some point in the future, build a utopia. The Bible knows better, but then so did the ancient mythographers. Man, the Bible attests, did not struggle upward from animism to pantheism to polytheism to monotheism to science, but fell away from an original monotheism into myriad forms of idolatry. In Hesiod's *Theogony* (lines 106-201) and Ovid's *Metamorphoses* 1, man's spiritual journey is not one of moral progress but of moral entropy.

Hesiod and Ovid did not have access to the biblical story of Eden, but they did look back to a golden age from which they believed man had fallen into successively less virtuous ages of silver, bronze, and iron. They did not need the prophet Jeremiah to tell them that "the heart is deceitful above all things, and desperately wicked" (Jeremiah 17:9).

At the core of both Judeo-Christian doctrine and Greco-Roman tradition lies the foundational belief that the problem with man is willful sin, disobedience, and rebellion. This understanding of man as a moral agent who chooses to commit vicious acts persisted until

Introduction 7

the eighteenth-century Enlightenment, when Rousseau argued, in *The Social Contract* and *Discourse on Inequality Among Men*, that the problem with man is not sin, disobedience, and rebellion but ignorance, private property, and inequality. The problem for Rousseau lay with society's corrupting influence, not with man's inbuilt propensity for evil and depravity.

Writing in 1908, before World War I and the outbreak of totalitarian regimes from the right and the left dedicated to building utopias through the purging of subversive social elements and the pedagogical reconditioning of the rest, Chesterton prophetically warned that if "we wish to pull down the prosperous oppressor we cannot do it with the new doctrine of human perfectibility; we can do it with the old doctrine of Original Sin" (*Orthodoxy*, chap. 9).

Or, to put it in the words of Chesterton's greatest disciple:

> I am a democrat because I believe in the Fall of Man [that is, original sin]. I think most people are democrats for the opposite reason. A great deal of democratic enthusiasm descends from the ideas of people like Rousseau, who believed in democracy because they thought mankind so wise and good that everyone deserved a share in the government. . . . The real reason for democracy is just the reverse. Mankind is so fallen that no man can be trusted with unchecked power over his fellows.[3]

What has this deep-seated Greco-Roman/Judeo-Christian truth about human nature to do with education? If it is neglected, education can too easily morph into an instrument of social engineering, blinding students from their own depravity while waking them to the ineradicable evil of individuals or groups chosen by those in power to play the role of scapegoat. Rather than appeal to classical or Christian bulwarks against depravity—virtue, wisdom, tradition, duty—educators who deny original sin in their students *and themselves* run the risk of setting up new, utopian values and then using

---

[3]C. S. Lewis, "Equality," in *Present Concerns*, ed. Walter Hooper (San Diego: Harcourt Brace Jovanovich, 1986), 17.

education to indoctrinate students in those values. Rather than put education in service to virtue, wisdom, tradition, and duty, those who deny human depravity are more likely to use education as a tool for conditioning and remaking, not restoring and strengthening, the souls and consciences of the next generation.

We Are Incarnational Beings

Man possesses a deep-set depravity that cannot be removed externally by the elimination of corrupt groups or individuals or internally by state-run education-as-conditioning. He also possesses an innate and essential dignity that must be respected by nations, governments, and schools alike. Still, even if we acknowledge both man's nobility and his depravity, the danger remains that we will falsely link the first to our soul and the second to our body.

The most central and distinctive doctrine of Christianity is the incarnation: the belief that Jesus was not half man and half God, nor a man with a God consciousness, nor a God who appeared to be human, but fully human and fully divine, 100 percent man and 100 percent God. In an analogous way, we who bear the image of God (*imago Dei* in Latin) are not souls trapped in bodies or bodies animated by souls but beings who are fully physical and fully spiritual: in a word, enfleshed souls.

To preserve the purity of the doctrine of the incarnation, the early church fathers had to fend off two equal and opposite heresies: Arianism, which denied Jesus' divinity, and Gnosticism, which denied his humanity. The second was particularly dangerous, for it promoted a worldview that not only rendered impossible the good news of God become man but deconstructed the unique nature of man and reality itself. For the Gnostics, the fall did not follow creation; creation *was* the fall. Matter, they believed, was intrinsically evil, the aborted handiwork of a lesser god.

Just as matter was inherently and irredeemably fallen, so was man's flesh. Salvation necessitated the freeing of the soul from the dark

Introduction   9

prison house of the body. The Gnostics rejected the incarnation, for they believed, in keeping with their low view of matter, that if God had literally taken on flesh, as John 1:14 proclaims, he would have become unclean and sinful. In the same way, they identified man's body as the source of the corruption of his soul.

Though doctrinaire Gnosticism is not particularly strong today, its low view of matter has helped to fuel an error—what I would call a soft heresy—that is ubiquitous across the Western world but especially in America. That error generally goes by the name of dualism; it consists of the—mostly unconscious—belief that our soul is good and our body is bad. Alfred Hitchcock's 1960 film *Psycho* shocked audiences by brutally killing off its star in the first third of the movie. But that was not the only shock it delivered. It was also the first American film to allow audiences to see and hear a flushing toilet.

Most Americans, then and now, get squeamish when two topics are discussed: sex and the bathroom. If you do not believe me, just watch how uncomfortable an American gets when a European, unaware that he is supposed to use the euphemism *bathroom*, asks if he may use the toilet. What do sex and the bathroom have in common? Both force us to face our own physical, bodily nature—that part of us that is most like the beasts.

Though most Americans would not say outright that their body is inherently bad, most are embarrassed by it, finding it somehow distasteful. Their body is something to be overcome by willpower, a somewhat mythical force believed to reside in the soul. When Paul speaks of overcoming the flesh (Romans 7:5, 18, 25; 8:1-10), he means not our skin but the sinful nature that exists in both our fallen body and soul. But that does not prevent Americans (again, mostly unconsciously) from equating Paul's "flesh" with our physical body and then setting out, futilely, to conquer it.

Consider what may be the best celebration of the American heart and ethos ever put on the silver screen: *It's a Wonderful Life*. Frank

Capra was by no means a heretical Christian, and yet in his film he dramatizes a commonly held misconception that directly contradicts the Christian doctrine of the resurrection of the body: namely that when we die, we become angels. Behind this misconception lies a belief that our true self is our soul, and that our body is just a covering that weighs us down now but that we will one day shuffle off. In heaven, we will be purely spiritual (angels); our "bad" body will no longer exercise dominion over our "good" soul.

Such dualistic thinking is not good for education, for it isolates the soul from the body, treating students as primarily mental beings who must beat their bodies into submission. This kind of thinking has proven particularly harmful to boys. As Christina Hoff Summers and Leonard Sax demonstrate in *The War Against Boys: How Misguided Policies Are Harming Our Young Men* (2000, 2015) and *Boys Adrift: The Five Factors Driving the Growing Epidemic of Unmotivated Boys and Underachieving Young Men* (2007, 2016), the public school system has hurt an increasing number of boys by seeking to repress their natural physicality and aggressiveness, even to the point of putting them on drugs that interfere with their developing brains and brand them unfairly as difficult students.[4]

Although the Department of Education's 2000 report *Trends in Educational Equity of Girls and Women* showed clearly that boys, and not girls, were in educational crisis, the results of the study, Summers writes, were initially ignored by most women's groups, journalists, educators, and public officials. Soon, however, the "phenomenon became impossible to ignore. Teachers observed male fecklessness and disengagement before their eyes, day after day in their classrooms. Parents began noticing that young women were sweeping the honors

---

[4]See Christina Hoff Summers, *The War Against Boys: How Misguided Policies Are Harming Our Young Men* (New York: Simon & Schuster, 2015), and Leonard Sax, *Boys Adrift: The Five Factors Driving the Growing Epidemic of Unmotivated Boys and Underachieving Young Men* (New York: Basic Books, 2016).

Introduction 11

and awards at junior high and high school graduations, while young men were being given most of the prescriptions for attention deficit/ hyperactivity disorder. College admissions officers were baffled, concerned, and finally panicked over the dearth of male applicants."[5] We are incarnational beings, not disembodied brains; any true education must take account of our physical/spiritual, amphibian nature. The war on boys that Summers and Sax document represents the bad fruit of a dualistic mindset that mistrusts the body and sees it as a hindrance to intellectual and spiritual growth.

How much better to envision a form of education that treats the bodies and souls of both boys and girls as integrally united: that treats them as whole people, not as immaterial persons contained in bodies that may or may not express their personhood. Such an education would not blind itself to the different temperaments and biological-hormonal makeups of its male and female students, nor would it excise gym class or recess time for utilitarian reasons. But it would do more than that. It would seek to teach wisdom, instill virtue, and promote growth in a way that joins word (logos) and action (praxis), belief and behavior, reason and volition. In such a school, life lessons would arise naturally out of discussions of literature, history, and philosophy.

WE ARE DUAL BEINGS

It is now time to consider Hamlet's full speech on the nature of man: "What a piece of work is a man, how noble in reason, how infinite in faculties, in form and moving how express and admirable; in action how like an angel, in apprehension how like a god: the beauty of the world, the paragon of animals. And yet, to me, what is this quintessence of dust."

Here, in this celebration that suddenly turns back against itself, we catch a glimpse of the strange creatures we are. Our dreams and accomplishments are rich with meaning and glory, yet our lives are brief

---

[5]Summers, *War Against Boys*, 18.

and futile and leave no trace behind. We are at once the jewel in the crown of creation and a destructive mole on nature. Our reason makes us the noblest of all the beasts while enabling us to be, as Mark Twain once lamented, the only animal that is cruel.

Pascal expressed it best in number 434 of his *Pensées* (*Thoughts*): "What a chimera then is man! What a novelty! What a monster, what a chaos, what a contradiction, what a prodigy! Judge of all things, imbecile worm of the earth; depositary of truth, a sink of uncertainty and error; the pride and refuse of the universe!"[6] Only if we understand and accept this paradox, only if we come to realize that we are a chaotic contradiction, a monstrous prodigy, will we be able to embrace the fullness of reality.

Although it is a dualistic heresy to identify our soul with goodness and our body with evil, it is nevertheless true that we possess a hybrid nature that partakes of the angelic as well as the beastly. It is further true that our soul bears a stronger similarity to the angels, as our body does to the beasts. We know deep down that we should be able to soar above this world of sin and depravity, but we also know that we cannot and that our physicality is part of what anchors us down. We are frustrated by our inability to align our body and soul toward a single good purpose, all the while feeling that we should be able to do so. How can this be?

Although the presence of injustice in the world is often used as an argument against God, it actually provides one of the strongest arguments *for* God's existence. If there were no God, there would be no absolute, transcendent standard for what is just and what is not. If that standard did not exist, we would not know the world was unjust because we would have no touchstone against which to measure it. In a world of pure natural selection, where the strong as a matter of course devour the weak, there can be no such thing as justice and therefore no such thing as injustice.

---

[6]Blaise Pascal, *Thoughts*, trans. William Finlayson Trotter, in *The European Philosophers from Descartes to Nietzsche*, ed. Monroe C. Beardsley (New York: Modern Library, 1960), 131.

Introduction 13

The ineradicable sense we have of our perpetually warring duality—of our simultaneous capacity for good and evil, altruistic desires and primal urges, self-sacrificing heroism and self-serving villainy—can be explained only if we have a communal memory of a time of innocence against which we can compare our corruption. Had we no memory of our former innocence, we would have no sense of our present corruption. We would be like the animals who kill and are killed in an endless cycle, untroubled by remorse or a stinging sense that the world should not be as it is. The melancholy truth expressed by Francesca in *Inferno* 5 is ultimately true for all of us who remember just enough of our prelapsarian state to feel its loss: "The double grief of a lost bliss / is to recall its happy hour in pain."[7]

In the same meditation from which I quoted above, Pascal argues that, although the mystery of original sin seems to us offensive and unjust, "Without this mystery, the most incomprehensible of all, we are incomprehensible to ourselves. The knot of our condition takes its twists and turns in this abyss, so that man is more inconceivable without this mystery than this mystery is inconceivable to man."[8] Nothing about our paradoxical, split-personality nature makes sense in the absence of a primal disobedience that tore us away from an original innocence and bliss that we cannot recover yet cannot shake off. Apart from that, we cannot account for the wrestling within us, the sense of our own duality as simultaneously creatures of the dark with a memory of our brief sojourn in the light, and creatures of the light who cannot untangle ourselves from the deeply woven darkness within.

If we ignore that duality, or, worse, try to explain it away as a psychological or sociological phenomenon, we will never truly face ourselves but will project our own sinful nature onto other people or parties or systems or ideologies. If we dwell on it overmuch, as Hamlet

---

[7]Dante Alighieri, *The Divine Comedy*, trans. John Ciardi (New York: New American Library, 2003), 50.
[8]Pascal, *Thoughts*, 132.

does, we will drive ourselves mad and lose the ability to act in a proper and healthy manner. If we take the middle course of acknowledging it but not brooding over it, we can make a move toward reconciling within ourselves the dark and the light, the beast and the angel.

Just so, educators who recognize the duality within their students and themselves will be better able to guide them along the path of wisdom and virtue. Rather than reduce knowledge to a bundle of facts or morality to a list of dos and don'ts, they will seek to align their students with the truth about our human nature. Education does not have the power to rip out the beast, nor should it. But it can and should appeal to (and draw out) what Abraham Lincoln, in his First Inaugural Address, called "the better angels of our nature."

WE ARE MORAL AGENTS

But what if we *could* remove the beast from ourselves? What if we could discover some kind of secret knowledge that would lift us out of our enslavement to the body, to the physical world, to ignorance, to mortality? Would it be wise and virtuous to do so? It would not. According to Genesis 3, our original parents sacrificed their innocence, immortality, and direct fellowship with God to taste of the forbidden fruit of the knowledge of good and of evil. Even those who do not believe in Adam and Eve must recognize the great truth here. I say they must, for the human race keeps telling the same tale of what happens to those who pluck such fruit.

Consider Prometheus, who steals the fire of creativity from the gods and is tormented for a thousand years; Faust, who makes a pact with the devil to gain alchemical knowledge and comes quickly to regret the bargain; Dorian Gray, who sells his soul to the devil so that his portrait will bear the marks of his age and his infamy and equally comes to lament the exchange; Dr. Jekyll, who invents a potion that will free him from his dark side, only to be overcome by the darkness within; Dr. Frankenstein, who brings down destruction on himself

Introduction 15

and his family because of his mad desire to possess the secret of life; Dracula and the mummy, whose lust for immorality dooms them to wander the night as living corpses; and Gollum, who thinks that the Ring will open his eyes to hidden mysteries but is enslaved and consumed by it instead.

In addition to these characters who specifically pluck forbidden fruit, there are many others who commit a similar taboo crime: Cain, guilty of fratricide; Oedipus, guilty of patricide and incest; Orestes, guilty of matricide; Macbeth, guilty of murdering a guest; Heathcliff, guilty of loving and destroying his stepsister; Ahab, guilty of impiety and blasphemy in his search for the whale; Captain Nemo, guilty of killing innocent sailors in the name of peace; Don Juan, guilty of defying God's laws in his adulteries; Richard Wagner's Siegmund and Sieglinde, guilty of incestuous love; and Samuel Taylor Coleridge's ancient mariner, guilty of killing the innocent albatross that saved his ship from the ice.

Romantic poet Lord Byron created so many of these characters that they are often referred to collectively as Byronic heroes. Manfred, Byron's greatest creation, is a Faust-like antihero guilty of incest with his sister, defiance of God, and a desire to possess the power and wisdom of the spirit realm. In the opening scene of the play that is named for him, Manfred sums up in three weary lines of poetry how the quest for that which is forbidden leaves one empty and alone: "Sorrow is knowledge: they who know the most / Must mourn the deepest o'er the fatal truth, / The Tree of Knowledge is not that of Life."

At the core of all Byronic heroes lies their failure to accept their dual nature. They try to surpass the limits of their flesh and/or their base, sinful nature only to find that in doing so they have cut themselves off from their fellow man and from their own humanity. In the process, they learn one simple truth about the sons and daughters of Adam and Eve: we are volitional beings, moral agents whose choices have short-term and long-term consequences. Free will, as we use it today, is too flimsy a phrase to capture how deeply we are shaped by our decisions and actions, how they determine the lives we lead and the people we become.

Body affects soul as soul affects body, a result of our incarnational nature as enfleshed souls and our duality as noble-but-fallen creatures whose twin capacities for goodness and wickedness are so closely woven together that they cannot be separated. Educational institutions that do not take seriously our moral nature and the consequences that follow on our choices will produce educators who think their role is to set their students free to think for themselves rather than to think prudentially. Neither teachers nor their students can rebel without ramifications or act without accountability. We live in a natural *and* moral world of cause and effect, where the consequences of our choices are as hard and real and concrete as the laws of gravity or of entropy.

The role of education is not to produce Byronic heroes who are unafraid to breach any and all social, sexual, and scientific mores but to instill in students a sense of their proper limits and of how the choices they make in school will determine the course of their lives.

We Are Habitual Beings

As moral agents, we are responsible for our choices. That is a great and vital truth, but it is not the whole truth. To say only that we are responsible for our choices is to cast our moral nature in negative terms. We are not only creatures meant to flee vice; we are meant as well to pursue virtue. Depraved and fallen we may be, but we continue to possess both the desire and the capacity for virtue. But what is virtue, and how does one become a virtuous person?

In *Nicomachean Ethics*, Aristotle famously argues that virtue does not come to us naturally but "comes about as a result of habit" (book 2, chap. 1).[9] A brave man is not someone who feels brave. He *becomes* brave by *acting* on the feeling; he acquires the *virtue* of bravery by

---

[9]All quotations from Aristotle's *Nicomachean Ethics* in this chapter follow Aristotle, *The Nicomachean Ethics*, trans. David Ross (New York: Oxford University Press, 1980), 28-32.

Introduction 17

doing so repeatedly. It is "by doing the acts that we do in the presence of danger, and being habituated to feel fear or confidence, [that] we become brave or cowardly." Effective "legislators make the citizens good by forming habits in them," for they understand how the human machine works. It is not our feelings but our habitual actions that form us into virtuous people.

The same is true of effective educators. In harmony with his great teacher, with whom he did not always agree, Aristotle argues, "We ought to have been brought up in a particular way from our very youth, as Plato says, so as both to delight in and to be pained by the things that we ought; for this is the right education" (chap. 3). It is the role of parents, teachers, and culture alike to build up in the young proper reactions to that which is virtuous and that which is vicious. Only once those reactions have become so ingrained in the student that they become habitual can the student be said to be virtuous.

One of the best signs that a student has been properly trained in virtue is that when he deviates from the path of virtue, he feels guilty. By proper use of this internal feeling of guilt, traditional teachers have strengthened the habit of virtue within their students. Sadly, this central element of proper teaching has been replaced by a belief that students, and people in general, can only become heathy, balanced, and integrated if they overcome their feelings of guilt. Whether that guilt comes from our parents, the clergy, God, the state, society, or our own superego, it prevents us from liberating our true selves and becoming fully self-actualized.

This demonizing of guilt, which has convinced psychologists and psychiatrists across the Western world that they must affirm their patients even and especially when they have violated a traditional moral, ethical, or religious code, may just be the most destructive lie to come out of our therapeutic culture. Guilt is not the problem. It is the signal that there is a problem.[10]

---

[10]In *Character and Culture* (New York: Collier, 1963), Sigmund Freud argues that people commit crimes and feel guilty because the crimes they commit are forbidden (Augustine confesses as

Although no one enjoys experiencing physical pain, pain is a blessing that prevents us, quite literally, from falling apart. Pain is our body's way of signaling to us that something is wrong with it that needs attention. If the pain is intense, it means that our body needs immediate attention. Only a fool would ignore intense pain coming from his head or chest or belly; only an incompetent doctor would wave off the pain without investigating for injury. If the doctor were unethical to boot and a lackey of the pharmaceutical companies, he might prescribe an expensive, self-perpetuating round of painkillers that would mask rather than cure the deeper medical problem.

Now, given that we are broken people living in a broken world, our body's pain alarm is not flawless. If we contract a terrible disease or bodily injury that causes a malfunction in our nervous system, we will experience successive waves of unhealthy, unnatural pain for which our doctor will prescribe pain medication. In this case, the prescription is correct, for the pain *is* the problem and not merely a signal.

The same goes for guilt. Because of the evil in our world, people will often suffer traumatic experiences that leave them with some form of posttraumatic stress disorder. In such cases, the patient will often suffer from unnatural and unhealthy feelings of guilt that will need to be treated with drugs, counseling, or both. But in the natural course of things, we feel guilt not because wrong has been done to us

---

much in *Confessions* 2.4 about his base motive for stealing pears). But Freud does not stop there. He goes on to argue that the cause/effect of crime/guilt is not what it appears. "Paradoxical as it may sound, I must maintain that the sense of guilt was present prior to the transgression, that it did not arise from this, but contrariwise—the transgression from the sense of guilt. These persons we might justifiably describe as criminals from a sense of guilt" (179-80). Freud then identifies the Oedipal complex as the ultimate origin of our (false sense of) guilt. He elaborates on this connection in chapter 21 of his *A General Introduction to Psychoanalysis*, trans. Joan Riviere (New York: Clarion, 1969). For two books that expose the dangers of a therapeutic view of man that frees us from guilt, see Carl Trueman's *The Rise and Triumph of the Modern Self* (Wheaton, IL: Crossway, 2020) and Paul. C. Vitz's *Psychology as Religion: The Cult of Self-Worship*, 2nd ed. (Grand Rapids, MI: Eerdmans, 1994). The second book directly addresses the dangers in education of the self-esteem movement. See also footnote 11, below. Modern educators and therapists sometimes distinguish between guilt and shame, but the dynamic of seeing guilt (or shame) as the problem rather than the signal that there is a problem remains.

Introduction 19

but because we have thought, said, or done something wrong: an act that causes injury to our soul the same way that a disease causes injury to our body. In such cases, and they represent the majority of cases, the therapist who attacks the guilt and ignores the sin that set it off is as incompetent or criminal as the doctor who treats the pain and ignores the actual condition that prompted it.

Just as the field of psychology has been deeply compromised by the war on guilt, so the field of education has been equally compromised by the self-esteem movement.[11] To prevent students from feeling guilt or shame when they have done something immoral or unethical is to breed monsters whose internal sense of right and wrong, virtue and vice has been dulled to the point of nonfunction.

When teachers and therapists seek to free those in their care from experiencing the proper shame and remorse that should accompany vicious behavior, they risk nurturing a generation of people with seared consciences. It is then that the beast that lurks within each of us will break free from his cage and wreak destruction on our mentors, our society, and ourselves.

WE ARE SUBCREATORS

Thus far, I have focused on man's moral (the good) and rational (the true) nature. It is time now to turn to his aesthetic (the beautiful) nature and consider his supernatural, metaphysical capacity for imagination and creativity. Man is the animal who dreams and who converts his dreams into works of beauty and wonder.

"Fantasy," J. R. R. Tolkien, author of The Lord of the Rings, once argued, "is a natural human activity. . . . We make in our measure and in our derivative mode, because we are made: and not only made, but made in the image and likeness of a Maker."[12] In sharp contrast to secular

---

[11]See Kenzo E. Bergeron, *Challenging the Cult of Self-Esteem in Education: Education, Psychology, and the Subaltern Self* (London: Routledge, 2015).

[12]J. R. R. Tolkien, *On Fairy-Stories*, in *Tree and Leaf* (Boston: Houghton Mifflin, 1965), 54-55.

and Christian critics who dismiss fantasy as frivolous or unnatural or even wicked, Tolkien believed that fantasy and imagination were part of the very fabric of what it meant to be human. We cannot help but tell stories and make up new worlds, for we were made in the image of a Maker, a God who creates and forms and takes joy in what he makes.

In order to capture that essential aspect of our nature, Tolkien coined the word "Sub-creator" and then wove it into a poem he wrote to defend our myth-making proclivities. Tolkien ends the poem by asserting that our right of sub-creation "has not decayed / We make still by the law in which we're made."[13]

As subcreators, we follow in the footsteps of the Creator, making on a smaller scale, and with the potential for misuse, but in the same mode and in accordance with our original commissioning. Though disgraced and dethroned, we continue to bear the image of the Creator and draw on him as the ultimate source of our creativity.

It is our joy and our right to create, to fashion worlds like our own but populated by creatures that exist only in our imaginations. We dare to build these things, for we remain confident that our creativity allows us to participate, if on a lower (sub) level, in the greater, divine creativity that rolled out the heavens like a scroll and set suns and moons, planets and stars in their celestial orbits.

If Tolkien is right, and I believe he is, then our impulse both to tell old tales and to fashion new ones is tied to our essential, fundamental nature. We yearn to be weavers of stories, even as we know in our bones that we are part of the grander weave of an overarching story that is greater than ourselves. Some might argue that our belief that we are part of a story comes from the fact that we as a human race love to invent stories. But I would respond that the truth of the matter is exactly the opposite; we invent stories because we are conscious of being a part of a story ourselves.

---

[13]Tolkien, *On Fairy-Stories*, 54.

Introduction   21

Although God's command to Adam and Eve to be fruitful and multiply and subdue the earth (Genesis 1:28) is specifically directed toward the bearing of children, we as a species have been just as prolific in our production of stories: myths and legends, folklore and fairy tales, epics and novels, poems and plays, songs and films. We are subcreators, characters in a story who create stories populated with characters like ourselves. Tolkien is right: we make because we were made in the image of a Maker.

Across time and place, the most effective way to teach children to pursue virtue and forsake vice has been to tell them stories where characters like themselves face dangers and respond to them in the right (or wrong) way. What would Jesus do? Yes, but also what would Achilles do? Or Odysseus? Or Aeneas? Or Antigone? Or Hamlet? Or Elizabeth Bennet? Or Huck Finn? Or Peter Rabbit? Or Winnie the Pooh? Or Frodo and Sam?

We are, if I may alter a line from Shakespeare, such stuff as tales are made on. We cannot help but create and pass down and live through stories; we narrate even as we seek to discern the narrative in and through which we live and move and have our being. We define ourselves against archetypes, which in turn shape and define our interactions with others, with the world, and with ourselves. Educators who do not take that essential human truth into consideration will miss the pedagogical power of storytelling to pierce to the heart and soul of students of all ages.

We Are Builders

Because I spent the last section waxing poetic about man's creative gifts and his compulsion to craft stories and to participate in them, I hope you will not think that I consider the species of which I am a member to be made up of feverish and frivolous dreamers. Man is also a builder. He can be and often is quite lazy, but he is driven nevertheless to raise monuments and to leave behind a legacy for future generations.

Across the globe, civilizations as diverse as the Greeks and Romans, British and French, Egyptians and Babylonians, Persians and Phoenicians, Chinese and Indians, and Mayans and Incas have erected structures that celebrate our genius for building. The Seven Wonders of the Ancient World offer a glimpse of the ingenuity of the cultures that dominated the Mediterranean, though, sadly, only the first remains: the Great Pyramid of Giza, the statue of Zeus at Olympia, the Colossus of Rhodes, the Lighthouse of Alexandria, the Mausoleum at Halicarnassus, the Hanging Gardens of Babylon, and the Temple of Artemis at Ephesus.

Let me consider briefly just a few of the accomplishments that have defined the Western world. Through a perfect fusion of natural elements and manmade ingenuity, the Romans created the most flexible and magical of materials, concrete, and then used it to erect structures that were at once functional and beautiful. Nothing is more elegant and graceful than the aqueducts that the Romans built to draw life-giving water to their city, and yet nothing is more practical and utilitarian. And the same goes for their forums and amphitheaters, baths and basilicas, bridges and roads.

Not to be outdone by antiquity, the medievals constructed massive Gothic cathedrals whose sacred, otherworldly splendor continues to pay silent tribute not only to man's nobility but to his humility before the power and holiness of God. As many of the cathedrals took a generation or more to complete, most of those who began the project did not live to see its completion. Inspired both by their medieval forebears and by the glory of the ancient Greco-Roman world, the sculptors, architects, and engineers of the Renaissance transformed Rome, Venice, Florence, and a dozen other cities in Italy and across Europe into testaments to man's desire to reach after goodness, truth, and beauty.

The quest to build, to invent and then realize permanent structures on a grand scale, continued unabated through the Enlightenment, Romantic, and Victorian periods, culminating with the gravity-defying skyscrapers of the twentieth and twenty-first century that yearn

Introduction 23

heavenward not only in the West but in cities around the world. Although the first human skyscraper, the Tower of Babel, was a product of pride, rebellion, and disobedience, and though vanity, ambition, and greed have all played a role in man's desire to build monuments, I do not believe that such base and sinful motives offer an adequate explanation for the desire itself. After all, for every monument built to honor a single individual or family, there are many more built to honor cities, peoples, nations, ideals, and God. Preserving our name and passing down our DNA to our children is not sufficient for most people. We harbor a deeper need and desire to foster order, balance, and symmetry, to fashion something that will endure.

Just as it is or should be the role of education to pass down the literature of our greatest subcreators, so must it keep alive the accomplishments of our greatest builders. Without hiding the fact that the pyramids were built by slaves, that the Colosseum featured gladiatorial fights to the death, that the Tower of London held political prisoners, and that man's ingenuity has supported warfare as much as it has worship, educators should encourage their students to see in our desire to build a deep-seated drive to impose form on matter, order on chaos. The educational enterprise, after all, includes the forming and ordering of the undisciplined minds, unruly hearts, and disordered souls of students. When educators abdicate that charge, they do more than leave their society prey to undisciplined, unruly, disordered citizens; they fail to pay tribute to one of the very things that makes us human.

WE ARE GROWN CHILDREN

While there is an integral part of humanity that looks forward to the brave new world that our ingenuity and passion for order would build, there is an equally integral part that looks backward to the emotional and psychological forces that shape us into creatures endowed with meaning and individual purpose. One of the chief explorers and celebrators of that backward glance was British Romantic poet William

Wordsworth. In his autobiographical poetry, Wordsworth took a deep dive into the fragile, mysterious world of the developing human psyche, focusing in particular on how the psyche is formed through its interactions with nature.

Here are the nine deceptively simple lines that comprise "My Heart Leaps Up," Wordsworth's brief sketch of human growth in nature:

> My heart leaps up when I behold
> A rainbow in the sky:
> So was it when my life began;
> So is it now I am a man;
> So be it when I shall grow old,
> Or let me die!
> The Child is father of the Man;
> And I could wish my days to be
> Bound each to each by natural piety.[14]

"So was it," "So is it," "So be it." These three linked phrases do not so much define past, present, and future in the sequential sense as they do the three stages of growth that unite boy to adult and adult to old man. That unity rests on the shared perception of boy, adult, and old man of the beauty of the rainbow and the effect that beauty has on their heart: that is, the core of their being.

The poet speaks as an adult, poised between memories of his childhood reactions to nature and anticipations that those reactions will continue into his twilight years. He describes the leaping of his heart as taking place in the present tense, a present he hopes will define all of his life from beginning to end. Though he does not fear growing older, he does fear that he might lose his spontaneous, childlike response to the beauty of the rainbow. Were he to do so, he would no longer be himself and would welcome death as an alternative to the loss of his true and authentic self.

---

[14]Russell Noyes, ed., *English Romantic Poetry and Prose* (New York: Oxford University Press, 1956), 309.

Introduction 25

Without denying the biological-genetic fact that man is father of child, Wordsworth upholds the child and his experiences as the base and foundation on which the perceptions of the man are constructed. Childhood is not just a stage of life that one must survive but a richly creative time when the matrix out of which the man will emerge is being formed.

Although it is not exactly true to say that the Romantics invented childhood, it is true that they put a heavier emphasis on it and came to appreciate it as the crucible out of which adult consciousness is born. It is not just that the child is a sponge, absorbing all the information he comes in contact with. It is that the delicate, finely spun web of the child's interactions with nature forms a cocoon that nourishes the child while it forms the embryonic adult.

That cocoon Wordsworth calls "natural piety." By this somewhat ambiguous phrase, the poet means the sense of awe and wonder that nature provoked in him when he was a child, still provokes in him now, and hopefully will continue to provoke in him when he is old. Without denying the role that tradition plays in instilling piety in the young, Wordsworth ascribes to nature, and our interactions with nature, an educative power that nurtures and refines the psyche.

Indeed, there *is* a kind of training and equipping that can only be done when we are young and supple, open to forces external to our psyche—but those forces must be allowed to be forceful. If we coddle and overprotect our children, we will prevent them from the necessary shaping that occurs in the face of the infinite and the sublime. We must not shield them from guilt and shame; neither must we shield them from those things in nature that are uncanny and menacing. The same goes for those aspects of fairy tales that inspire terror and dread. They need to be protected, of course, from real dangers, but not from their capacity to experience fear of the numinous and the unknown.

For Wordsworth, adulthood is a product of the experiences— physical, spiritual, emotional, perceptual—that we have as children. Educators must not ignore those experiences and focus *solely* on

26 *Introduction*

reading, writing, and arithmetic. That is why, though I will be defending classical Christian education in this book, I will embrace as well romantic methods of pedagogy that emphasize experience and the cultivation of imagination, wonder, and awe.

WE ARE POLITICAL ANIMALS

In *Politics*, Aristotle argues, "It is evident that the state is a creation of nature, and that man is by nature a political animal. And he who by nature and not by mere accident is without a state, is either a bad man or above humanity."[15] To call man a political animal is to say that it is natural for him to join a city (*polis* in Greek). The Latin equivalent of *polis* is *civitas*, from which we get such words and concepts as *civic*, *civility*, *citizen*, *citizenship*, and *civilization*.

The one who does not need and is not naturally attracted to a *polis/civitas* is, for Aristotle, either less than or more than a man. Beasts do not need such societies; neither do gods. "A social instinct," Aristotle goes on to explain in the same chapter, "is implanted in all men by nature, and yet he who first founded the state was the greatest of benefactors. For man, when perfected, is the best of animals, but, when separated from law and justice, he is the worst of all."[16] We are not made to live on our own. There is no such thing as a noble savage, for a savage in the wild, cut off from the laws and justice of the polis, will quickly resort to savagery.

Anglo-Irish statesman and member of Parliament Edmund Burke had many reservations about the French Revolution. He was most troubled, however, by the revolution's seeming contempt for the traditions and rituals Burke believed made us human and bound us together as political creatures made in the image of God but fallen. "This sort of people are so taken up with their theories about the rights of man, that they have totally forgot his nature. Without opening one

---

[15]Aristotle, *Politics*, trans. Benjamin Jowett (New York: Modern Library, 1943), 54 (book 1, chap. 2).
[16]Aristotle, *Politics*, 55.

Introduction 27

new avenue to the understanding, they have succeeded in stopping up those that lead to the heart. They have perverted in themselves, and in those that attend to them, all the well-placed sympathies of the human breast."[17]

Man the political animal is not an abstract idealogue but a living, breathing human being with a rational, emotional, and spiritual life that refuses to be reduced to impersonal theories that know nothing of his individual loves and desires and fears. Burke believed that the reason the British Glorious Revolution of 1688 succeeded in a way that the French Revolution of 1789 did not is that the British maintained a traditional view of man-as-political-animal while the French revolutionaries tried to remake man altogether. It is because they stayed true to the traditional view, Burke argues, that the British "have real hearts of flesh and blood beating in our bosoms. We fear God; we look up with awe to kings, with affection to Parliaments, with duty to magistrates, with reverence to priests, and with respect to nobility."[18]

In chapter eight of *A Preface to "Paradise Lost,"* C. S. Lewis, in the tradition of Burke, warns against the modern erosion of the rectitude ("straightness") of our responses to such things as pride and treachery, death and pain, love and children, nature and virtue: "That elementary rectitude of human response, at which we are so ready to fling the unkind epithets of 'stock,' 'crude,' 'bourgeois,' and 'conventional,' so far from being 'given' is a delicate balance of trained habits, laboriously acquired and easily lost, on the maintenance of which depend both our virtues and our pleasures and even, perhaps, the survival of our species."

There is nothing phony or hypocritical, superstitious or ignorant about stock responses. They are what make our communal existence as political animals possible. They are the prudently ingrained habits and

---

[17]Edmund Burke, *Reflections on the Revolution in France*, ed. Thomas H. D. Mahoney (New York: Macmillan, 1986), 74.
[18]Burke, *Reflections on the Revolution*, 98.

judiciously refined emotions that should and must drive our actions and feelings. They protect us from what is harmful to our individual and communal body and poisonous to our personal and national soul.

When Burke speaks of the fear, awe, affection, duty, reverence, and respect we owe to God, kings, parliament, magistrates, priests, and nobility, he speaks precisely of the stock responses that should and must guide our hearts and minds. When they are absent or have been artificially reprogrammed, society loses its center, and all things spin out of control. We may be by nature political animals, but if we are to continue to be so, we must first enlighten ourselves in all that is good, true, and beautiful, and then pass that torch to our children.

The role of education is not to teach children to ridicule and feel superior to Burke's sympathies and Lewis's stock responses but to instill those sympathies and responses in those who will preserve civilization and civilized behavior.

❍━❍━❍━❍

If I were in possession of a Stradivarius but did not know its function, I might very well use it to pound a nail into my floorboard. As a result, I would mar irreparably one of the finest instruments for making music ever created. In the same way, educators who do not know who and what their students are and how and for what they were made will run the risk of misusing and marring their true potential. With apologies to John Locke, our children are not blank slates. They, like ourselves, are noble-but-fallen creatures endowed with reason, driven by purpose, and hungry for meaning. They must not be herded or manipulated to serve a purpose foreign to their essential ontological being. Rather, they must be nurtured in a proper education, equipped with the proper virtues, challenged by the proper reading, and entrusted with the proper legacy.

A shorthand way for expressing all four of those "propers," one I will use often in this book, is to say that our children must be educated in the good, the true, and the beautiful. These three, which find their

Introduction   29

source in Plato but which were equally central to medieval Catholicism and Renaissance humanism, are referred to as the three transcendentals. I will speak of the transcendentals at length in chapter six; for now, I will simply say that goodness, truth, and beauty should, by rights, be spelled with capital letters. The Good, the True, and the Beautiful are the Platonic Forms of the compromised good, relativistic truth, and partial beauty that we encounter in our fallen, fragmented world. They point beyond our world to the absolute standards of moral and ethical behavior, philosophical and theological reality, and aesthetic balance and harmony against which classical Christian education shapes and molds its students.

PART 1

THE NATURE OF EDUCATION

ONE

LIBERAL ARTS VERSUS VOCATIONAL

WHAT KIND OF EDUCATION, we are now ready to ask, is fitting for volitional, incarnational beings who possess innate, essential worth but are inherently rebellious and disobedient, who build and create, and whose better angels impel them to form communities and practice virtue? We are, as I attempted to show in my introduction, creatures who struggle within ourselves, against nature, and against our fellow man. Our capacity for nobility, kindness, integrity, and self-sacrifice is matched only by our proclivity for depravity, cruelty, deceit, and selfishness. How is one to educate so strange and contradictory a creature?

As far back as the golden age of Athens, the birthplace of humanism in the West, the answer to that question has been clear: by means of a liberal arts education that frees ("liberates") the mind from the idols of the agora (the marketplace) and equips it to think critically, contemplate creatively, and act virtuously. Such an education was initially reserved for the aristocratic children of the wealthy; tradesmen, servants, and slaves, in contrast, would receive a servile education whose purpose was merely to teach a skill: *technē* in Greek, from which we get our words *technique* and *technology.*

There is, of course, nothing wrong with learning a trade; vocational schools have always performed an important function in society, ensuring that the skills necessary for the survival of the community are preserved. Vocational education, however, does not address the whole person; it concerns itself with neither shaping the mind nor molding the character. Vocational education is functional rather than formative; it trains the body without transforming the soul. As such, it does not provide the kind of holistic paideia that a society needs if it is to pass down its culture to the next generation.

Built on the same Greek root (*pais, paidos,* "child") from which we get our words *pedagogy* and *pediatrics, paideia* means "education," but in a much fuller sense than we typically ascribe to the word. In addition to meaning "training," "instruction," and "discipline," *paideia* connotes "rearing," "fostering," "nurturing," "breeding," and "cultivating." Paideia was the process by which the proper virtues of wisdom, courage, justice, and self-control were instilled in aristocratic children via an education in such "liberal" subjects as grammar, logic, rhetoric, math, philosophy, music, and gymnastics.

In the Roman period, Cicero used the Latin word *humanitas* to describe this process of rearing just and philanthropic citizens through, in part, a study of classical literature, art, and philosophy. From *humanitas* we get the words and concepts *humanity* (the quality possessed by people who behave in a benevolent and civilized manner) and *humanities* (the core liberal arts disciplines that shape and form virtuous citizens).

In the New Testament, paideia connotes the process of nurture, instruction, and discipline by which Christians are formed in the image of Christ:

> And, ye fathers, provoke not your children to wrath: but bring them up in the nurture [*paideia*] and admonition of the Lord. (Ephesians 6:4)

> All scripture is given by inspiration of God, and is profitable for doctrine, for reproof, for correction, for instruction [*paideia*] in righteousness: That the man of God may be perfect, thoroughly furnished unto all good works. (2 Timothy 3:16-17)

> Now no chastening [*paideia*] for the present seemeth to be joyous, but grievous: nevertheless afterward it yieldeth the peaceable fruit of righteousness unto them which are exercised thereby. (Hebrews 12:11)

For Greek, Roman, and Christian alike, man's dual nature makes paideia a necessity as well as a possibility: for we are creatures for whom discipline is as compulsory as it is profitable. It may not seem pleasant at the time, but its rewards are great, leading the pupil—which is what *disciple* means in Greek—into righteous living by drawing him into relationship with divine standards of Goodness, Truth, and Beauty (Greco-Roman) or a personal God who is himself Goodness, Truth, and Beauty (Judeo-Christian).

Throughout most of human history, only the elite had the resources and the leisure to pursue a liberal arts education. In America, that is no longer the case, at least on the precollegiate level. Granted, not everyone can or should get a four-year liberal arts college degree, particularly between the ages of eighteen and twenty-one, but there is no reason why all American students cannot receive at least a partially liberal arts paideia in grade school, middle school, and high school. Once they graduate from twelfth grade, many young people will choose to go directly into the workforce or to a vocational school. I am in no way opposed to that.

But we are a rich nation with vast resources, and there is no reason why the classical Christian vision I will be discussing and defending in this chapter and those that follow cannot be implemented, in whole or in part, in public schools across the nation. We live in a democracy, not a monarchy or aristocracy; that is why it is vital that all future citizens be given the opportunity to wrestle with the great ideas that shaped our cultural, political, economic, and social systems. Although it is possible for the elite class of a nation to preserve most of its cultural riches, in a democracy of (at least theoretically) equal citizens, the passing down of culture is best effected by a broad base of citizens who are invested in its preservation.

I am aware that many today maintain that it is unfair, inegalitarian, and ethnocentric to expect students with Asian, African, and Latin American backgrounds to be expected to immerse themselves in the civilization and culture of the West, and I can sympathize with their concerns. But it must not be forgotten that the American system that has drawn people from all over the world to our shores is the product of a serendipitous crossing of the Greco-Roman and the Judeo-Christian. Our country has been greatly enriched by the immigrants who have flocked here from every corner of the globe—all four of my grandparents emigrated here from Greece around 1930—but the bedrock ideals of freedom and democracy, equality of dignity and opportunity, private property and social responsibility, individual initiative and communal sacrifice are gifts of our tradition that have made it possible to assimilate so many different cultures and religions into our body politic.

That does not mean, of course, that people cannot or should not retain their ethnic identity. I proudly consider myself a Greek American, even though my family has been in this country for almost a century. As an American, I have learned, respect, and abide by the traditions on which this country was founded. As a Greek, which identity complements and enriches my primary identity as an American, I keep alive as best I can the ethnic traditions of my immigrant grandparents. I believe that dual identity has strengthened me, as I believe it has the many Honduran American, Indian American, Vietnamese American, Nigerian American, and Filipino American students I teach each semester. Indeed, when I conduct my master of fine arts students through the Greco-Roman myths and biblical stories that have inspired and influenced art in the West, I encourage my dual identity students to integrate their ethnic background into their artwork. Over the years, I have had Mexican American artists fuse a Greek myth with a Mayan myth to produce a highly original painting, Iranian American artists contrast biblical and qur'anic

Liberal Arts Versus Vocational 37

stories to create a dialogical work of art, and Chinese American artists refract Eastern folk tales through the lens of Western myth. There is much value in encouraging dual identity students to study their own ethnic heritage, but that should not be the primary or central role of classical Christian education.

I am also aware that many readers of this book will be concerned that I am advocating for the proselytizing of Christianity in our public schools. I am not. Public schools are not the proper arena for the sharing of the gospel of Christ; that is the work of churches and of private Christian schools. However, those aspects of Christianity that are foundational to the worldview on which our civilization rests—the history of Israel and the church; the essential dignity and essential depravity of man; our dual, enfleshed-soul nature; the ethical teachings of Moses and Jesus; transcendent notions of goodness, truth, and beauty; the reality of purpose, design, and meaning—form a legacy that must be passed down in our schools if we hope to preserve the ideals and freedoms our nation cherishes and, when we are worthy of ourselves, shares.

By no means have we lived up to all the ideals and freedoms championed in our tradition, but that is why we must continue to wrestle with the founding documents, people, and events that have shaped the soul of our nation. I will have more to say on these matters in chapters to come. For now, I return to my discussion of the meaning and history of paideia in the West.

<hr>

Though the concept of paideia has long been known by defenders of the liberal arts, it was given prominence on the eve of World War II, when the first volume of German classicist Werner Jaeger's *Paideia: The Ideals of Greek Culture* was published (1939, with volumes 2 and 3 following in 1943 and 1944). Jaeger's exhaustively researched trilogy definitively identified the ancient Greeks as the founders of paideia, of a system for passing the torch of culture to their children and grandchildren.

Beginning with Homer in the eighth century BC and reaching its zenith in the fifth-century teachings of Socrates and the fourth-century writings of his star pupil, Plato, the goal of paideia was to form and mold the next generation of gentlemen-knights (in its aristocratic form) or citizens (in its democratic form) in accordance with universal patterns and ideals. Its focus was simultaneously on the individual and the community. The worth of each student was acknowledged and upheld, but the goal of paideia was not to make that student into an autonomous individual who cared only for his own pleasure and advancement but into an active and virtuous member of the *polis*.

One of the foundations of the Greek paideia was the study of Homer's *Iliad* and *Odyssey*. Modern readers might find it difficult to understand how virtuous citizens could be shaped by a close reading of Homer's epics, but that is because we have artificially separated the aesthetic from the ethical. Homer offers something far greater than a pretty poem; he delves into and then wrestles with the very spirit of man. Poetry, Jaeger explains, "cannot be really educative unless it is rooted in the depths of the human soul, unless it embodies a moral belief, a high ardour of the spirit, a broad and compelling ideal of humanity. And the greatest of Greek poetry does more than show a cross-section of life taken at random. It tells the truth; but it chooses and presents its truth in accordance with a definite ideal."[1]

For the Athenian democracy, that ideal was embodied in the law; for Plato, in the Forms. Homer, the fountainhead of paideia, found his (aristocratic) ideal in the person of the hero: a view that was revisited by Aristotle—whose standard of virtue was not Plato's abstract Form of Virtue but a flesh-and-blood virtuous man—and the New Testament writers, who held up the incarnate Christ himself as the

---

[1]Werner Jaeger, *Paideia: The Ideals of Greek Culture*, 2nd ed., trans. Gilbert Highet (New York: Oxford University Press, 1945), 1:36.

ideal. All understood that true paideia does not and cannot thrive in a virtue-free, morally relative vacuum; a fixed standard grounded in truth must exist, or there will be nothing against which to measure the goal and the quality of the instruction.

Jaeger points to two places (one in the *Iliad*, one in the *Odyssey*) where a young man of about nineteen years (Achilles; Telemachus) is challenged by a teacher figure (his tutor Phoenix; Athena in the guise of a mortal man) to heed the example of a hero. In the former case, Achilles refuses to be guided, and it leads to his destruction. In the latter, Telemachus accepts and abides by the touchstone held up before him, and he is victorious. Whereas Achilles will not allow himself to be shaped and formed by the paideia of Phoenix, Telemachus eagerly embraces the process.

Achilles's moment of testing comes in book nine of the *Iliad*. Several days earlier, he pulled out of the Trojan War because Agamemnon stole his war prize. But now the tide of war has turned against the Greeks, and Agamemnon is forced to offer innumerable war prizes to convince Achilles to put on his armor and fight. Along with the ransom, Agamemnon sends Odysseus, Ajax, and Phoenix to convince Achilles to accept it and return. When Achilles rejects the more-than-generous offer, Phoenix attempts to instruct him by way of a story of a hero from the past generation: a pure, Achilles-like warrior named Meleager.

Meleager, like Achilles, lived for the battlefield, but when he felt dishonored by his leaders, he pulled out of the fighting. Knowing they could not win without Meleager's strong right arm, the leaders of his people offered him countless war prizes if he would return. Although he refused the offer, the sounds of battle around his camp eventually stirred his blood and forced him to return. But Meleager had delayed for too long, and those who had offered the gifts would no longer make good on their promise. As a result, Meleager, though he saved his people, was robbed of the honor the war prizes would have given him.

The lesson Phoenix attempts to teach Achilles is grounded in the cultural understanding that soldiers fight for war prizes: not because they are materialistic in the modern sense of the word but because war prizes signify honor, and they are all, Greek and Trojan alike, driven to gain as much honor as they can before death takes them. Since Achilles knows from his immortal mother, Thetis, that he is destined to live a short but glorious life, it is even more vital that he accumulate as many prizes as his brief years will allow him.

But Achilles will not be persuaded by the paideia of his tutor. Some of his reasons for refusing to accept the prizes and return are, from a Christian point of view, admirable. Achilles wonders aloud whether honor is such an important thing: perhaps honor is an internal gift shared alike by the coward and the brave man; perhaps our value cannot be counted in gold and weapons and concubines but is something we possess merely because we are alive. Admirable ideas, indeed, ones that will someday reform the world, but Achilles is not listening carefully enough to his tutor. It is not that we can never have new ideas or that society can never change, but that, being the kinds of creatures we are, we must hold in tenuous balance the dreams of the individual and the needs of the community, the passions of the heart and the demands of the moment, high ideals and earthly realities, the desire to build and the duty to preserve.

Christians ask, "What would Jesus do?" Achilles would have done well to follow the lead of the wise Phoenix and ask, "What would Meleager do?" Or, in this case, "What *should* Meleager have done?" One must not simply throw off one's culture and traditions. Paideia teaches us our possibilities and our limits, the superhuman greatness to which we can aspire and the tragic folly into which we can fall. Rather than fulfill his proper role and use the gifts he was given to defend the Greeks, Achilles allows his best friend Patroclus to fight in

Liberal Arts Versus Vocational 41

his place. When Patroclus is killed, Achilles reacts by rejecting utterly his noble ideas of intrinsic human value and embracing instead a nihilistic ethic of revenge and despair.

In the end, he finds some balance and reconciles with King Priam, the father of his friend's killer, but he knows he has made a mess of things and that his own death will soon follow. To cast off the paideia of one's culture is to remove oneself from the vine that nourishes, the circle that protects, and the template that gives shape.

In contrast, Telemachus, the untested son of Odysseus, profits by the paideia offered him by Athena. Disguised as a mortal man named Mentor—the origin of our word—Athena gently but firmly mentors Telemachus as he transitions from a timid boy who dreams that his father will return and set things to right into a confident young man who understands and accepts his role in his family, his culture, and his troubled island kingdom of Ithaca. Over the course of *Odyssey* 1-4, Athena-Mentor guides Telemachus into embracing his full duty and identity. Her chief method for doing so is holding up before the eager eyes of Telemachus a role model who, like himself, is the son of a famous Trojan War hero to whom fate has been unkind.

The name of that role model is Orestes, son of Agamemnon and Clytemnestra. Seven years after his father is treacherously killed by his wife's lover, Orestes returns to his father's house and exacts revenge on the usurper. Athena challenges Telemachus to live up to the courage, loyalty, and determination of Orestes, no matter the cost to himself. Though Homer would have been aware of a darker version of the myth, in which Clytemnestra kills her husband and Orestes kills his mother, he wisely leaves out those taboo crimes so as to provide an ethical paideia within the bounds of traditional moral standards. Athena could hardly have held up a matricide as a role model for Telemachus, whatever the strength and gravity of Orestes's motives.

The Orestes of Homer is a hero, for he risks all to save his *oikos*: the Greek word for a household that functions not merely as a dwelling for a single nuclear family but as an economic and political unit. Orestes recognizes his role within the *oikos* once led by his father and does what he must to restore it to its original state. Telemachus has never seen his *oikos* in its proper working form, but he trusts the paideia of Athena and the role model she offers him. He receives the story Athena tells him about Orestes as a standard of proper filial duty and courage against which he can test and measure his own decisions and actions.

To reinforce the story and its hero–role model, Athena then sends Telemachus on a journey to the restored households of two Trojan War heroes, Nestor and Menelaus, who knew and fought alongside the father whom Telemachus himself has never known. By so doing, she offers her pupil a liberal arts education—exposing him to the great tales, deeds, and figures of the past and exhorting him to live up to their legacy.

Writing in the first century BC, the great Roman historian Livy offers a similar rationale for why a culture must study its past. In the introduction to his epic, 142-book history of the Roman Republic, Livy explains with admirable precision the essence and purpose of a liberal arts education grounded in man's dignity and depravity and his moral nature: "The study of history is the best medicine for a sick mind; for in history you have a record of the infinite variety of human experience plainly set out for all to see; and in that record you can find for yourself and your country both examples and warnings; fine things to take as models, base things, rotten through and through, to avoid."[2]

Telemachus imitates the good example of Orestes and matures into a pillar of his civilization; Achilles ignores the bad example of Meleager and comes close to tearing down the foundations of his own.

---

[2]Livy, *The Early History of Rome*, trans. Aubrey de Sélincourt (New York: Penguin, 1971), 34.

Liberal Arts Versus Vocational   43

Fast-forward eight centuries to the golden age of Athens, where the paideia of Phoenix and Athena-Mentor took on new forms while retaining the same basic function. Sophocles, the playwright of *Oedipus* and *Antigone*, dramatized myths that predated the Trojan War as a vehicle for compelling his fellow Athenians to wrestle with ideas and issues that were more relevant to the fifth century than the thirteenth. Pericles, Athens's greatest statesman, guided those same Athenians to be involved, loyal members of the *polis*. Phidias, the artist who carved the statues of Athena in Athens and Zeus in Olympia, shaped ivory, gold, and marble into objects of timeless beauty.

All three, Jaeger explains, used their specific paideia to sculpt the soul of the citizens of Athens the way gymnastics sculpts the body. Both Sophocles and Phidias pierced through the surface to reveal the deeper, essential spirit of man. There is a strange serenity and equanimity that gazes at us through the heroic characters of Sophocles and the noble statues of Phidias. In both, we catch a glimpse of the true nature and mission of paideia: culture deliberately guiding and forming human character in harmony with an ideal sense of balance and proportion. Meanwhile, in Pericles, as in Sophocles, we encounter the true gentleman-citizen of the golden age who possessed a kind of urbanity and inner peace one rarely sees elsewhere.

Pericles believed firmly that the laws of Athens played the role of tutor to her citizens, a political paideia that shaped the soul of the *polis*. He says as much in the famous funeral oration he gave in 431 BC, after the first year of the Peloponnesian War, a speech on which Lincoln closely modeled his Gettysburg Address:

> Let me say that our system of government does not copy the institutions of our neighbours. It is more the case of our being a model to others, than of our imitating anyone else. Our constitution is called a democracy because power is in the hands not of a minority but of the whole people. When it is a question of settling private disputes, everyone is equal before the law: when it is a question of putting one person before another in positions of public

44 PART 1—THE NATURE OF EDUCATION

responsibility, what counts is not membership of a particular class, but the actual ability which the man possesses. . . . We are free and tolerant in our private lives; but in public affairs we keep to the law. This is because it commands our deep respect. We give our obedience to those whom we put in positions of authority, and we obey the laws themselves, especially those which are for the protection of the oppressed, and those unwritten laws which it is an acknowledged shame to break.[3]

At the core of Greek cultural and political paideia lay the belief that freedom and obedience, private autonomy and public duty, proper pride and proper shame were not at odds. Democracy does not mean a relativistic free-for-all but a deep respect for the law and a tolerance for others who hold themselves to the same laws.

In the paideia of Pericles, as in those of Sophocles and Phidias, a concerted attempt is made to shape and form man as he ought to be. In sharp contrast to the finally antihumanistic project of the modern utopian progressive, who seeks to remake man in his own image, the Greeks sought to mold their citizens in accordance with objective, transcendent standards of goodness, truth, and beauty. The Greeks first discerned those standards in the ordered structure and design of the cosmos and then later applied them to the agora, the law court, the theater, the workshop, and the schoolroom. The golden age architects of the Greek paideia, Jaeger explains, did not see the human soul "as a chaotic flow of inner experience, but subjected it to a system of laws, as the only realm of being which had not yet incorporated the ideal of cosmos. Like the body, the soul obviously had rhythm and harmony."[4]

Even the Sophists, who were cultural relativists and tended toward materialism, recognized the connection between the design in the cosmos and the design in the soul. They knew that there could be no properly working *polis* or system of punishment and reward if

---

[3]Thucydides, *History of the Peloponnesian War*, trans. Rex Warner (London: Penguin, 1972), 145.
[4]Jaeger, *Paideia*, 279.

Liberal Arts Versus Vocational   45

citizens were not able to be educated in virtue and so be empowered
to choose or reject that which was noble and good. That could only
be accomplished by passing down the treasure of their culture to the
next generation.

Indeed, Jaeger gives the Sophists a central role to play in making
the Greeks conscious of their culture and their need to pass it down:

> Originally the concept paideia had applied only to the process of education.
> Now [under the tutelage of the Sophists] its significance grew to include the
> objective side, the content of paideia—just as our word *culture* or the Latin
> *cultura*, having once meant the *process* of education, came to mean the *state*
> of being educated; and then the *content* of education, and finally the whole
> *intellectual and spiritual world* revealed by education, into which any indi-
> vidual, according to his nationality or social position, is born. The historical
> process by which the world of culture is built up culminates when the ideal
> of culture is consciously formulated. Accordingly it was perfectly natural for
> the Greeks in and after the fourth century, when the concept finally crystal-
> lized, to use the word *paideia*—in English, *culture*—to describe all the artistic
> forms and the intellectual and aesthetic achievements of their race, in fact the
> whole content of their tradition.[5]

Though Jaeger does not use the phrase "liberal arts" in this passage,
the way he describes culture and paideia provides a perfect gloss of
the methods ("the process of education"), goals ("the state of being
educated"), tools ("the content of education"), and ethos ("the intellectual and spiritual world") of a classical liberal arts education.

Such an education should be national rather than global, committed to training up students in "all the artistic forms and the intellectual and aesthetic achievements of their race." It should uphold
and instill truths that are universal and that have relevance to all
cultures at all times; nevertheless, it must be grounded in the traditions, sacred and secular, of a people. It should promote *our* heritage,
but in such a way that that heritage embodies and illuminates the
struggles of all humanity.

---

[5]Jaeger, *Paideia*, 303.

When I say "our," I mean the common heritage that all immigrants, including my grandparents, agreed to be a part of when they came to America. That agreement does not mean the forfeiting of one's native culture or religion, but it does mean a willingness to abide by the laws of our nation and to study, understand, and respect the traditions out of which those laws arose and on which they were built. Indeed, a citizen, whatever his place of origin, who does not study, understand, and respect those traditions will be prevented from participating fully in the ongoing experiment that is our democratic republic: what Lincoln, in his Pericles-inspired speech, called "government of the people, by the people, for the people."

But what are the parameters of that tradition? On what list of canonical works does it rest? And how can such works form the backbone of a liberal arts education that would do justice to the full and essential nature of man?

TWO

CANONICAL VERSUS IDEOLOGICAL

In "The Function of Criticism at the Present Time," the opening essay of his *Essays in Criticism* (1864), Victorian poet and man of letters Matthew Arnold—son of the headmaster of the prestigious Rugby School and himself an inspector of schools—famously defines criticism as "a disinterested endeavor to learn and propagate the best that is known and thought in the world." By *disinterested*, he does not mean uninterested or apathetic but free from all pragmatic concerns and political ideologies. The works that are to be learned and propagated are not to be chosen for their utilitarian or propagandistic value but as ends in themselves.

The role of the true critic, like that of the true educator, is not to indoctrinate the young in works that fit his own individual agenda but to expose them to timeless and time-tested works that have proven themselves to be worthy of long and careful study and contemplation. It is precisely such works that make up the Great Books of the Western intellectual tradition—or "canon" for short—and that have long formed the backbone of any liberal arts education worth its salt.

The Great Books are those that take up universal issues that all human beings must wrestle with in their lives. They ask the big questions about life and purpose, goodness and beauty, truth and justice,

48 PART 1—THE NATURE OF EDUCATION

and they do so by carrying on a three-thousand-year-old conversation into which our own Founding Fathers entered when they conceived our nation. Far from parroting the status quo, these are the books that both established the ideas that defined the status quo and criticized those ideas once they became enshrined. They are the books that have preserved the past while pushing forward to the future. They represent, as Arnold makes clear, the best that has been known and thought in the world.

The canon includes such works as the epics of Homer, Virgil, Dante Alighieri, and John Milton; the tragedies of Aeschylus, Sophocles, Euripides, and William Shakespeare; the philosophy of Plato, Aristotle, Cicero, Marcus Aurelius, René Descartes, Blaise Pascal, and Friedrich Nietzsche; the theology of Athanasius, Augustine, Thomas Aquinas, Martin Luther, John Calvin, and Jonathan Edwards; the history of Herodotus, Thucydides, Livy, and Plutarch; the political science of Niccolo Machiavelli, Thomas Hobbes, John Locke, Edmund Burke, the authors of the *Federalist Papers*, Alexis de Tocqueville, John Stuart Mill, and Karl Marx; the novels and short stories of Miguel de Cervantes, Jane Austen, Charles Dickens, Herman Melville, Nathaniel Hawthorne, Mark Twain, William Faulkner, Victor Hugo, Fyodor Dostoevsky, Leo Tolstoy, James Joyce, Ernest Hemingway, and Flannery O'Connor; the poetry of Chaucer, John Donne, Alexander Pope, William Wordsworth, John Keats, Alfred Tennyson, Walt Whitman, Emily Dickinson, T. S. Eliot, and William Butler Yeats; the math and science books of Euclid, Ptolemy, Copernicus, Galileo Galilei, Charles Darwin, and Albert Einstein; the social commentary of Jean-Jacques Rousseau, Mary Wollstonecraft, Frederick Douglass, George Orwell, and Martin Luther King Jr.; and, of course, the Bible.

Many today think that the best window into what it means to be human is empirically grounded, double-blind, statistic-driven psychological, sociological, and physiological studies. Though I will concede that these studies have taught us much about the diverse

Canonical Versus Ideological

groups that make up our nation and the world, I would yet argue that they have yielded very little lasting insight into the mystery that is man. To the contrary, such studies have tended to increase confusion as to the nature of truth, goodness, and beauty; love, friendship, and happiness; the family, sexuality, and gender. Where the social sciences have faltered, however, in unpacking these perennial mysteries, the Great Books have excelled—and have done so for three millennia.

If we want to understand the wonder and terror that is love, discovering what area of our brain lights up when we think of our beloved will do us little good. We must turn instead to Sappho and Ovid, Dante and Petrarch, Shakespeare and Donne, Percy Bysshe Shelley and Keats, Robert and Elizabeth Browning. If we want to understand what faith in God *is* and how it changes us at the core, scouring through epistemological studies of religious experience will leave us none the wiser. We must immerse ourselves in Augustine's *Confessions* and Dante's *Paradiso*, Julian of Norwich's *Revelations of Divine Love* and John Bunyan's *Pilgrim's Progress*. If we want to understand the essential nature of the world in which we live, the physicists and geologists and biologists can only tell us so much. To break through to the reality that lies behind what we perceive with our senses, we need Plato and Boethius, Descartes and Pascal, Milton and Samuel Taylor Coleridge.

In some ways I have already demonstrated in the introduction how central and indispensable the canon is to understanding and wrestling with our humanity. That is why I framed much of it around direct interactions with such canonical writers as Shakespeare and Sophocles, Plato and Aristotle, Augustine and Dante, Wordsworth and Byron, Burke and Chesterton, Lewis and Tolkien, not to mention the writers of the canonical Scriptures.

Please do not think I first formulated my views on the nature of man and then borrowed passages from these writers to illustrate my views. Quite to the contrary; it was from these writers and many more that I gained and honed my ideas about myself and my neighbor, nature and nature's God. It was in dialogue with them that I forged a sense of my own unique identity, purpose, and destiny within the wider identity, purpose, and destiny of the human race. Indeed, I would argue, along with the founders of the Athenian democracy, the Roman Republic, the British Empire, and the United States of America, that a vigorous reading and wrestling with the Great Books provides the best paideia for shaping virtuous, morally self-regulating citizens.

In what follows, I will consider what American students living in a modern democracy can gain from a close dialogue with the epics, tragedies, philosophy, theology, history, and political science of the classical Christian canon.

Anyone who has the desire and the courage to wrestle with the core questions of humanity—What does it mean to be mortal? Where is my true home? What is my purpose, my duty, and my vocation? How do my choices shape my character and my fate? How do I chose between duty and disobedience?—must engage the epics of Homer, Virgil, Dante, and Milton. There is no better proving ground for asking and engaging these questions than by immersing oneself in the epic journeys of Achilles and Hector, Odysseus and Telemachus, Aeneas and Dido, Dante the poet and Dante the pilgrim, Adam and Eve, Jesus and Satan.

One of the most effective ways to pass down the wisdom and traditions of our classical Christian heritage is to have students wrestle with the human conflicts and timeless struggles that run rampant through the *Iliad, Odyssey, Aeneid, Commedia,* and *Paradise Lost.* In the previous chapter, I discussed how Achilles in *Iliad* 9 and Telemachus in *Odyssey* 1-4 received a paideia when their tutor/mentor held up before each of them a role model whose choices led him to a very different destiny. When students are invited into a Great Books, liberal arts education that brings them face to face with the struggles,

Canonical Versus Ideological

external and internal, of Achilles and Telemachus, they participate in that paideia.

That Achilles and Telemachus "lived" over three thousand years ago and Homer composed his epics over twenty-five hundred years ago is irrelevant to the nature of the paideia. For it is the *same* paideia, the same that shaped and molded the best and brightest of Periclean Athens, Augustan Rome, Renaissance Italy, and Elizabethan England. In fact, it is precisely because they participated themselves in the paideia of Homer that Virgil, Dante, and Milton wrote their epics, preserving and carrying on the tradition, even as they added to it something of their own. Just as Virgil, Dante, and Milton lived and wrote in dialogue with Homer, so students today who receive a liberal arts paideia in the Western canon join in that great conversation as well, keeping alive and pushing forward the perennial issues and struggles that glow and shimmer at the heart of the *Iliad*, *Odyssey*, *Aeneid*, *Commedia*, and *Paradise Lost*.

One of the things that makes these epics unique is that they fuse together the genius of an individual poet with the culture of a great nation and people. The Greek, Roman, Florentine, or Englishman who reads them will feel a special thrill of pride, but the national elements that inspire those patriotic feelings do not take away from the universality of the message. All the facets of man that I discussed in the introduction are sounded and delved into in these supreme products of the human imagination. Each highlights in a slightly different way man's glory and his depravity, his triumphs and his failures; each explores the internal wrestling match between our angelic and bestial natures.

The *Iliad* presents heroes in pursuit of the virtues of the battlefield but who refuse at the moment of crisis to be persuaded by sound advice. The *Odyssey* gives us father and son heroes who are both committed to building—or, to be more accurate, rebuilding—the broken *oikos* of Ithaca. They strive not for war prizes but for something that will last. Aeneas, like no hero before or after, learns what it means to be a political animal, that man cannot reach his fullest potential apart from a polity, a republic of citizens called to bring peace and justice to the world.

Dante as poet is perhaps the supreme subcreator of all time, fashioning an aesthetic universe in imitation of the cosmos of God; Dante as pilgrim explores man's moral agency and the consequences that follow on his choices. Milton, while illuminating all aspects of creation and fall, sin and salvation, good and evil, infuses his epic with a deep psychological sense of how our consciousness and our conscience grow. Every Romantic poet who gazed within to study the growth of his soul from infancy to adulthood owed a literary and spiritual debt to *Paradise Lost.*

In the title to this chapter, I have, at the risk of sounding too polemical, set the canonical in opposition to the ideological. By *canonical*, I mean works that have stood the test of time because of their ability to speak to those parts of our humanity that cannot be circumscribed by a particular social-cultural-political milieu. By *ideological*, I mean works that, far from being disinterested, have an agenda that supersedes that which is common to humanity, that seeks primarily to set right a real or presumed injustice rather than explore what it means to live in a world that is good but broken.

I am aware that some will reject this distinction, reminding me that the *Aeneid* is a work of propaganda meant to praise and justify the newly created Roman Empire of Caesar Augustus, and the *Divine Comedy* and *Paradise Lost* partisan celebrations and defenses of Roman Catholic Christendom and the Protestant Reformation and Puritan revolution. I concede that these epics have a message, a moral, and a purpose, but all three rise above the narrow limits of ideology by treating their heroes as both concrete individuals and universal types rather than as amorphous members of groups whose chief function is to oppress or be oppressed.

Canonical Versus Ideological 53

The search for glory, for home, for destiny, for salvation, for truth transcends distinctions of race, class, gender, age, and culture. That does not mean that they shy away from conflicts between those who have power and those who do not; but it does mean that the external and internal conflicts that drive the heroes to their glory or ruin are not reduced to categories of political, social, economic, or sexual power. The view of man in these epics is expansive rather than reductive, humanistic rather than mechanistic. The heroes are shaped and influenced by their milieu, but they are not determined by it.

Many other long, narrative poems were written in the Greek, Roman, medieval, and Renaissance periods, but these are the ones we still read, study, and debate because they have proven to embody the fullness of those periods, enshrining and critiquing what they most valued while pointing a light backward and forward, and carrying on a vigorous dialogue about what it means to be human.

❦

In his great work of literary criticism, *Poetics*, Aristotle hails epic and tragedy as the two highest genres. In the end, however, he ranks tragedy above epic (see chap. 26), for it is more concentrated and unified and better achieves its goal of bringing about a catharsis in its audience. According to Aristotle, our experience of the catharsis—a Greek word transliterated into English—is linked to our emotions of pity and fear. When we watch or read a tragedy, we are simultaneously drawn toward the hero out of pity and repelled out of fear—the fear that the same might happen to us.

No one fears that he will discover, as Oedipus does, that he has killed his father and married his mother. But we all *do* fear, often unconsciously, that we may one day stumble upon a hidden truth that will shatter our sacred, carefully guarded illusions about ourselves, God, and the world. No one fears he will be put in a situation where he must choose whether to sacrifice his daughter or kill his mother, as Agamemnon and Orestes are in the *Oresteia*. But we do fear we will be thrust into a dilemma that will test every ounce of our moral fiber. No one fears he will be deceived and destroyed by the Greek god of wine, women, and song, as Pentheus is by Bacchus. But we do fear that we will be torn apart by our own repressed or rejected desires and passions.

Greek tragedy explores, even as it reveals, the tragic nature of the human condition. We journey along life's path as if on a razor's edge, with folly awaiting us on the one side and catastrophe on the other. Unless we balance courage with prudence, ambition with self-control, and justice with mercy, we will stumble and fall, to our own ruin and that of those in our orbit. What harms the individual harms as well the family, the tribe, the state, the nation. We are volitional, moral-ethical beings, but we are not totally free. We must navigate the forces of destiny and necessity that lie just outside our grasp and just beyond our sight.

The tragedies of Aeschylus, Sophocles, and Euripides seem strange to us, but that is as it should be. They would have seemed almost as strange to their original audience, for the plays do not dramatize current events but legendary tales that occurred in the dim reaches of time, nearly a millennium before the golden age of Athens. By displacing the difficult decisions we all must make (and endure) onto ancient tales seemingly remote from the troubles of today, the Athenian playwrights drew their audience—intellectually, emotionally, and spiritually—into the heart of the drama before waking them up to the realization that *they* were Oedipus and Antigone, Orestes and Electra, Pentheus and Medea.

That is precisely the kind of paideia we need today, when so many of us live trapped in a contemporary bubble, assured that our age is one of pure Enlightenment, free from the prejudices and superstitions of the past. The awakening is often a rude one, but it is as instructive as it is humbling. It is especially so for Americans living in a two-and-a-half-century-old political experiment. Tragedy, we must not forget,

Canonical Versus Ideological 55

is an invention of Athenian democracy; it appeared nowhere else in Greece. It is in fact the democratic genre par excellence, for it merges the voices of the old aristocracy (embodied in the major characters) with those of the common citizen (embodied in the chorus).

Kings and other rulers may think they can keep their lives and choices secret, but those secrets are inevitably exposed in the public square. Blood will out, and the strength and resilience of citizens and *polis* alike are tested and tried by the ordeal like gold in the fire. As students participate in Orestes's desperate quest to find legal, moral, and psychological expiation for the guilt he incurred when he obeyed Apollo and killed the mother who killed his father, or Antigone's fearless crusade to stand for piety over political expediency, or Hippolytus's anxious wrestling between forbidden lust and unhealthy prudery, they become aware of their own internal struggles and the implications of those struggles for society as a whole—particularly one that claims to be of the people, by the people, and for the people.

Though scores of playwrights have tried to achieve the same level of intensity, the same spiritual and civic engagement with the fullness of the human condition, only Shakespeare has succeeded in sounding the depth and breadth of Greek tragedy. No paideia is complete that does not bring its students into dialogue with Shakespeare. Every character type, every conflict, every degree of triumph and despair finds its echo in one or more of his timeless comedies, tragedies, histories, and romances. To deny that is to deny the very essence of man as a player on this earthly stage.

This is not to suggest that Shakespeare is the only playwright one should read. The Spanish will also want to study the plays of Miguel de Cervantes and Lope de Vega, the French Molière and Jean Racine, the Germans Johann Wolfgang von Goethe and Friedrich Schiller, the British Oscar Wilde and George Bernard Shaw, the Scandinavians Henrik Ibsen and August Strindberg, the Americans Eugene O'Neil and Arthur Miller. Still, Shakespeare must play a part in the shaping of the young as they develop a sense of themselves as individuals and as members of a culture, a polity, and a tradition.

It is true that a good vocational school can help students to determine what role they will play in the workforce and teach them skills for being productive members of society. From a liberal arts education, however, they will also learn what it *means* to be a member of society and to make the kinds of choices one must make to balance one's individual desires with the needs of the community.

As Athens gave birth to tragedy, so she gave birth to philosophy. True, there were thinkers before Socrates who pondered the riddles of the universe, but it was Socrates who united metaphysics (What is the nature of reality?) and ethics (How should one behave?) to give us philosophy in its fullness. It was Socrates as well who compelled his pupils to define their terms: What do you mean by Justice? Beauty? Goodness? Courage? He did not ask his questions to make money or gain political power or even to win applause. He asked because he believed that the unexamined life was not worth living, that it was the duty of all rational beings to seek to know themselves and their world.

An educated person need not read every dialogue by Plato and treatise by Aristotle, but he should be familiar with the key questions and how the answers philosophers have offered to those questions have exerted a strong, if invisible, influence on the types of things we believe and the kinds of actions we perform. It is not enough that students memorize the key propositions of the major philosophers; they must enter into the dialogue *between* the philosophers. Only citizens educated in such a dialogical manner will possess the knowledge, the skills, and the *attitude* necessary to maintain a deliberative representational democracy.

It is precisely because the great philosophers deal with questions about God, man, and the universe; justice, freedom, and duty; ethics, aesthetics, and linguistics as ends in themselves that a vigorous education in those questions and the variety of answers they have generated can yield results that are concrete, practical, and life changing. Because philosophy is, to borrow Arnold's trenchant phrase from the start of this chapter, a "disinterested endeavor" to explore the nature of reality, it has more often than not arrived at ideologically neutral solutions that have wide applicability to different times, places, and cultures and that are not primarily driven by a political agenda. Young minds trained by and in a dispassionate, impartial, unbiased wrestling match with philosophical ideas become honed and sharpened, and thus better able to make wise decisions in personal, pragmatic, and political matters.

Please recall the distinction I made a moment ago between canonical and ideological. No one in our depraved and fragmented world has pure motives; no one can achieve complete objectivity. The quantum physicists have even demonstrated that our perception of the physical world plays a role in forming the seemingly concrete external things that we see. The great writers of the canon *do* write from the point of view of their specific moment, but they nevertheless strive to transcend their moment to touch on those parts of themselves, and ourselves, that are the most essential and unchanging. As fallen creatures, we are inherently biased and egocentric. We were, however, made in the image of a God who is "the same yesterday, and to day, and for ever" (Hebrews 13:8), and there are therefore aspects of our humanity that endure beyond the vicissitudes of history, politics, and economics. No book or author can tap in full purity those permanent things that endure, but canonical books come closer to doing so than ideological ones—that is why we still read and study them today.

I would extend this same line of reasoning to the great theologians, whose struggles with and meditations on mercy and justice, grace and works, salvation and damnation, heaven and hell cannot simply be sequestered in a religious corner cut off from all other areas of life. We are enfleshed souls, holistic beings who cannot arbitrarily separate soul from body, spiritual from physical, without leaving ourselves disjointed and fragmented. The restlessness of the human heart and the yearning of the human spirit demand a grappling with transcendent, metaphysical realities. The ethical call to treat our neighbor as we would be treated ourselves cries out for a supernatural reference point.

Throughout the Middle Ages, theology was considered the queen of the sciences, not just because the Catholic Church was central to the life of Europe but because it was understood that the study of the Creator gave form, meaning, and purpose to all the varied pursuits and strivings of the creature. While it is true that the need to pass down the cultural torch from one generation to the next gives focus and unity to that culture's paideia, the existence of a divine dimension secures the universality of what is taught and the persistence of goodness, truth, and beauty within those universal teachings.

In a public school setting that includes diverse people from different (or no) faith backgrounds, it is certainly appropriate that the Bible not be taught as the authoritative Word of God. But it does need to be studied, and studied carefully, for what it has to teach us about origins and destinations, moral law codes and self-destructive behaviors, life and death, wisdom and folly, joy and lament, the problem with man and the problem of pain. People who are trained in the high moral call of the Bible will make better citizens, and will more readily honor their parents, teachers, and community leaders, and will preserve and transmit the inheritance of their ancestors and their sacred tradition.

Let me add here that a classical Christian curriculum grounded in the Great Books would be well served by having its students interact with the Qur'an as well. Much of the Christian Middle Ages is defined by the West's interactions with Islam, positive and negative.

Canonical Versus Ideological 59

Studying the ways in which the Qur'an both agrees and disagrees with the Bible will deepen students' understanding of the choices that the architects of European (and American) culture made relative to the nature of God, man, and the universe. Discussions of the Hindu *Gita* and *Analects* of Confucius would also be helpful, though less so than the Qur'an, for the clash of civilizations between Christendom and Islam has been more formative than those with Hinduism, Buddhism, and other world religions. Even more formative has been the Christian dialogue with Plato and his heirs and with such Epicurean and Stoic writers as Lucretius, Cicero, Seneca, Epictetus, and Marcus Aurelius.

<hr />

Still, the Bible is and must be the core religious text for any liberal arts curriculum that would call itself classical, whether or not that curriculum is specifically Christian. In the introduction I listed some aspects of Christianity that are central to classical education. The Bible, on account of its ethical teachings and its exploration of all areas of the human story, cannot be left out of the curriculum. But there is another reason it must be included that is no less vital to the Western paideia: it details the history of the Jews, arguably the most remarkable people group that has ever lived. They did not create a multifaceted culture, like Greece, or build great monuments, like Egypt, or rule a mighty empire, like Rome. What they did was survive, and they survived because of their faith in God and their adherence to the law. They remain today, having retained a remarkable, if not miraculous, cultural continuity with their past.

Their sacred Scriptures stand as a witness to providential history: to the belief that history is not random or arbitrary but moves forward in accordance with a divine plan that works in synergy with the ethical decisions and behaviors of nations and their leaders. The historical books of the Bible do more than provide a chronology and a list of major figures and events; they offer a moral reading of history that attributes the rise and fall of Israel and Judah to the righteousness or unrighteousness of her judges and kings.

Though the great historians of Greece and Rome, of the Middle Ages and the Renaissance, and even of the Enlightenment, Romantic, and Victorian periods are less deliberate than the Hebrew Scriptures in connecting individual or national sin and repentance to the flow of history, they nevertheless look for cause-and-effect patterns in the events they record. From the landing of the *Mayflower* to the present day, Americans have continued to debate whether we are a chosen nation and to what extent our successes and failures, our exceptionalism and our arrogance are coincidences or acts of providence influenced by our virtues and our vices.

Teachers who guide their students through Herodotus and Xenophon, Polybius and Plutarch, Livy and Tacitus, Eusebius and Bede, Edward Gibbon and Thomas Babington Macaulay should not feel it their duty to take a definite position on providential history. They should, however, encourage students to study the fluctuations and undulations of nations with an eye for meaningful design in the warp and weft of history. It is a natural human instinct to search for such meaning, and an education that does not assist in that search is not fulfilling its purpose of equipping citizens.

To aid further in that equipping, a paideia grounded in the canon will also introduce its students to the classic works of political science. If providential history illuminates interactions between the natural and supernatural spheres, then political science illuminates interactions between those who govern and those who are governed. It too looks for patterns, but those patterns concern the themes of justice and expediency, freedom and tyranny, social contracts and the divine right of kings.

Rather than move directly into practical concerns, these Great Books begin with theoretical questions: What is the nature of the good life, the good citizen, and the good state? From where does

Canonical Versus Ideological

political power originate? How are the tasks of a *polis* to be most fairly and/or efficiently distributed? Are justice and equity the same thing? Do we have inalienable rights to life, liberty, and property? Only by wrestling with such abstract questions about the nature of government and society will citizens possess the necessary foundational knowledge to make decisions about specific political issues.

Epic and tragedy, philosophy and theology, history and political science help exercise and equip the mind to function and find meaning in a world of earth-shattering events and life-changing ideas, a world where fate struggles perpetually with free will, mortality with immortality, and power with freedom. But what of the less grand aspects of our lives? What of our subtler emotions, our quieter struggles with self-identity and memory, with family dynamics and personal relationships?

For that the canon offers a treasure trove of lyrical poems and novels that have explored and unpacked, often with stunning psychological precision, the interior lives of men and women. These are the works that, when we read them, make us feel strangely exposed, as if the poets and novelists had been reading our mail or peering into the windows of our home. They are those who have stared deeply into the abyss of the self and returned to teach us what they saw and heard. By reading and reflecting on their work, we are challenged to put in order our own wandering thoughts and feelings and to recognize that many of them are more universal than we had imagined.

The time-tested poems and novels of the canon draw us into the wider human community, helping us to see where we are similar and where unique to our fellow travelers on the road. They hone down our edges, refining and polishing what would otherwise be rough, sharp, and jagged or clumsy, dull, and ungainly.

Such are the Great Books and the ways they have been used by educators for the last twenty-five hundred years to build up the hearts, souls, and minds of the young. To them, an ambitious educator will also add the art of Leonardo da Vinci, Michelangelo, Raphael, Caravaggio, Peter Paul Rubens, Rembrandt, J. M. W. Turner, and Vincent van Gogh and the music of Johann Sebastian Bach, Ludwig van Beethoven, Wolfgang Amadeus Mozart, Frédéric Chopin, and Pyotr Ilyich Tchaikovsky.

This is our legacy, and it is our duty to pass the torch to each new generation.

⊙▬▬▬⊙

It remains to say a few words as to why the canon I have put forward as the centerpiece of a liberal arts education is Western (though it does include works from the Near East and the northern coast of Africa). The answer is simple. We live in the West, not only geographically but in terms of the culture that has shaped our nation. It is true, and thanks be to God for it, that our country continues to draw immigrants from around the world. But that is all the more reason why the canon must be preserved and taught.

For over a century and a half, an almost endless stream of immigrants have left or fled from their home countries and emigrated to America. They did so at great cost, risk, and hardship because they believed in the vision of America, a vision that is grounded in and inseparable from the Western canon. Our cherished notions of freedom, individualism, equality, justice, law, private property, democracy, and humanitarianism are all gifts of the Great Books. They arose out of the dialogue that still reverberates within and across the canon.

A growing number of people today are disturbed by the Whiteness of the canon, even leveling claims of racism and colonialism against those who would "impose" White culture on non-White people. Such critics, however, overlook an important fact of history. As late as the 1950s, if not later, immigrants from Southern and Eastern Europe (Greeks, Italians, Poles, Romanians, Armenians, Jews), not

Canonical Versus Ideological 63

to mention the Scotch and the Irish, were not considered White. Whites were those who came from England, France, Germany, Holland, and, sometimes, Scandinavia. The distinction here is vital, for the first people to be colonized by the Great Books were the northern Europeans. When Greco-Roman, Judeo-Christian, Mediterranean culture was at its height, the British, French, Germans, and Vikings were barbarians. It was precisely the Great Books and the ideas that flowed from them that civilized those barbarians, leading to their cultural ascendancy.

If that is (Mediterranean) cultural imperialism, then the (northern European) objects of that imperialism benefited mightily from it—so much so that, in time, they spread it to other nations. Without in any way denying the atrocities that were committed by Western colonial powers over the past five centuries, the fact remains that the movements for reform and liberation in India, South Africa, Algeria, and Latin America, among others, have been couched in the language of the classical Christian canon. The European colonists who spread the Great Books to their colonies did many things that violated the ideals they claimed to represent; but their misuse of the tradition could not cancel the power of that tradition to ennoble man and to help him build a freer, more just society. Those in America who would dethrone the Western canon in the name of diversity, equity, and inclusion seem to have forgotten that those values have only been successfully expressed and guaranteed in countries founded on the virtues and principles passed down by the Great Books.

In his posthumously published *Memoirs* (1974), Chilean communist poet Pablo Neruda included a haunting prose poem titled "La Palabra" ("The Word"); in it, he grapples with the legacy of the conquistadores who brought the Spanish language to the shores of Latin America. He does not shy away from the fact that they stole much from the native peoples: their food, land, culture, and gold. Yet, even

64 PART I—THE NATURE OF EDUCATION

as they stole, they left behind a priceless treasure. Here is how he ends
his poem:

> Wherever they went, they razed the land. . . . But words fell like pebbles out
> of the boots of the barbarians, out of their beards, their helmets, their horse-
> shoes, luminous words that were left glittering here . . . our language. We
> came up losers. . . . We came up winners. . . . They carried off the gold and left
> us the gold. . . . They carried everything off and left us everything. . . . They
> left us the words.[1]

The words that Neruda celebrates with such gratitude are the foundation of the Great Books. Those luminous words, contained in those
luminous books, gave the West—and through the West, much of the
world—a new and richer way to think about our human lives and
goals and yearnings, about the good and the true and the beautiful,
about how one can be free in mind, body, and spirit, about what it
means to strive for virtue and justice and love.

However, the best argument for an education in the Great Books is
to be found in Martin Luther King Jr.'s "Letter from Birmingham Jail"
(1963), an essay that offers a logically and rhetorically flawless argument for integration in America. By dialoguing carefully and consciously with the full breadth of the canon—the Old and New
Testament (including Amos, Jesus, and Paul), Socrates, Augustine,
Aquinas, Abraham Lincoln, and Thomas Jefferson, as well as twentieth-
century Jewish philosopher Martin Buber and Christian philosophers
Reinhold Niebuhr and Paul Tillich—King decisively argues that racial
equality is woven deeply into the Greco-Roman, Judeo-Christian
roots of our country. While his essay does not mount an apology for
classical Christian education, it demonstrates powerfully how the canonical Great Books offer the surest foundation for what I would call
a good ideological cause. By "good," I mean a cause that unites rather
than divides, that affirms the inherent worth of all people rather than

---

[1]Pablo Neruda, *Memoirs*, trans. Hardie St. Martin (New York: Penguin, 1978), 54.

Canonical Versus Ideological

sets one group against another, that strikes a balance between our dignity and depravity.

Instead of dismissing or attacking the Catholic, Protestant, and Jewish clergymen who wrote to him encouraging him to slow down his struggle for civil rights, King has a conversation with them over the real virtues and beliefs that built our nation. He concedes that their concern over his willingness to break segregation laws is valid and then argues that there is a distinction between just and unjust laws.

> I would agree with Saint Augustine that "An unjust law is no law at all." Now what is the difference between the two? How does one determine when a law is just or unjust? A just law is a man-made code that squares with the moral law or the law of God. An unjust law is a code that is out of harmony with the moral law. To put it in the terms of Saint Thomas Aquinas, an unjust law is a human law that is not rooted in eternal and natural law. Any law that uplifts human personality is just. Any law that degrades human personality is unjust. All segregation statutes are unjust because segregation distorts the soul and damages the personality.[2]

Note that King, as a custodian of and participant in the Western canon, does not vilify or deconstruct that canon but gets to its heart—just as Jesus himself does when he fulfills rather than destroys the true spirit of the law (Matthew 5:17). King takes for granted, as do Augustine and Aquinas, that humans have inherent dignity and that they are moral agents: but that is only because all three have accepted a classical Christian understanding of man. Though one could argue that King quotes Augustine and Aquinas only because he knows that his audience will recognize their authority, I would respond that King quotes them because they are central figures in the best—I would argue only—world tradition that can make such a distinction between just and unjust laws without giving way to moral and ethical relativism.

---

[2]Martin Luther King Jr., *A Testament of Hope: The Essential Writings and Speeches of Martin Luther King, Jr.*, ed. James Melvin Washington (New York: HarperSanFrancisco, 1991), 293.

King is successful in his defense of integration because he writes and thinks within the classical Christian tradition. But he does more than that. He also wrestles within that tradition. In answer to complaints that he is a troublemaker and disturber of the peace because he creates tension, King compares himself to Socrates, who, though he did not begin the Western canon, was central to initiating its dialogical nature.

> Just as Socrates felt that it was necessary to create a tension in the mind so that individuals could rise from the bondage of myths and half-truths to the unfettered realm of creative analysis and objective appraisal, we must see the need of having nonviolent gadflies to create the kind of tension in society that will help men to rise from the dark depths of prejudice and racism to the majestic heights of understanding and brotherhood.[3]

The Great Books that I am arguing must serve as the chief foundation of classical Christian education are more than a reading list; they are an arena for dialogue. Those who accuse the canon of being elitist are sadly mistaken. Far from being elitist, it has proven to be one of the greatest tools of liberation the world has ever known. Far from being totalitarian, it contains within itself the methods and the worldview necessary for self-correction. King does not throw out the accomplishments of our Founding Fathers; he completes their work by drawing out what is latent in the Western tradition.

The canon offers the best weapon for fighting for true equality (not sameness), true freedom (not license), and true individuality (not individualism). But it cannot fight for itself. We must continue to defend and teach it or its hard-won, dearly bought lessons will be lost to humanity. The barbarians are ever at the gates, and a single generation of neglect can bring back the dark ages. We must be vigilant and keep the torch burning bright and clear.

---

[3]King, *Testament of Hope*, 291.

THREE

BOOKS VERSUS TEXTBOOKS

ALTHOUGH I DEVOTED the previous chapter to defending (and championing) the Great Books as the proper centerpiece of a liberal arts, classical Christian education, I feel the need to append to that defense a shorter but no less vital chapter on the proper use of the Great Books in the classroom. Too often, schools pay lip service to the canon and then quietly replace the books themselves with textbooks.

Not all textbooks, of course, are problematic. There is a need for course packs that gather under one cover essays or short stories or poems or excerpts from longer works. Such course packs allow students to survey a given genre or theme without having to purchase a dozen different books. It is also helpful to have anthologies of historical periods that include editorial notes that set the excerpts in their proper context.

Textbooks are also appropriate, if not necessary, for classes in the hard sciences. I would, however, argue that the social sciences of psychology, pedagogy, sociology, and anthropology would be improved if they devoted more time to reading and discussing the actual works of Sigmund Freud and Carl Jung, Jean-Jacques Rousseau and John Dewey, Karl Marx and Herbert Spencer, Max Weber and Émile Durkheim, George Herbert Mead and Claude Lévi-Strauss, Ferdinand de Saussure and Noam Chomsky. Better yet would be if they read such modern figures in light of Plato, Aristotle, Augustine, and Aquinas.

68　　　　　　　　　　　　　　　　　　　PART I—THE NATURE OF EDUCATION

Still, with a few exceptions, textbooks have more often than not hindered the preservation of our cultural traditions and the instilling of them in the young. The reason for this is simple: most textbooks bend the past to make it fit our own modern prejudices and blind spots. Sometimes they patronize the past; sometimes they demonize it. At other times, they sanitize it or purposely misinterpret it to suit an agenda that would have been foreign to the original authors. In all cases, they replace a direct encounter with the Great Books of the past with an ideological filter that ensures that no student or teacher will be confronted or transformed by the wisdom of our ancestors.[1]

The problem is best articulated by a senior devil in a series of letters meant to educate his nephew in the fine art of temptation. In number 27 of C. S. Lewis's *Screwtape Letters* (1942), Uncle Screwtape explains to Wormwood that if humans really read the Great Books of the past, they would see through most of their temptations with ease. As long as the dialogue between the people of today and the writers of the past remains open and accessible, the danger remains that our modern weaknesses will be lessened (and lessoned) by their ancient strengths.

Thankfully, exclaims Screwtape with glee, the devils have so cut off the citizens of the modern West from their past that no one actually reads the old books anymore. Well, almost no one. There are a

---

[1] In chapter 12 I discuss C. S. Lewis's *Abolition of Man*, which begins by critiquing a school textbook that, while appearing to be neutral, indoctrinates its young readers in an emotivist view of the world that reduces the sublime and the beautiful to subjective feelings rather than objective realities. Perhaps the best-known example of an American textbook that bends the past to fit an agenda is Howard Zinn's bestselling *A People's History of the United States* (New York: Harper Perennial, 2005). A more recent and even more controversial example is Nikole Hannah-Jones's equally bestselling *The 1619 Project: A New Origin Story* (New York: One World, 2021). Textbooks that bend the past to fit a modern ethos or agenda are not new. Edward Gibbon's Enlightenment-minded, multivolume *History of the Decline and Fall of the Roman Empire* (1776–1788) paints a very negative view of the church, essentially blaming it for the fall of Rome. Steven Runciman's three-volume *A History of the Crusades* (1951–1954) helped promulgate a negative view of the Crusades that has lasted almost until today. H. G. Wells wrote an influential, highly read *Outline of History* (1920) that imposed a Darwinian perspective on human history (G. K. Chesterton's *Everlasting Man* was written in part to refute Wells's *Outline*). Wells was influenced by the French *Encyclopedia* (1751–1772), which was edited by Diderot and enshrined the Enlightenment's biased and historically inaccurate view of the Middle Ages as a dark age of ignorance and superstition.

Books Versus Textbooks

particularly annoying group of scholars who live in a land called academia and devote their lives to studying the old books. Still, they pose only a minor threat, for they are precisely the people who are incapable of learning anything from the canon.

Screwtape's explanation of this ironic phenomenon is worth quoting in full, for it cuts to the heart of the problem with textbook-driven education:

> Only the learned read old books, and we have now so dealt with the learned that they are of all men the least likely to acquire wisdom by doing so. We have done this by inculcating the Historical Point of View. The Historical Point of View, put briefly, means that when a learned man is presented with any statement in an ancient author, the one question he never asks is whether it is true. He asks who influenced the ancient writer, and how far the statement is consistent with what he said in other books, and what phase in the writer's development, or in the general history of thought, it illustrates, and how it affected later writers, and how often it has been misunderstood (specially by the learned man's own colleagues) and what the general course of criticism on it has been for the last ten years, and what is the "present state of the question." To regard the ancient writer as a possible source of knowledge—to anticipate that what he said could possibly modify your thoughts or your behavior—this would be rejected as unutterably simple-minded. And since we cannot deceive the whole human race all the time, it is most important thus to cut every generation off from all others; for where learning makes a free commerce between the ages there is always the danger that the characteristic errors of one may be corrected by the characteristic truths of another. But, thanks be to Our Father [Satan] and the Historical Point of View, great scholars are now as little nourished by the past as the most ignorant mechanic who holds that "history is bunk."

Neither I nor Lewis would disparage the hardworking scholars who, beginning with the textual critics of the Library of Alexandria in the second and third centuries before Christ, have carefully edited, annotated, and preserved the Great Books of the Western intellectual tradition. Their work is necessary and foundational, and they are to be commended for their dedication. Apart from accurate texts, chronologies, translations, and patterns of influence, the great conversation cannot be carried out effectively.

Still, once textual purity and linguistic understanding have been achieved, the time comes when professors must challenge themselves and their students to wrestle honestly and humbly with the books themselves. The *Iliad, Oedipus, Republic, Ethics, Aeneid, Confessions, Inferno, Hamlet,* and *Paradise Lost* are more than artifacts to be preserved. They are fountains to be drunk, prophets to be heeded, obstacles to be confronted. Until and unless students and their teachers are willing to ask whether what Homer, Sophocles, Plato, Aristotle, Virgil, Augustine, Dante, Shakespeare, and Milton wrote is true, their encounter will not change their beliefs or alter their behaviors.

Too often, modern textbooks fall prey to the historical point of view. Rather than encourage students to have their beliefs and behaviors tested by a grappling with the words and ideas of the Great Books, they shield them from any words or ideas that run counter to our own modern sense of moral, intellectual, and aesthetic superiority. It is not enough to mention Dante, Shakespeare, and Milton in the table of contents or the index; their work must be treated as a lathe against which students can shape and hone their attitudes and actions. That does not mean students should not disagree with what they read in the Great Books. It does mean, however, that they should take the Great Books seriously, with an equal dose of gravity and gratitude, and that they should be prepared to have their own shortcomings exposed by the searching eye of the canon.

I regret to say that the same historical-point-of-view approach that has prevented our schools and colleges from freeing their students from the narrow confines of contemporary agendas and prejudices has become entrenched in seminaries across Europe and America. Too often, our best Christian scholars, together with their best students, stand in judgment over the Bible, rather than allow the Bible to guide, judge, and convict them. Rather than treat the Bible as the

Books Versus Textbooks

supreme repository of transcendent, crosscultural truths, more and more seminaries treat it as an artifact to be weighed, assessed, and ultimately bent to fit and even to uphold our own fashionable, "progressive" notions. To imagine that what the biblical writers wrote in their pre-enlightened, pre-industrial age could convince us to question what we now "know" is true about morality or miracles, marriage or gender would be naive, reactionary, obscurantist, and atavistic.

To stand naked and face to face with the Great Books is to have our thoughts tested and our actions altered. Those same works, when they are filtered through a textbook that defangs, deconstructs, and domesticates them, only reinforce our feelings of smugness, self-satisfaction, and self-righteousness.

⊙━▫━▫━⊙

How different is Screwtape's historical point of view from the "historical sense" that the great poet and critic T. S. Eliot celebrates as one of the attributes of the properly educated man. In his provocatively titled essay "Tradition and the Individual Talent" (1917), Eliot privileges the weight of tradition over the private inspiration of the individual poet. Whereas Romantic poet-critics such as Wordsworth and Shelley celebrated those parts of a work that were the most original, Eliot counters that "not only the best, but the most individual parts" of a poet's work are often those "in which the dead poets, his ancestors, assert their immortality most vigorously."

This is not to say that a poet honors the tradition by following it blindly and timidly. To the contrary, he must exert great labor to wrestle with it and to find his place within the stream of the tradition:

> The historical sense involves a perception, not only of the pastness of the past, but of its presence; the historical sense compels a man to write not merely with his own generation in his bones, but with a feeling that the whole of the literature of Europe from Homer and within it the whole of the literature of his own country has a simultaneous existence and composes a simultaneous order.

Although Eliot speaks here with reference to poets, all that he says describes students who have been trained and enculturated in a liberal arts, classical Christian paideia. Students so taught grow into mature people who know where they came from and therefore where they are going. Whatever they do, whether writing or speaking, working or playing, they do it with the full tradition reverberating in their bones.

Such students possess what Eliot calls a "historical sense," a perception of the pastness of the past and of its presence, of its temporal and its timeless nature. To engage in direct dialogue with the Great Books is to achieve a higher vision of one's own place in time, to perceive that the epics of Homer, Virgil, Dante, and Milton, though they were written long ago, are contemporaneous with the student's own day and age. They were written then, but they live now; they and the student who reads them exist for a moment in a sublime, even mystical spiritual-aesthetic space that transcends time and distance.

The poet or student who achieves such a state of illumination realizes, in a flash of insight,

> that art never improves, but that the material of art is never quite the same. He must be aware that the mind of Europe—the mind of his own country—a mind which he learns in time to be much more important than his own private mind—is a mind which changes, and that this change is a development which abandons nothing *en route*, which does not superannuate either Shakespeare, or Homer, or the rock drawing of the Magdalenian draughtsmen.

Although, Eliot admits, we know more than the past, the reason for our greater knowledge is that we have acquired it precisely by studying the past.

A direct, unfiltered encounter with Shakespeare and Homer—not to mention the cave drawings—should breed in us wisdom as well as humility. Even as we celebrate our growth and achievement, we are, or at least should be, struck with a sense of awe, wonder, and gratitude at the legacy that has been passed down to us. Once again, we only

Books Versus Textbooks 73

know more than the great writers of the past because they are what we know.

Textbooks tend to cut us off from the mind of Europe or America by disrupting the dialogue, along with the humility and gratitude that should accompany it. When we travel with Odysseus, Aeneas, and Dante and share in the struggles of Antigone, Orestes, and Telemachus, we become one with the past and the mind of the past. When we are instructed instead to analyze these heroes under a microscope and judge them by our own modern standards, we turn the dialogue into a monologue or a sermon and dissociate our mind from the mind of Europe that made us who we are.

What, then, is the proper way to read and interact with the Great Books? A vivid answer comes down to us from the Renaissance. Machiavelli, who was certainly unafraid to critique the past, nevertheless approached the Great Books with respect and even reverence. In his December 10, 1513, letter to Francesco Vettori, he describes the four hours per day he spends reading the authors of the canon as a stately conversation.

> In the evening, I return to my house, and go into my study. At the door I take off the clothes I have worn all day, mud spotted and dirty, and put on regal and courtly garments. Thus appropriately clothed, I enter into the ancient courts of ancient men, where, being lovingly received, I feed on that food which alone is mine, and which I was born for; I am not ashamed to speak with them and to ask the reasons for their actions, and they courteously answer me. For four hours I feel no boredom and forget every worry; I do not fear poverty, and death does not terrify me. I give myself completely over to the ancients.[2]

The first time I read this passage, I thought that Machiavelli was describing a dinner party, that he was sitting with a group of aristocratic

---

[2]Niccolo Machiavelli, "Letter to Francesco Vettori," trans. Allan Gilbert, in *The Norton Anthology of World Masterpieces*, 6th ed., ed. Maynard Mack et al. (New York: Norton, 1992), 1:1706.

friends around a rich, well-laden table in a majestic banqueting hall. Only when I read it more closely did I realize that Machiavelli was sitting alone in his library with a bevy of his beloved books resting gently on his lap. His dinner conversation was not with living, talkative guests but dead, silent books. Or maybe not so dead or silent.

For Machiavelli, these books and their authors were his friends, confidantes, and sparring partners. As he dialogued with them, he entered Eliot's spiritual-aesthetic zone where time ceases to gnaw and mortality loses itself, for a suspended moment, in eternity. If only we could invite students of all ages into this zone, their enthusiasm for learning would be greatly increased. Then would they learn to respect the tradition while also having the courage, as Machiavelli did, to question it. Then would they wrestle themselves into wisdom.

FOUR

HISTORY VERSUS
SOCIAL STUDIES

I ATTENDED MIDDLE SCHOOL IN THE 1970s. Even by that decade, the teaching of real history had been edged out by something they called social studies. An amalgamation of sociology and anthropology, with touches of psychology, pedagogy, and linguistics, the class introduced us to some very fine myths and legends as well as the practices and rituals of various tribal groups, but it taught us precious little about history.

Worse yet, it did not instill in us any sense of our debt to the past, of what our ancestors accomplished so that we could have what we have and be who we are. We did learn about the civil rights movement in America, and I am grateful that we did, but the sense of debt did not go much further back than that. The history of freedom in the West that lays the foundation for Martin Luther King Jr.'s "Letter from Birmingham Jail" and gives it its logic and its power was mostly absent.

We learned about democracy, but it was more as an abstract, ahistorical synonym for "all people are created equal" or "the majority is always right" than as a political system invented, experimented with, and refined by the long, slow labor of Athenian democrats and Roman republicans, medieval Catholics and reformed Protestants, British Parliamentarians and American Founding Fathers. It was not just the historical context that was missing; it was the human cost and the human drama.

Sometimes there was an overarching theme, a narrative thread, but it was always some version of the myth of evolution. The people of the past were ignorant or prejudiced or superstitious, and we were wise, bias-free, and scientific. Far from bringing the past alive and instilling humility and gratitude, this tired myth removed us even further from the heroes and martyrs and geniuses of the past. They became caricatures to patronize rather than flesh-and-blood people whose struggles and choices, whose fight to bring order out of chaos and beauty out of discord, laid the foundation for our world.

The primary problem with the evolutionary (or progressivist) myth is that it is demonstrably untrue. Can our age really claim to have produced philosophical or creative minds that surpass those of Plato and Aristotle, Augustine and Aquinas, Virgil and Dante, Luther and Calvin, Michelangelo and Leonardo, Shakespeare and Milton? Though time will be the ultimate judge of such things, the thinkers and artists of our day have not, to borrow T. S. Eliot's word, superannuated the work of Plato and others. We have made our contributions, but we have not effected a demonstrable leap forward in aesthetic beauty, philosophical truth, or moral goodness. Despite its great technological advances, the twentieth century was the bloodiest on record. With all the great strides we have made in transportation and communication, we have not really gotten closer or understood each other better. I do not say this to disparage the present but to stop the present from disparaging the past.

That leads to the secondary problem with the cherished myth of progress that has undergirded modern education since the Enlightenment: it impedes any real dialogue with the past. The past is not to be learned from but to be overcome or ridiculed or swept under the rug. History itself is reduced to an impersonal machine, a train whose telos is to get us to the twenty-first-century station, rather than an arena and a crucible that formed and shaped our ancestors, just as it continues to shape and form us today.

History Versus Social Studies

Things have devolved at an alarming rate since I was in grade school, so much so that of all the liberal arts, the one that my incoming freshmen are weakest in is history. They sometimes recognize the names of battles or historical figures, but they do not know how to arrange those battles in any kind of meaningful chronology or how to match up the names they have heard with their historical contributions. The second subject area I have found them to be particularly weak in is geography, a knowledge of which is essential to understanding the major events of history and the ramifications of those events. While Screwtape's historical point of view has prevented students from learning eternal and enduring truths from literature, philosophy, and theology, history has been increasingly effaced from the curriculum of required knowledge.

When I speak with my colleagues from other schools, they make the same complaint. Students have lost their historical sense, a loss that makes it difficult for them to judge and measure the beliefs and actions of our current moment against those of the past. As far back as 1987, E. D. Hirsch noticed and documented this phenomenon in *Cultural Literacy*, which I discuss and dialogue with in chapter fourteen. Although Hirsch demonstrates that modern Americans are weak in a number of different knowledge areas (literature, science, art, philosophy, etc.), all of those areas revolve around history, for it is history that arranges them in time, as geography arranges them in space.

In chapter two I spoke briefly about providential history. In this chapter I will zero in on the more general discipline of history and explain why a firm grounding in it is essential to a classical Christian paideia committed to passing down the traditions and virtues of the past. Without that grounding, students—who grow into citizens—are left adrift: doomed to repeat the errors of the past while gaining nothing of value from its wisdom. Worse yet, they lose a sense of themselves as participants in the flow of history and the choices of their ancestors.

The ideal Greco-Roman, Judeo-Christian paideia would conduct students three times through the eras of Western history. The first sweep through the classical, medieval, Renaissance, Enlightenment, Romantic, Victorian, and modern eras would emphasize key dates, places, figures, and conflicts (grammar school). The second would build on that framework by offering fuller biographies of the central heroes and villains, focusing on their moral choices and motivations (middle school). The third would analyze the patterns of force that converge around the major events that have defined each era (high school). Military, diplomatic, intellectual, and political history should be emphasized, but with a healthy sprinkling of social history to provide students with a feel for what life was like in those eras.[1]

A balance must always be struck between the natural and the human, general lessons and specific details, the historical stage and the individual actors on that stage. Questions of who and why must be asked as often as questions of what and how, and an attempt must be made to discern causes, purposes, and meanings.

Let us take a quick look, then, at each of the historical eras or periods listed above and what students can and must learn from the record they have left.

In chapter one I borrowed several insights from the first volume of Werner Jaeger's *Paideia*. It is significant that Jaeger concludes that volume by making a bold claim: the funeral oration of Pericles recorded in Thucydides's *Peloponnesian War* is not a transcript of the speech but "a free composition by the historian himself," written several decades after the death of Pericles.[2] Why would Thucydides

---

[1]This concept of a three-stage paideia by which students progress from grammar to middle to high school is referred to as the trivium, the "three paths" of grammar, logic, and rhetoric. I discuss and defend the classical trivium in chaps. 10 and 13.

[2]Werner Jaeger, *Paideia: The Ideals of Greek Culture*, 2nd ed., trans. Gilbert Highet (New York: Oxford University Press, 1945), 1:408.

History Versus Social Studies 79

do such a thing? Does Jaeger's claim strip away from the ancient historian his claims to objectivity, sincerity, and veracity? It does not!

As one of the founders, along with Herodotus, of the discipline of history, Thucydides considered it his duty to extract from historical events principles to instruct and guide his readers. Apart from that extraction and instruction, history becomes little more than a collection of random facts and figures, names and dates. Although history should not be reduced to a board to hang moral precepts on, if we do not attempt to learn something from the choices and consequences of our ancestors, then we are merely playing with history rather than engaging and honoring it. One of those key unifying themes is the metanarrative of West versus East. Starting with Herodotus, Thucydides, and the writers of the Old Testament, the civilizations of Greece, Rome, and Israel (what we would now call the "West") understood themselves to be islands of freedom, law, and human dignity in a sea of Eastern nations that had little regard for personal freedom, allowed tyrants to break the law at will, and rejected the equal intrinsic value of all people. The nations grouped under that general heading included the Egyptians, Babylonians, Assyrians, Persians, Philistines, Canaanites, Phoenicians, and Carthaginians.

The pattern became long-running. In the Middle Ages and Renaissance, the West/East culture war manifested itself in terms of an on-and-off struggle between Western Christendom and Eastern Islam—with the Christian Byzantine Empire sometimes aligning with one and sometimes the other. For over a thousand years, the West grappled successively with Arabs, who nearly defeated France in 732; Moors, who controlled Spain for eight hundred years; Saracens, who fought waves of European Crusaders for two centuries; and Turks, whose Ottoman Empire conquered the Byzantines and threatened Europe. In the age of colonialism, Europe sought to extend the benefits of Western culture and civilization to the other continents of the world. In the twentieth century, the Cold War marked yet another incarnation of the culture wars for Western observers, with a totalitarian East represented by the Soviet Union, the Eastern European satellites, and communist China, Korea, Vietnam, and Cuba. Today, while Russia and China continue to enact policies that compromise freedom, law, and human dignity, the Eastern role has also been assigned to terrorist groups and the nations that sponsor them.

I do not mean to overlook the atrocities perpetrated by the West, from the Roman Empire to the present. Just as great ideas and inventions were gifted to the world by the Egyptians, Persians, Chinese, Indians, and Ottomans, so Europeans and Americans have often violated the very principles enshrined in the Great Books. My point is not to advocate oversimplifying the history of West and East but rather to counter the intrinsic "hermeneutics of suspicion" of the West that Paul Ricoeur identified in the work of the three masters of suspicion: the West's own Sigmund Freud, Karl Marx, and Friedrich Nietzsche.

When academics and the students they teach study the West through the lens of suspicion, skepticism, and cynicism, they see only hypocrisy, aggression, oppression, and realpolitik. In a classical Christian paideia, the goal is not to deconstruct the canon but to discern and celebrate the wisdom, justice, courage, and temperance that it held up as ideals. Only once those classical virtues are understood and respected can students identify and critique those people and periods that violated them. Students must not point to American slavery and end the discussion. They must so wrestle with the Great Books and American history as to determine (1) precisely how and why America strayed from the values she claimed to uphold in her founding documents, and (2) how she was able to use those documents and the ideas they embodied to self-correct and eradicate the evil of slavery.

The point is not to present the West as perfect. It was not, and it is not. Nevertheless, the Greco-Roman, Judeo-Christian tradition that underlies the classical Christian paideia set a high bar for freedom, law, and human dignity. It often fell short of that bar, but when it did it possessed the resources to try again. It also shared those resources with other nations. If we lose faith in our tradition, or worse, seek to tear it down in the name of equality or social justice, then we will lose the one tradition that has brought the most real equality and justice into the world.

The claim to exceptionalism is a claim about ideas and institutions, not people. I teach in Houston, the most diverse city in the nation, a diversity that is represented in my university. I have learned from experience that for every White family I meet that embodies the values on which the classical Christian paideia is founded, I meet two (or three) Chinese, Colombian, Nigerian, Pakistani, Mexican, Vietnamese, Filipino, and Indian families that do so to an even greater degree. Most of those families would not have succeeded as well in their home countries as they have here because their home countries do not embody Greco-Roman, Judeo-Christian values the way our country still (mostly) does.

With that as prologue, I will survey some of the things that a historical knowledge of the West/East dichotomy can teach the next generation—if they, and we, will have ears to hear.

<hr />

Through the funeral oration of Pericles, Thucydides reveals his conclusion that Athens—the model for all democracies to come—was successful because she combined equality under the law with a robust meritocracy that allowed brilliant dark-horse candidates such as Pericles to rise up and guide the state. While fighting for justice, she did not give way to the kind of envy and suspicion that forces all people to be the same. Her citizens loved pleasure and beauty, but that love did not make them soft. Great in peace as well as war, her citizens enjoyed their possessions while being willing to sacrifice them for freedom and honor. It is for such reasons that Pericles, Thucydides,

82   PART 1—THE NATURE OF EDUCATION

and Jaeger all hail Athens as the "school of Greece"—which phrase, in the original Greek, is the "paideia of Hellas."

It should come as no surprise that Abraham Lincoln, a dark-horse candidate himself who was well versed in the history of democracy, patterned his "Gettysburg Address" on the funeral oration of Pericles. The question of whether "government of the people, by the people, for the people shall not perish from the earth" has reverberated across Europe and America for twenty-five hundred years. Lincoln, like Thucydides, had a keen understanding of political science and of how power manifests itself in various polities.

Writing a generation before Thucydides on the wars between Greece and Persia rather than the civil war between Athens and Sparta, Herodotus discerned in his study of history not power politics but a clash of civilizations between West and East. Unlike the Egyptians, Babylonians, and Persians, whose cultural history Herodotus describes with the sharp insight of an anthropologist, the Greeks valued freedom, self-determination, and the sanctity of the individual. While he does not demonize the East, he does demonstrate how the democratic city-states of Greece were able to defeat the much more powerful Persian Empire because their free institutions equipped them with free hearts and wills.

Before recounting the exciting battles and Greek heroics of the Persian Wars, Herodotus surveys the cultural and institutional foundations of Greece and Persia. Before that, however, he tells a memorable tale in which the founder of Greek democracy, Solon, meets Croesus of Lydia, a king whom Herodotus presents as an embodiment of all those Eastern vices that stand opposed to freedom, law, and human dignity. In book 1, he has the poor but free-souled Solon visit the ostentatious court of Croesus (chaps. 30-33). After giving Solon a tour of his palace, Croesus asks him whom he considers to be the most fortunate of all men.

Rather than tell the old tyrant what he wants to hear—that he, Croesus, is the most fortunate man—Solon tells two stories of an

History Versus Social Studies 83

obscure Greek man and two obscure Greek brothers who had little money and no power but who died well, having served their family and state with dignity and honor. Croesus is angered by Solon's answer, but the Greek sage tells him that he should count no man lucky until he is dead—for no one knows what strange twists fortune might take before the end.

As it turns out, Croesus falls victim to just such a twist and is almost executed by Cyrus, founder of the Persian Empire. He is saved from being burned at the stake only when he calls out the name of Solon, and Cyrus halts the execution to ask him who this Solon is. Croesus tells the tale, and Cyrus makes him one of his chief advisers, leading to several situations where Croesus's advice saves him from death. Thus, Herodotus concludes, did the poor but free-souled Solon save the lives of two Eastern tyrants.

This story remains in the mind of the reader as Herodotus works his way through his lengthy history, serving as a sort of motif to the clash of civilizations that unfolds before our eyes. Though modern historians might accuse Herodotus of simplifying that clash or of being an ethnocentric jingoist, his history provides a window into an ongoing struggle between liberty and tyranny, the rights of the individual and the oppression of the masses, freedom of religion and of speech and social-political conformity.

<hr>

The same struggle that Herodotus explores between Greece and Persia can, as I explained a moment ago, be discerned in the struggles between the Jews and the Egyptians (Exodus), Philistines (Judges), Canaanites (Joshua), Assyrians, and Babylonians (1–2 Kings), the Romans and the Carthaginians, the Crusaders and the Saracens, the Venetians and the Ottoman Turks, the Western democracies and the Eastern Soviet bloc.

Although Polybius, the great historian of the Punic Wars who witnessed Rome's final defeat of Carthage in 146 BC, was Greek, his careful study of nations and their characters convinced him that Rome embodied the highest virtues of Western culture and the best political institutions for civilizing the world. These virtues and institutions allowed her to defeat not only the Carthaginians but, in the same year, the Greek leagues that had devolved and lost their way in the two centuries since Alexander the Great.

The crowning achievement of Polybius's *Histories* comes in book 6 when he unpacks the mixed constitution of the Roman Republic and shows how the political checks and balances instituted by Rome provided her with a strong but supple government structure that enabled her to defeat and absorb tribe after tribe and nation after nation. The framers of the American Constitution and the writers of the *Federalist Papers* learned from Polybius and successfully integrated similar checks and balances into our own fledgling democracy. It is no exaggeration to say that Polybius's analysis of Roman history helped America's Founding Fathers, all of whom were nurtured in a classical Christian paideia, to avoid the mistakes of the past.

A century after Polybius, the Roman historian Livy, while not contradicting Polybius's reading, located Rome's strength in another dimension of her historical development. In book 1 of his *Histories*, Livy argues that Rome had two foundings: the first by her first king, Romulus the man of war; the second by her second king, Numa the man of peace. Whereas Romulus taught the surrounding tribes of Italy to fear Rome for her military prowess, Numa taught them to reverence her for her piety and devotion. Under Romulus, Livy explains, "Rome's neighbours had considered her not so much as a city as an armed camp in their midst threatening the general peace; now they came to revere her so profoundly as a community dedicated wholly to worship, that the mere thought of offering her violence seemed to them like sacrilege."[3]

---

[3]Livy, *The Early History of Rome*, trans. Aubrey de Sélincourt (New York: Penguin, 1971), 56.

History Versus Social Studies

Which is not to say that Western historians are mere propagandists lavishing uncritical praise on their own nations and cultures. Livy himself censures his fellow Romans for their slow slide into decadence in the century following their defeat of Carthage. Plutarch, while praising such great military and political leaders as Alexander the Great and Julius Caesar, uncovers their flaws of vanity and ambition. Suetonius and Tacitus spare no punches in their scorn for Nero's excesses and indulgences.

Luke, one of the finest historians of the ancient world, records a sermon by the first Christian martyr, Stephen, in which he surveys the history of the Jewish people from Abraham to Christ (Acts 7). Though Stephen cleaves closely to the major figures and events of the Old Testament, in the closing lines of his sermon, he offers an interpretative analysis of that history that convicts and then enrages the Pharisees and the Jewish mob:

> Ye stiffnecked and uncircumcised in heart and ears, ye do always resist the Holy Ghost: as your fathers did, so do ye. Which of the prophets have not your fathers persecuted? and they have slain them which shewed before of the coming of the Just One; of whom ye have been now the betrayers and murderers: Who have received the law by the disposition of angels, and have not kept it. (Acts 7:51-53)

Hardly a celebration of God's chosen people, Stephen's pointed commentary exposes a running theme of rebellion and disobedience that the Jewish leaders were unable to see and unwilling to acknowledge. Had they done so, they would not have crucified the very Messiah whose coming had been foretold by priest, prophet, and king.

The mission of the historian, the fruit of which he passes down to each new generation of readers, is to discern in the flow of events patterns to which the common man is blind. The historians of the canon are like the magi of Matthew 2, Gentiles who saw in the star over Bethlehem a portent and a prophecy missed by the keenest eyes of God's people. Once the historian (or the magus) points out the pattern and its meaning, however, that knowledge becomes the shared wealth of the nation that preserves and studies his work. The last several generations of Americans have squandered that wealth; more disturbingly, they have failed to bequeath it to their children and grandchildren.

Eusebius in the fourth century and Bede in the eighth wrote ecclesiastical histories: the former of the early church; the latter of Britain's early medieval period. Both offer providential histories of the spread of the gospel through pagan Rome and pagan England. To read their works is to gain insight into a historical process that is overseen by God's hand yet subject to the obedience and obstinacy, sacrifices and sins of counselors and kings, missionaries and martyrs.

In Dante's *Commedia*, we get not only history told poetically but a powerful plea for the value of *knowing* history. Many modern readers think Dante's contemporaries would have recognized all the poet's historical allusions without the need of notes. In fact, *The Divine Comedy* was almost immediately annotated by various editors. By lacing his epic with layer upon layer of historical references, Dante hoped to force his readers to engage more fully with the ebb and flow of historical events.

Indeed, part of the problem with the neutrals, or opportunists, who are condemned to spend eternity in the vestibule of hell (*Inferno* 3), is that they removed themselves from the struggles and decisions of history. Because they refused to take sides on earth, their punishment is to dwell neither in heaven nor hell, perpetually chasing after a flag they can never reach. For Dante, God is an active, involved God who participates in the flow of history. To be ignorant of that flow, or, worse, to remain passively on the sidelines, is to exempt oneself from the sacred drama whose playwright is God.

As the Middle Ages gave way to the Renaissance, new dangers and challenges arose, calling for new heroes to meet them and new

History Versus Social Studies 87

historians to make sense of them. One of those historians identified and analyzed a new type of hero who was neither soldier, nor politician, nor priest. His name was Giorgio Vasari, and in his *Lives of the Artists* (1550, 1568), he hails such artistic geniuses as Giotto, Lorenzo Ghiberti, Donatello, Fra Angelico, Sandro Botticelli, Michelangelo, Leonardo da Vinci, Raphael, and Titian as the supreme representatives of their age. The great artists are lifted above other men, not by power or wealth but by magnificence of soul and vision, fidelity to nature, and virtuous living.

Contrast Vasari's vision with that of his older contemporary, Machiavelli, both of whom were patronized by the Medici family. In the latter's *Prince* (1532), the heroes of the Renaissance are those who know how to ride the waves of fortune and seize control of political power. While Vasari's artists harvest the zeitgeist and incarnate it in timeless works of art, Machiavelli's political leaders use violence as well as virtue, deceit as well as truth to seize power and establish, by patronage and fiat, what that zeitgeist will be.

Just as Renaissance historians Vasari and Machiavelli offer two different kinds of heroes with contrasting virtues and talents, so Enlightenment historians Edward Gibbon and Alexis de Tocqueville offer opposing readings of the relationship between a healthy state and the Christian religion. In the former's *Decline and Fall of the Roman Empire* (1776), Christianity is made to carry much of the blame for the unraveling of the Roman Empire. In the latter's *Democracy in America* (1835), it is the Christian faith that provides the glue to hold together the American colonies: unlike in France, where church and state are at odds, in America, liberty and religion support each other.

In nineteenth-century England, John Ruskin looked back to the period of the Gothic cathedrals to find man at his most creative and free, while Thomas Carlyle praised charismatic leaders as the force that propels history forward. In contrast to these romantic readings of history and its heroes, Thomas Babington Macaulay offered a

Victorian Whig interpretation that presented history as leading unstoppably toward liberal democracy and constitutional monarchy.

In the closing decade of the twentieth century, Francis Fukuyama, channeling Georg Wilhelm Friedrich Hegel and Marx as well as Macaulay, published a book, *The End of History and the Last Man* (1992), that carried the Whig interpretation of history to its logical end, with a prophecy that liberal democracy would prove triumphant across the globe. Although the destruction of the Twin Towers on September 11, 2001, by Islamic terrorists cast Fukuyama's thesis into serious doubt, his progressivist reading of history as an evolution from religious superstition to scientific enlightenment continues to hold sway in many social studies classes today.

◀━━▶

I could give more examples, but I hope this will suffice to demonstrate how vital the discipline of history is to a liberal arts education that would preserve and pass on its traditions to the next generation. In order to interpret the leaders and movements that defined the past and thus the future, the factors that caused the rise and fall of great nations, and the nature of human purpose and destiny, students must be provided with a firm grounding in history. They will not be able to assess or understand the various readings of battles and heroism, culture and civilization that I surveyed above unless they have at least a working knowledge of the eras of history and the nations, people, and ideas that dominated them.

Indeed, I hope that close readers of this chapter experienced a fresh engagement with history as they made their way through my survey. One of the greatest joys of an education grounded in the Great Books is that it forges connections between multiple eras, genres, and disciplines. It enables students to trace patterns of cause and effect, influence and outcome, necessary skills for reading the times. I hope readers will notice that I included at the end of my survey several historians—Machiavelli, Gibbon, Macaulay, Fukuyama—whom I do not altogether agree with. Critique, comparison and contrast, and disputation are all essential elements of a classical Christian paideia.

In the opening paragraph of this chapter, I lamented the displacement of history by social studies. I did so for three reasons. First, sociological-anthropological approaches to teaching tend to press the volitional human element out of its study of the past. Second, they tend to brush over the facts of history—names, dates, battles, successions, and so on—that students must learn if they are to understand the past at all. Third, they downplay, dismiss, or demonize the unique and lasting achievements of the West, inspiring smugness rather than gratitude in students and leaving them incapable of sifting good ideas from bad. Ideologies *have* risen out of the study of history, but social studies classes, like textbooks, too often *begin* with an ideological position on the nature of man and then evade and elide the kind of vigorous study of history that would allow that ideology to be put to the test. I believe that the difficulty many modern European and American academics and social commentators now have in seeing value in Western civilization can be traced to the eclipse of traditional history and the rise of progressive social studies.

That leads me to the next chapter, where I will argue that the overall pedagogical shift from the humanities to the social sciences has compromised education, leaving students adrift with no sense of themselves as human beings who are part of a tradition and no fixed standards of goodness, truth, or beauty.

FIVE

HUMANITIES VERSUS SOCIAL SCIENCES

HERODOTUS, THUCYDIDES, SOCRATES, PLATO, Aristotle, and Cicero laid the foundations for psychology, sociology, anthropology, political science, pedagogy, and linguistics. Nevertheless, the social sciences as we know them today are firmly rooted in the secular Enlightenment of the late eighteenth and early nineteenth centuries (Jean-Jacques Rousseau, Immanuel Kant, Auguste Comte, Henri de Saint-Simon, etc.) and saw their flowering in the late nineteenth and early twentieth centuries in the works of such thinkers as Karl Marx, Sigmund Freud, Charles Darwin, Friedrich Nietzsche, Herbert Spencer, John Dewey, Émile Durkheim, Max Weber, and Ferdinand de Saussure.

By identifying the social sciences as coming out of the secular Enlightenment, I do not mean to imply that all social scientists are atheists who harbor an anti-God animus. I do, however, very much mean to imply that the modern social sciences rest on a worldview that runs counter to the traditional Judeo-Christian, Greco-Roman view of man—and therefore education—on which this book is based. Although many, if not most, individual social scientists believe that each of us was created in the image of God (and therefore possesses innate and essential value) but is broken and depraved (and therefore needs the kinds of limits embodied in the institutions of church and family), the presuppositions on which the social sciences are founded

Humanities Versus Social Sciences 91

ultimately stand at odds with and even contradict the dual nature of man as inherently good but intrinsically fallen.

The methodological naturalism that undergirds the social sciences does not preclude the existence of God, but it does demand natural explanations grounded solely in physical, material processes. This limitation also undergirds the modern—post-Enlightenment, rather than post-Renaissance—natural sciences, but at least there the objects being studied are not noble-but-sinful creatures who are as fully spiritual as they are fully physical. The social sciences treat man as an object stripped of supernatural design and purpose in a manner analogous to how the modern natural sciences treat nature and the animal kingdom.

Again, most social scientists do not interact with flesh-and-blood human beings in such a manner, but that is because they do not live out the presuppositions on which their disciplines, at least in their modern iterations, rest. That is also the case with most Darwinians, who, despite the evolutionary theory to which they pay allegiance, do not treat their fellow men as products of a blind, undirected process of natural selection that cares little for the individual. Of course, in the death and/or reeducation camps of Adolf Hitler, Joseph Stalin, Mao Zedong, and Pol Pot, not to mention the eugenic labs of early twentieth-century America, the foundational tenets of Darwinian natural selection (survival of the fittest) were put into practice with ruthless scientific precision. Thanks to the brutality of those doctrinaire Darwinians, most modern people have been cured of the desire to enact in the real world the logical consequences of Darwinian evolution.[1]

Still, the social sciences as disciplines, as opposed to those who study and teach them, are shaped by and founded on Darwin's rejection of the *imago Dei* (man is not a special creation of God but a product of random physical forces and material processes) coupled

---

[1]See Richard Weikart, *Darwinian Racism: How Darwinism Influenced Hitler, Nazism, and White Nationalism* (Seattle: Discovery Institute, 2022).

with Rousseau's rejection of the fall (man is not born with original sin or natural depravity but is corrupted by social institutions). Although it would be false to accuse the social sciences of being Marxist in any doctrinaire sense, the understanding of man, and therefore education, that they uphold comports with the view Marx propounds in the "Author's Preface" to his *A Contribution to the Critique of Political Economy*.

Marx is a reductionist, for he reduces the intellectual, emotional, and spiritual complexity of man to simple physical, material causes. For Marx, all things, and he means *all* things, are determined by the economic modes of production:

> The mode of production in material life determines the general character of the social, political and spiritual processes of life. It is not the consciousness of men that determines their existence, but, on the contrary, their social existence determines their consciousness. At a certain stage of their development, the material forces of production in society come in conflict with the existing relations of production, or—what is but a legal expression for the same thing—with the property relations within which they had been at work before. From forms of development of the forces of production these relations turn into their fetters. Then comes the period of social revolution. With the change of the economic foundation the entire immense superstructure is more or less rapidly transformed. In considering such transformations the distinction should always be made between the material transformation of the economic conditions of production which can be determined with the precision of natural science, and the legal, political, religious, aesthetic or philosophic—in short ideological forms in which men become conscious of this conflict and fight it out. Just as our opinion of an individual is not based on what he thinks of himself, so can we not judge of such a period of transformation by its own consciousness; on the contrary, this consciousness must rather be explained from the contradictions of material life, from the existing conflict between social forces of production and the relations of production.[2]

---

[2]Karl Marx, *A Contribution to the Critique of Political Economy*, ed. and trans. N. I. Stone (Chicago: Charles H. Kerr, 1904), 11-12.

Humanities Versus Social Sciences

For Marx and his heirs, man is not a free, moral agent who chooses and stumbles, builds and destroys, loves and deceives. He is a product of a socioeconomic milieu over which he has no control. Not only are our legal, political, religious, ethical, and philosophic systems ideological products of economic transformations; our very consciousness is a construct of those same transformations.

The disciplines that make up the social sciences may not state the situation quite so baldly and crudely as Marx, but they nevertheless ascribe to a reductionist view of man that treats us as products of economic or biological or sexual forces that ultimately determine our beliefs, our institutions, and our perceptions of ourselves, our world, and our Creator. We are not unique individuals endowed with the potential for personal goodness but perennially guilty of personal evil, but members of groups that often stand over against each other as oppressors and oppressed, victimizers and victims.[3]

Again, most social scientists do not view people this way; some have even suggested changes to society that have brought about real freedom and justice. My contention is not with individual social scientists but with the (generally unstated) presuppositions on which the modern social sciences rest. While the foundational tenets of Marx and Darwin threaten to strip human beings, especially students, of their agency and inherent value, those of Rousseau too often blind us to our innate, universal capacity for greed, prejudice, and disobedience. These twin (false) tenets about man's nature, I would argue, have led to three pedagogical initiatives that have either prevented schools from fulfilling their proper mission or turned that mission awry.

First, social science–driven schools inevitably place too heavy a focus on classroom management. As a result, students end up being more herded than taught, controlled than nurtured. It is and has

---

[3]See Neil Shenvi and Pat Sawyer, *Critical Dilemma: The Rise of Critical Theories and Social Justice Ideology—Implications for the Church and Society* (Eugene, OR: Harvest House, 2023).

94 PART 1—THE NATURE OF EDUCATION

always been necessary to keep order in the classroom; but the utilitarian science of management, which applies the same methods to schools, cafeterias, hospitals, factories, prisons, and asylums, rests on a very different view of man.[4] Too often, classroom management becomes less about order for the sake of learning and virtue and more about the objectification of children for motives that may or may not enhance that learning and virtue. Because such objectification flows naturally out of the kind of reductive thinking to which the social sciences are ever susceptible, classroom management easily sinks into regimentation, coercion, and regulation for its own sake.

Second, schools grounded in the theories of Darwin and Marx can easily morph from safe spaces where traditions are passed down and virtues instilled to sites of social engineering where whatever ideas or causes are fashionable at the time are indoctrinated into students. Here are some of the causes that were pressed on me as a public school student in the 1970s, my children in the 2000s, and my incoming college freshmen in the 2020s: antidrinking, antismoking, hygiene, evolution, family planning, feminism, safe sex, environmentalism, gay rights, multiculturalism, equity, identity politics, and transgenderism. Though I will admit that some of these causes are admirable, I object to the centrality such causes have played and continue to play in public schools. More specifically, I am troubled by the tone that too often accompanies the promotion of these causes. Rather than be taught in conjunction with Judeo-Christian virtues—do unto others as you would have them do unto you; care for your body as the temple of the Holy Spirit; keep the marriage bed pure; be a steward of God's creation—they are offered as substitutes for traditional religion and morality. Worse yet, rather than work together with parental authority,

---

[4]Ironically, Michel Foucault, a postmodern heir of Marx and Nietzsche, exposes this social regimentation in his *Discipline and Punish: The Birth of the Prison*, trans. Alan Sheridan (New York: Vintage, 1995).

Humanities Versus Social Sciences 95

students are too often taught to feel morally superior to their backward, superstitious parents.[5]

Third, schools that take their cue from Rousseau and Freud will adopt a therapeutic, utopian approach to education that seeks to set students free from the social, ethical, aesthetic, and sexual inhibitions of their parents, churches, and cultures. Expressive-autonomous individualism, not courage, wisdom, self-control, justice, faith, hope, and love, will be the goal and purpose of education. Rather than cultivate the virtues, train the affections, and order the desires of students, such schools will teach students to construct their own values, think for themselves, and be true to who they are. Above all, students will not be allowed to feel guilt or shame when they do something that is wrong or shameful. It is always someone else and not the student who is at fault. As long as the student feels good about himself, then the actual content being taught is secondary. Reason and logic, not to mention ethics and morality, must take second place to sincere feelings and authentic emotions.[6]

I am aware that I have written in strong, hyperbolic, even polemical terms in this chapter. Let me repeat again that my criticism is of ideas, not people. Most teachers are hardworking public servants who do their best with what they are given. Likewise, most undergraduate and graduate students who major in sociology, anthropology, psychology, and education are trying to better understand humanity and to serve the public good. Still, I maintain that the ideological and pedagogical line I have attempted to draw from social-scientific presuppositions to educational practice is not far off the mark. Classroom management, social engineering, and therapeutic utopianism not only dominate the school day but drive out the true mission

---

[5] Abraham Lincoln famously expressed the power of public schools to set the tenor of society thus: "The philosophy of the school room in one generation will be the philosophy of government in the next."

[6] See Greg Lukianoff and Jonathan Haidt, *The Coddling of the American Mind: How Good Intentions and Bad Ideas Are Setting Up a Generation for Failure* (New York: Penguin, 2018).

of education: to pass the torch of tradition and create virtuous, morally self-regulating citizens.[7]

Choices, and ideas, have consequences.[8]

As the title of this chapter suggests, I will be arguing that for education to fulfill its true mission, it needs to be removed from the control of the social sciences and returned to the humanities. Unfortunately, a disturbing trend that has accelerated over the last half century has rendered this move highly problematic. Increasingly since the 1960s, the humanities have been absorbed by the social sciences and have traded in their humanistic methods, purposes, and view of man for ones that are essentially Marxist.

As an English professor, I would like to be able to claim that the fault for this lies solely with the social scientists, that they consciously and aggressively defeated and colonized us. Alas, the last several generations of English, history, government, philosophy, and theology professors have initiated and welcomed the takeover, desperate to gain the "scientific" prestige that comes with the social sciences.

In much of academia, humanities professors have so lost their humble confidence in and grateful respect for the canonical writers that they are no longer willing or able to learn anything from them. All they can do is appropriate social-scientific methods to make themselves feel superior to the authors and texts they have purportedly devoted their lives to studying. They have done so by reading and teaching the Great Books through the interpretive and appropriating lens of literary theory.

Please do not confuse literary theory with the age-old genre of literary criticism, which has been practiced by such sage critics as Aristotle,

---

[7]For a book that sets itself a task parallel to my own—to trace the negative influences of Marx and the Frankfurt school on the modern evangelical church—see Voddie Baucham, *Fault Lines: The Social Justice Movement and Evangelicalism's Looming Catastrophe* (Washington, DC: Salem Books, 2021).

[8]For the classic study of how the faulty, antihumanistic presuppositions I critique in this chapter have born bad fruit, see Richard Weaver, *Ideas Have Consequences*, expanded ed. (Chicago: University of Chicago Press, 2013).

Horace, Longinus, Sir Philip Sidney, John Dryden, Alexander Pope, Samuel Johnson, William Wordsworth, Samuel Taylor Coleridge, Percy Bysshe Shelley, Matthew Arnold, T. S. Eliot, John Crowe Ransom, Cleanth Brooks, and Northrop Frye. For all of these writers, many of whom were poets as well, criticism was a tool for opening up literature and enhancing its influence on readers. Since the social-scientific seizure and annexation of the humanities, literary theory has been used to empty the Great Books of their authority and lay them open to modern and postmodern scrutiny. Marxist, feminist, postcolonialist, deconstructionist, and queer theories dominate the teaching of the humanities in most of America's Ivy League and state universities and even in many small private colleges, including ones that identify as Christian.

Traditional schools place Shakespeare at the center of the curriculum on account of the purity of his poetry, but that is not the only reason. Shakespeare is studied because his plays take up and wrestle with universal, crosscultural themes and characters that are vital to what it means to be human. As contemporary playwright Ben Jonson said of his poetic rival: "He was not of an age, but for all time!" Most readers today, I believe, would agree with this assessment. Not so theory-based critics who treat Shakespeare not as a man whose genius allowed him to transcend his time and place but as a product of Elizabethan power politics. Do not get me wrong. The more we know about Shakespeare's age, the better we can understand his plays. The problem is when historical study gives way to historicism, and the poet is reduced to his socioeconomic milieu or to his race, class, and/or gender.[9]

And the same goes for Homer, Virgil, Dante, and Milton; Plato, Aristotle, and Cicero; Augustine, Thomas Aquinas, and Martin Luther.

---

[9]In *A Glossary of Literary Terms*, 6th ed. (Fort Worth, TX: Harcourt Brace Jovanovich, 1993), 249, M. H. Abrams lists the following presupposition as one shared by nearly all proponents of the theoretical school of new historicism: "Literature does not occupy a 'trans-historical' aesthetic realm which is independent of economic, social, and political conditions and is subject to timeless criteria of artistic value. Instead, a literary text is simply one of many kinds of texts—religious, philosophical, legal, scientific, and so on—all of which are subject to the particular conditions of a time and place, and among which the literary text has neither unique status nor special privilege."

An educational system driven by the social sciences will eventually and inevitably rob the Great Books of their power to transmit from one generation to the next the accumulated wisdom of our ancestors. It will treat those seminal thinkers as artifacts of the past, creations of a less-enlightened age who cannot really teach us anything. Needless to say, the theorists who reduce the authors of the canon to products of their socioeconomic milieu believe that they themselves have the power to study all ages, including their own, with a removed, critical eye unfettered by the social ideologies and economic modes of production that define their own milieu.

My apologies if I am sounding more polemical here than in previous chapters, but education cannot perform its job of preserving civilization and building character as long as it is chained to a worldview that reduces human beings to physical forces and material processes. Education must be liberated from its century-long enslavement to the social sciences *and* from its half-century-long embrace of antihumanistic humanities programs if it is to thrive again and accomplish the goals for which it exists.

Only once the humanities are restored to their proper identity, mission, and methods as well as to their central role in the curriculum of grade schools and liberal arts colleges alike will education (paideia) be able to resume its true function and raison d'être. Only then can viable alternatives, such as classical Christian education, be offered to counter the regime of classroom management, social engineering, and therapeutic utopianism that shapes education today and prevents it from fulfilling its civilization-preserving purpose.

First, the antidote to classroom management must come from within and not from without. Utilitarian methods of regimentation are powerless to change the heart. For students to be engaged fully in their education, they must have instilled in them a love and joy for learning. But that instilling can only be accomplished by teachers (and professors) who themselves take love and joy in what they teach:

not resentment or grievance or self-righteousness but real love and joy, accompanied by humility, wonder, awe, and gratitude.

The humanities, when set free to perform their traditional pedagogical ministry, have the power to invite students of all ages into a dialogue with the canonical writers, into that great conversation that has been going on since the Five Books of Moses and the *Iliad* and *Odyssey* of Homer. Though there have always been critics who have accused the Great Books of being elitist and exclusivist, when the humanities are properly taught, they are truly democratic, for they equip and empower students of all backgrounds to enter into the dialogue and even add their own voices to it.

That is not to say that the humanities cannot be and have not been taught in a dry, legalistic manner. But the fault therein lies not with the Great Books themselves but with teachers who have not been transformed by their reading of them, who have used them as a stick to beat down the enthusiasm and individuality of their students rather than as a ladder to help them ascend to better versions of themselves. Students who perceive that their teachers are invested in the dialogue and that they have been convicted and changed by it will themselves come to feel invested in the dialogue—and when that happens, they will need less management.

Second, an education that is firmly grounded in the humanistic Judeo-Christian understanding of man as made in God's image but fallen will not be lured in by fashionable causes that treat people as members of groups rather than as individuals. Such an education will be too focused on universal issues and enduring truths to be sidetracked by this or that cause célèbre. Its goal will not be to indoctrinate children or to set them in opposition to their parents. To the contrary, it will equip them with the proper grammatical, logical, and rhetorical skills to construct and defend their own arguments.

It will neither incite them to dismiss the authority of their parents out of hand nor force them to blindly kowtow to it. Rather, it will

provide them with objective tools to analyze the wisdom of their ancestors and to assess those aspects of the tradition that need to be
maintained and those aspects that could do with a cultural tweak. The
goal of education is not to teach students to think for themselves but
to teach them to think rightly, not to encourage them to be true to
what they think they are but to challenge them to be true to what they
truly are. Such a goal is not achieved by reading newspapers and ob-
sessing over current events; it is achieved by studying and wrestling
with works that have passed the test of time and that have shown
themselves to be relevant across multiple ages and cultures.

Third, a humanities-driven curriculum that honors the wisdom of
the past will help teachers and students alike to recognize the perils of
utopian thinking. Sociology and psychology may provide students
with a scientific nomenclature for discussing what it means to be
human, but only a firm knowledge of the literature, history, and philosophy of the past will allow students to study the successes and
failures of real people living real lives in real time. Apart from that
grand perspective, students, and society itself, risk forgetting what hap-
pened in the past when people and nations threw off the reins of tradition to experiment with the ethical limits and moral boundaries that
make us human and prevent us from committing social suicide.[10]

Civilization is not a given; it is a beautiful but delicate garden that
needs to be cultivated and weeded if it is to survive and thrive. Our
children are gardens as well, and we who teach them are the gar-
deners. Will we honor their true nature, or, in our desire to manage
and control, will we turn them into something they were never meant
to be?

---

[10]A recent book that sounds a similar warning is Rod Dreher's *Live Not by Lies: A Manual for
Christian Dissidents* (New York: Sentinel, 2020). Arthur Koestler's 1940 novel, *Darkness at Noon*
(New York: Bantam, 1984), and George Orwell's 1949 novel, *1984* (New York: Signet, 2023), also
connect totalitarian ideas to totalitarian rule.

SIX

GOODNESS, TRUTH, AND BEAUTY VERSUS RELATIVISM

AT THE END OF MY INTRODUCTION, I noted that I would be referring often to Plato's three transcendentals: the Good, the True, and the Beautiful. Whereas the goodness, truth, and beauty that we encounter in our fallen, broken world are partial and relative, Goodness, Truth, and Beauty point to absolute standards of moral and ethical behavior, philosophical and theological reality, and aesthetic balance and harmony. Classical Christian education puts a heavy emphasis on these standards, for it understands that one of its primary goals is to shape and mold students in accordance with such standards. Rather than reinterpret the transcendentals to accommodate the cultural and political causes of the day—as progressive education (and progressive Christianity!) too often does—it instructs and challenges students to use the transcendentals as a lens through which to interpret the key issues and struggles of the day.

One way to frame this vital distinction is to look back to the *Protagoras* of Plato, which takes up a question that is central to assessing the proper nature and function of paideia: Can virtue be taught? If it can, who is the best type of teacher? Jaeger explains that Plato distinguishes carefully between "the sophist, who crams people's minds indiscriminately with all sorts of knowledge . . . and Socrates, the physician of the soul, who holds that learning is 'the food of the soul' and begins by asking whether it does good or harm."[1] Whereas the Sophists measured what they taught against fragmented and relativistic standards that altered from *polis* to *polis* and culture to culture, Socrates held up fixed standards of virtue and vice, good and evil, justice and injustice to which the soul must be taught to conform itself.

For Socrates and Plato, it "is knowledge of the true standard which inevitably dictates our choice and determines our will."[2] It is the role of the teacher and the goal of paideia to clarify and reinforce that standard. What Socrates's age needed, argues Jaeger, "was to recognize one supreme standard, which was binding on all alike because it expressed the innermost nature of man, and on which education could attach its highest task, the molding of men to the pattern of true areté. All the skill and knowledge of the sophists could never lead to areté—the only thing that could was the deeper 'knowledge' about which Socrates so constantly enquired."[3]

Although I do not mean to claim that today's educators are Sophists, I would argue that much modern, progressive education is sophistical in nature. Just as the Sophists of ancient Greece were moral and cultural relativists who shunned and often denied fixed, transcendent truths, so our public schools have too often ridden the moral-cultural bandwagon of whatever happens to be in vogue or cutting edge at the time. Classical Christian education, in contrast, seeks to pass down and preserve time-tested standards that are strong and perennial, that ride above the waves of cultural change and compromise.

If education is to regain its soul and fulfill its telos, it must move from the sophistical back to the Socratic. I do not mean that all classes must be taught by a dialectical method of question-and-answer.

---

[1] Werner Jaeger, *Paideia: The Ideals of Greek Culture*, trans. Gilbert Highet (New York: Oxford University Press, 1943), 2:109-10.
[2] Jaeger, *Paideia*, 122.
[3] Jaeger, *Paideia*, 124.

Goodness, Truth, and Beauty Versus Relativism

I mean, rather, that schools and teachers must reclaim the centrality of definition to the educational enterprise. Most of Plato's dialogues involve the exploding of definitions that are culturally and temporally relative (justice, courage, love) to arrive at definitions that are absolute and transcendent (Justice, Courage, Love). If students are not pressed to locate and make their decisions in accordance with absolute standards of Goodness, Truth, and Beauty, Justice, Courage, and Love, they will live their lives, and society with them, in a dim, debilitating haze of moral, philosophical, and aesthetic relativism.

As I will discuss in chapter eleven, John Dewey, generally hailed as the father of modern (progressive/pragmatic) education, had, like Rousseau before him, a strong aversion to ready-made truths: truths, that is, that have been inherited from the past rather than arrived at through experience. While I concede the importance of experience to the educational enterprise and the need for students to analyze and critique the errors of the past, I nevertheless maintain that individuals and societies need ready-made truths if they are to survive. Truth is not a negotiable thing that is constantly up for grabs; circumstances *do* influence our decision making, but that does not mean situational ethics should or can take the place of fixed, transcendent ethical standards. To follow the "always reforming" motto of the Protestant Reformation does not necessitate or legitimize the abandonment of the theological orthodoxy handed down by the ecumenical councils and creeds.

As I argued in the introduction to this book, man is a moral agent who organizes, builds, and civilizes. But he must do so within parameters, or he will destroy himself and his society. To find the proper balance between his glory and his depravity, his physical and spiritual nature, the raging inner beast that pulls down and the better angel within that draws up, he needs precisely those ready-made truths that come to him from revelation and tradition. Though our consciousness develops over time, and though social contracts often need to be renegotiated, that development and renegotiation must be carried out within proper limits if they are to lead to emotional-spiritual health and political-social stability.

The shift from classical Christian education to progressive-pragmatic (not to be confused with liberal-commonsensical) education began slowly in the late eighteenth century, was achieved in the late nineteenth, and accelerated in the late twentieth. As I will discuss in part two, progressive-pragmatic education privileges experience over authority, prefers child-centered classrooms to teacher-centered ones, and dismisses established (ready-made) curricula as flawed, backward looking, and reactionary. The answer to this shift is not to return to an overly authoritarian classroom that refuses to question the ancient pronouncements of an Aristotle or Aquinas, that crushes the initiative and individuality of students, and that looks with suspicion on any changes to teaching methods.

Instead, there needs to be a reclamation and rehabilitation of the verities, the eternal principles, the transcendentals of Goodness, Truth, and Beauty. Transcendentals, in philosophy, in logic, in education, are not things we argue *for* but things we argue *from*. They are the starting place, the foundation, the groundless ground on which rational thinking and ethical behavior are built. Apart from them, there can be vocational training in specific skills, but there can be no liberal arts education: no education, that is, that frees the mind from the idols of the marketplace.

Sophistical education may seem to free the mind by disconnecting it from absolutes; instead, it enslaves it to whatever fashion or trend is currently in vogue. Progressive education cannot provide the necessary ground for instilling reason and virtue in students, because progress is not a fixed quantity. It is too slippery to function as a standard for measuring growth, because it is constantly changing. One cannot *achieve* progress, for once it is achieved, it itself becomes a ready-made truth from which we must progress.

Progressive education is inherently unstable, for to privilege experience over authority is to favor ephemeral experiences over the collective wisdom that is gained through multiple generations of individual and communal experiences. To fashion the classroom around the student rather than the teacher is to place education in the hands of young people with no experience instead of people who have had the double experience of being students and teachers; it is tantamount to inviting patients to choose the drugs that look best to them rather than the ones recommended by experienced physicians.

Worse yet, to replace the Great Books with contemporary works fueled by the latest fad or cause or grievance is to so narrow the scope of education as to leave students unprepared to react to the universal human challenges that we all must learn to wrestle with. An engineer who only knows how to use hammers and nails will not be able to construct a home; a liberal arts student who can only respond to and be fashionably outraged by the latest media sensation will not function well in a human world fraught with concerns and crises that transcend the political passions of the moment.

All of this is not to say that students or teachers can claim a firm understanding or possession of the Good, True, and Beautiful. Our status as fallen creatures living in a fallen world, together with the deep and unavoidable influences of our time, culture, and socialization, guarantee that we cannot grasp all that is Good, True, or Beautiful. Still, by setting our sights on absolute standards and by wrestling with the great authors who wrestled with those standards, we can establish moral, philosophical, and aesthetic boundaries that will keep teachers, students, and schools on track. If we do that faithfully, we will find that our students *will* take up social causes, perhaps even progressive ones. They will do so, however, from a position of wisdom, for they will be able to set those causes in a proper historical and ethical framework and apply to them recurring principles of cause and effect, choice and consequence.

My favorite vision of what a student thus educated would look like comes from the image of the well-educated gentleman that the great Victorian critic, philosopher, and theologian Cardinal Newman describes in *The Idea of a University* (discourse 7, chap. 10). Originally delivered in 1852 as part of a series of nine lectures intended to help lay the groundwork for a Catholic liberal arts university in Ireland, discourse 7 ("Knowledge Viewed in Relation to Professional Skills") distinguishes, as I do in chapter one above, between the kind of narrow, practical education offered at a vocational school and the more wide-ranging, well-rounded education offered at a liberal arts university. Whereas, in the former, students are equipped only to perform a certain trade, in the latter they are taught to think critically about many different subjects, not just those in their specific discipline.

In the final paragraph of the discourse, Newman describes the kind of student who will be the fruit of a liberal arts education grounded in "true principles" and "fixed aims":

> A University training is the great ordinary means to a great but ordinary end; it aims at raising the intellectual tone of society, at cultivating the public mind, at purifying the national taste, at supplying true principles to popular enthusiasm and fixed aims to popular aspiration, at giving enlargement and sobriety to the ideas of the age, at facilitating the exercise of political power, and refining the intercourse of private life. It is the education which gives a man a clear conscious view of his own opinions and judgments, a truth in developing them, an eloquence in expressing them, and a force in urging them. It teaches him to see things as they are, to go right to the point, to disentangle a skein of thought, to detect what is sophistical, and to discard what is irrelevant. It prepares him to fill any post with credit, and to master any subject with facility. It shows him how to accommodate himself to others, how to throw himself into their state of mind, how to bring before them his own, how to influence them, how to come to an understanding with them, how to bear with them. He is at home in any society, he has common ground with every class; he knows when to speak and when to be silent; he is able to converse, he is able to listen; he can ask a question pertinently, and gain a lesson seasonably, when he has nothing to impart himself.

Democracies and republics, whether representational or parliamentarian, are neither made great nor maintained by a handful of heroic geniuses. They are conceived and sustained by a body of citizens who possess the skills enumerated by Newman. Those skills can only be instilled in a large body of citizens by means of an education that shapes and trains its students against and in accordance with standards of Goodness, Truth, and Beauty that rise above the propaganda of leaders and the madness of crowds.

Apart from a fixed measure of truth, teachers cannot raise "the intellectual tone of society" or cultivate "the public mind." In the absence of a transcendent sense of beauty, no school can hope to purify "the national taste" or supply "true principles to popular enthusiasm." Where a normative understanding of goodness does not exist, education is powerless to facilitate "the exercise of political power" or refine "the intercourse of private life." Only an education grounded in universal ideas can bring "enlargement and sobriety to the ideas of the age."

When education is cut off from physical and metaphysical reality, it cannot teach students "to see things as they are"; when it absorbs and mimics the sophistry of the day, it cannot teach them "to detect what is sophistical"; when it loses the power (and the will) to measure, rank, and discriminate, it cannot teach them "to discard what is irrelevant." Effective teaching demands a hierarchy of that which is good, that which is true, and that which is beautiful; only then can students have the firm foundation necessary to allow them to be "at home in any society" and to have "common ground with every class." The relativism of the Sophist traps pupils in a constricting, inflexible contemporary box.

Travelers need signposts, or they will go astray. But they also need a destination, or they will wander endlessly, lost in a no man's land between the old home they can no longer return to and the new home they cannot imagine. It is the role of the teacher and the school

108   PART 1—THE NATURE OF EDUCATION

to provide signposts and destinations for their students that have passed the test of time and that square with that which is most eternal in man.

<hr/>

Although I will devote the second part of this book to dialoguing directly with a kaleidoscope of different thinkers in the field of education, I would like to consider here a brief but incisive work that, though influential in the modern classical Christian movement, has waned in popularity. *The Seven Laws of Teaching* (1886) is the brainchild of John Milton Gregory (1822–1898), an American minister, editor, educator, superintendent, and university president who felt confident that he had hit upon pedagogical laws that were as systematic and scientific as the laws of nature.

Though convinced that there were universal standards of reason and virtue that needed to be taught to students, he was concerned that those standards could not be effectively conveyed unless teachers accommodated their teaching to the language and experiences of their students. That is to say, Gregory advocated a partly student-centered classroom, not to advance a relativistic philosophy of education but to ensure that the collective wisdom of the past could be passed down to each successive generation.

Gregory's first two laws call for teachers who have a deep and comprehensive knowledge of their subject and students who are active and attentive learners. These two laws come together when teachers attract students by eager delight rather than compelled obedience. The best teachers, aware that apathy and distraction are the worst foes of education, will awaken the intelligence of their students by shocking them with a new idea or a startling question.

With the third law, which he calls "the law of the language," Gregory makes the essential connection between the "authoritative" teacher equipped with wisdom from the full liberal arts tradition and the "progressive" student who demands information that is relevant to

Goodness, Truth, and Beauty Versus Relativism

himself and his age. The language we use as teachers, Gregory explains, must be held in common with our students. If we use words they do not recognize, they will not be able to learn. They may imitate our words, but they will not understand them and therefore will not be able to grasp the truths we are trying to teach them.

As educators, we must be aware of the shape and size of our students' storehouse of words and express ourselves as much as possible through those words. Ideas do not come alive for students (or teachers) until they are incarnated into words; human beings of all ages can only master truth by expressing it in the right language.

But we must not stop there. The end goal is not merely to speak their language but to use the medium of their language to draw them up into a fuller knowledge of the tradition. The fourth "law of the lesson" moves students, step by step, from what they already know to what they do not. Only once we establish common linguistic and philosophical ground with our students can we guide them over that pedagogical bridge.

Everything is a mystery for us until we know what it is and can express what we know in words. That is why figurative language is as vital to poetry as it is to good teaching: it allows students to understand new words and concepts by comparing them to things they already know. That sudden moment of connection, especially when instigated by teachers deeply immersed in their subject matter, causes the light-bulb flash that moves students up the steps from the known to the unknown.

So far, so good, but Gregory does not stop there. The "law of the teaching process" charges teachers to excite and direct their students to learn for themselves: to take what they have been taught and re-think and re-cognize it in their own words. Only by arousing in students a spirit of inquiry will we train them to be truth seekers and friends of wisdom. Students who fail to develop the power to continue acquiring their own knowledge will never be fully educated.

If, however, teachers can wake the minds of their students, then the sixth "law of the learning process" will follow, and students will seek to reproduce in their own minds the truths they have learned. It *is* good for young students to memorize their lessons word for word, but only if they are eventually moved to understand the thinking behind the lesson, to re-express it in their own words, to seek out evidence for it through their own research, and to find practical applications for it in their own lives.

Gregory ends his book by pressing home the necessity of a continual process of review to ensure that students fully understand the material. Still, what remained in my mind as I closed his book were the last four of ten practical rules Gregory suggests for helping the student to achieve the "law of the learning process":

> 7. Help him to test his conceptions to see that they exactly reproduce the truth taught, in its widest aspects and relations, as far as his powers permit.

> 8. Inculcate constantly a profound regard for TRUTH as something noble, enduring and divine—something that God loves and all true and good men revere.

> 9. Let it be seen and felt that truth in facts, truth in feeling, truth in words, and truth in action all come under the same eternal and divine law, and that the honest truth-seeker will seek them all alike earnestly.

> 10. Teach the pupil to hate all falsehoods, sophistries, and shams as things that are odious, hurtful, dishonoring, shameful, cowardly, and intensely mean and wicked. Make him to dread a false answer to a problem as a lie from the lips.

The teaching of facts is not sufficient for the proper education of the young. Those facts must be connected to enduring and divine truths, truths that students must be taught to seek, to revere, and to use as the touchstone for their beliefs, feelings, and behaviors. At the same time, they must be taught to hate that which is false and sophistical, spurning it as they would an object or person or action that was mean or wicked or shameful.

Teachers serve society by being caretakers of what T. S. Eliot calls the permanent things, the transcendent truths against which individuals and nations must shape themselves if they are to survive and flourish. Only by guiding students to identify and internalize Plato's transcendentals can teachers succeed in cultivating the virtues, training the affections, and ordering the desires of those entrusted to their care.

SEVEN

VIRTUES VERSUS VALUES

I BEGIN THIS CHAPTER where I ended the previous one, by identifying one of the nonnegotiable tasks of classical Christian schools and teachers: to cultivate the virtues, train the affections, and order the desires of their students. There can be no true liberal arts education that does not include an education in virtue; there can be no true study of the Great Books that does not lead at least in part to the moral improvement of the student. An education in the Great Books does not, of course, guarantee an increase in virtue, but it holds up such an increase as one of its proper goals.

"If men were angels," writes James Madison in *Federalist* 51, "no government would be necessary. If angels were to govern men, neither external nor internal controls on government would be necessary." What Madison argues here about government, I would extend to education. Were our students angels, we would not need to labor to form their character, shape their affections, and properly direct their desires. If they were beasts that lacked discourse of reason, we would likewise cease our virtue-building labors, for they would be incapable of benefiting from them.

That we are not mere animals but moral agents made in the image of God not only renders us capable of an education in both reason and virtue but argues against strict behaviorist models—think B. F. Skinner and Pavlov's dogs—that would train children the way we train horses and monkeys. Classroom management, as I discussed in chapter five,

Virtues Versus Values

has its uses, but it can easily devolve into the regimentation and objectification of children. Students deserve and are capable of more than a simple regimen of rewards and punishments; they are to be taught, not conditioned. When taken to their extreme, both rigid traditional-authoritarian models and fluid progressive-pragmatic models can fall into the pedagogical black hole of behaviorism.

Still, because we are not angels, we need moral limits and ethical yardsticks. It is one of the chief duties of education to teach students the difference between good and evil, right and wrong, virtue and vice. And not just taught the difference in terms of word, thought, and deed; students must also be taught the proper way to *feel* when they perform a virtuous or vicious action. Some might argue that the fact that we must teach students how to be virtuous is proof that Plato's transcendental Good is a manmade construct. But we must teach those same students the mathematical tables, and there are precious few educators or philosophers who would claim that math is manmade.

Virtue, like math, is not something we invent but something we discover. We argue *from* it, not for it. Values, in contrast, are ephemeral social constructs.

"It was in the 1880s," Gertrude Himmelfarb explains in her prologue ("From Virtues to Values") to *The De-moralization of Society* (1994),

> that Friedrich Nietzsche began to speak of "values" in its present sense—not as a verb, meaning to value or esteem something; nor as a singular noun, meaning the measure of a thing (the economic value of money, labor, or property); but in the plural, connoting the moral beliefs and attitudes of a society. Moreover, he used the word consciously, repeatedly, indeed insistently, to signify what he took to be the most profound event in human history. His "transvaluation of values" was to be the final, ultimate revolution, a revolution against both the classical virtues and the Judaic-Christian ones. The "death of God" would mean the death of morality and the death of truth—above all, the truth of any morality. There would be no good and evil, no virtue and vice. There would be only "values." And having degraded virtues into values,

Nietzsche proceeded to de-value and trans-value them, to create a new set of values for his "new man."[1]

To replace absolute virtues with relativistic values is tantamount to killing off God, for God is the center and ultimate source of all transcendent standards of good and evil, virtue and vice, truth and error. Whether Greco-Roman (classical) or Judeo-Christian, virtues are the ground of truth and morality; apart from them, society quickly becomes unmoored. But then that is precisely what Nietzsche wants. To create a new kind of man, he must first detach humanity from fixed virtues.

"'Values,'" Himmelfarb goes on to argue,

> brought with it the assumptions that all moral ideas are subjective and relative, that they are mere customs and conventions, that they have a purely instrumental, utilitarian purpose, and that they are peculiar to specific individuals and societies. . . . One cannot say of virtues, as one can of values, that anyone's virtues are as good as anyone else's, or that everyone has a right to his own virtues. Only values can lay that claim to moral equality and neutrality.[2]

I would hope that the negative implications of this distinction for the education of the young are obvious. How can the character of students be shaped against standards that are "subjective and relative," "mere customs and conventions"? If all values are morally equivalent, if my values are my values and your values are yours, there can be no real progress in virtue from point A to point B; there can only be social conformity to the ever-shifting values of the moment.

In a footnote, Himmelfarb makes clear the impact that the ascendancy of values over virtues has had on education: "The 'values clarification' technique currently used in 'moral education' courses typifies the new mode of thinking. The teacher in such a course is enjoined from any pronouncements that might intimate that something is right

---

[1] Gertrude Himmelfarb, *The De-moralization of Society: From Victorian Virtues to Modern Values* (New York: Vintage, 1996), 10.
[2] Himmelfarb, *De-moralization of Society*, 11-12.

Virtues Versus Values

or wrong. Instead the students are assigned the task of discovering their own values by exploring their likes and dislikes, preferences and feelings."[3] To repeat what I wrote in chapter five, the goal of education is not to encourage students to be true to what they think they are but to challenge them to be true to what they truly are. Though classical Christian teachers often play the role of facilitator in high school Socratic discussions, when it comes to virtue, facilitation is not enough.

Although the popularity of values clarification has waned since Himmelfarb wrote her book, I maintain that its spirit lingers and that it has in great part been responsible for what I consider public education's abdication of its responsibility to instill virtue in students.[4] That abdication has been hidden from the public, however, as it has from most teachers, by the allure and appeal of values. From diversity to equity, tolerance to inclusivism, environmentalism to multiculturalism, schools speak loudly and often of the values they want their students to adopt and enact. Sadly, those values bear little resemblance to traditional virtues.

Virtues are universal principles written into the cosmos as much as they are into the nature of man; values are socially constructed and alter from nation to nation, region to region, subgroup to subgroup. The former is finally objective; the latter is ultimately subjective. Perhaps the best way to understand the essential difference between virtues and values is to compare it to the difference between a person's sex and a person's gender. Sex is an objective reality that we are born with; gender is a social construct that is both culturally fluid and personally subjective. Virtues, like a person's sex, confront us with an external measure and rule to which we must conform ourselves;

---

[3]Himmelfarb, *De-moralization of Society*, 12.
[4]The classic study is Sidney B. Simon, Leland W. Howe, and Howard Kirschenbaum, *Values Clarification: A Handbook of Practical Strategies for Teachers and Students* (New York: Dodd, Mead, 1984).

values, like a person's gender, are measured by internal, fluctuating standards of approval or outrage.

The shift from virtues to values in public and most private American education has prevented teachers from passing down and imparting the virtues necessary for civilization, particularly democratic civilization, to endure. Here are four reasons that shift has been a deleterious one.

First, the values I listed above have never stood at the center of moral education. That place has long been held by the four cardinal (or classical) virtues that are defined and discussed in Plato's *Republic* and Aristotle's *Nicomachean Ethics*: courage (or fortitude in Latin), wisdom (prudence), self-control (temperance), and justice. Around that core, other virtues have clustered: honesty, integrity, diligence, loyalty, hospitality, responsibility, obedience, and gratitude. To these, the tradition has added the specifically Christian (or theological) virtues of faith, hope, and love (charity), along with those that St. Paul includes under the fruit of the spirit: joy, peace, patience, gentleness, goodness, and meekness (see 1 Corinthians 13:13 and Galatians 5:22-23).

Our job as educators is not to enlist students for our pet causes but to train them so well in the classical and theological virtues that they will be able to make their own reasoned decisions on the hot-button issues of the day. Far from guiding and equipping students to be free moral agents, values-based education transforms them into partisans and lobbyists, confining them within the narrow parameters of approved speech codes and behaviors. It is true that the traditional model of education was often guilty of restricting speech and behavior; however, by exposing students to the Great Books and the classical virtues, it left an opening for them to develop their own character. Modern education often fails to provide, or appropriates and contextualizes, the kind of universal, time-tested material that empowers students to think outside the approved values box.

Virtues Versus Values

Second, whereas virtues are positive and take the focus off the person who has them, values are negative and direct the focus inward. Love reaches out toward the other; tolerance steps away and then pats itself on the back. The trouble with the values-driven practice of virtue signaling is that it does not change a person's core or align him with standards that transcend the self. To the contrary, it allows him to feel superior while doing nothing to bring himself, or the person he is tolerating, within the healthy and human boundaries of the classical and theological virtues.

This leads to the third distinction between virtues and values, one that takes us back to my discussion of Aristotle in the introduction. Virtue, Aristotle taught, is not a feeling but a habit, one that is developed by a long and slow process of performing virtuous actions. The habit drives the feelings, not vice versa. Feelings of charity rarely lead to actual charitable behavior; to the contrary, the habitual action of charity builds in people charitable feelings for others. That is not to say that feelings are unimportant; they are, as I said a moment ago, essential to an education in virtue. But the feelings must be tied to active habits and concrete virtues, not virtue signaling and hazy values.

As for the virtues themselves, they embody the mean between the extremes and cannot be reduced to a simplistic list of dos and don'ts. Although schools need to institute various rules of conduct and to forbid behaviors that are illegal or unethical or disruptive, they must not fool themselves into thinking that such rules make students virtuous. Virtue is built on discernment, the wisdom that allows people to distinguish extremes and so identify and embody the mean between them.

Authoritarian, legalistic Christian schools that define virtue in fully negative terms—don't drink, smoke, curse, or indulge in public displays of affection—inevitably fail to instill virtue in their students. The same goes for extreme progressive schools that focus on negative values that collapse all distinctions and withhold reasoned moral judgment. While the former ends up enslaved to a nondiscerning list of don'ts, the latter ends up enslaved to an equally nondiscerning list of dos. Neither group of graduates develops into virtuous, morally self-regulating citizens. Rather than acquire carefully cultivated habits, they end up being controlled by fear, social (as opposed to moral) guilt, and emotional, knee-jerk responses. They align themselves to shifting social expectations rather than to enduring, transcendent standards of virtue.

Fourth, I have found—more anecdotally than in my research—that the values promoted by progressive schools and educators can be quite slippery, even to the point of disguising themselves as functional equivalents of traditional virtues.[5] The value of tolerance as taught in public schools today does not, I have found, mean respecting all people because they bear the image of God and so possess essential worth. It means that no one has the right to judge anyone else in accordance with standards grounded in the Bible or in natural law. Diversity *should* mean giving everyone a voice; in practice, it has led to a campus regime of shutting down or shouting down voices that are deemed, by contemporary standards, to be intolerant.

If equity meant affording all people the same opportunities in life, I would be in favor of it. Too often, however, it means that certain groups are given special privilege over others, with the goal of replacing equality of opportunity with equality of outcome. If environmentalism meant teaching children to be stewards of creation, it would line up well with a classical Christian paideia. Instead, I have found, it means treating nature as sacred and human beings as the problem. The value of multiculturalism does not, as far as I can tell, square with a virtuous duty to treat all cultures with equal respect. More often, it has meant

---

[5]As an example of this slipperiness, consider the ubiquitous sign that began to appear on house lawns all over America in 2016: "In this house, we believe: Black Lives Matter. Women's rights are human rights. No human is illegal. Science is real. Love is love. Kindness is everything." Rebecca McLaughlin offers a powerful but irenic critique of some of these secular progressive pillars in *The Secular Creed* (Austin, TX: Gospel Coalition, 2021).

Virtues Versus Values

encouraging young people to view Western culture through the lens of cynicism, skepticism, and deconstruction.

To educate students in values is to build their moral house, and thus the moral house of society, on shifting sand; to educate them in virtue is to found them and the civilization of which they are a part securely on the rock. The storms of change will rage against them, but they will not fall (see Matthew 7:24-27).

<hr />

In 1993, William Bennett, the third person to hold the office of secretary of education, caused something of a publishing sensation with his bestselling *The Book of Virtues: A Treasury of Great Moral Stories.* What I found ironic about Bennett's timely and well-conceived compilation of moral stories that celebrate such traditional, classical Christian virtues as self-discipline, friendship, courage, and honesty, while warning against the opposing vices, is that, had he published it one hundred years earlier, it would have passed by unnoticed.

Until quite recently, it was understood by nearly all educators that the best way to instill virtue in young people was to embody those virtues in stories. Whether sacred or secular, fictional or nonfictional, historical or allegorical, legendary or mythic, stories have for thousands of years been used to please as well as to teach, to entertain as well as to instruct. As I hope I demonstrated in the introduction, man is by nature a storyteller, a subcreator who longs to find his place in the metanarrative.

One of the classic examples of a story that inspired generations of Roman citizens to live virtuously was Cicero's *Dream of Scipio* (ca. 51 BC). In the story, which borrows heavily from Plato's Myth of Er from the end of *Republic,* Cicero has Scipio Aemilianus, the hero of the third Punic War, receive a heavenly vision in which he meets with the hero of the second Punic War, his grandfather (by adoption) Scipio Africanus. In addition to being given a tour of the cosmos, Scipio is afforded a brief Roman paideia:

120　　　　　　　　　　　PART I—THE NATURE OF EDUCATION

There is a sure place prepared in heaven for all who have cared for their fatherland, preserved it, contributed to its growth; increased it: a place where they may enjoy eternal life and everlasting bliss. There is nothing more acceptable to the chief of the gods who rules over the cosmos, of all the things that happen on earth, than the councils and gatherings of men who associate together in respect for law and justice, that is, the organizations called states. Their rulers and preservers have come from heaven and will return here.[6]

The purpose of Africanus's exhortation to his grandson is twofold: to teach him the virtues appropriate to a citizen of Rome and to show him the proper path to heaven. As it turns out, the two lessons are one and the same. The virtues that align the soul to its earthly duties also align it to its heavenly rewards.

Many today would protest that teaching students by means of such stories will turn them into blind patriots, arrogant jingoists with no cultural sensitivity. In fact, the Great Books balance praise with criticism, love of country with a greater love of truth. Cicero's story, for all its Roman pride, is careful to put the fame of Rome and of Scipio in its proper cosmic perspective:

Train your eyes ever on the heavenly realm and banish human thoughts from your mind. After all, what renown, what fame worth seeking can you gain from the lips of men? You see how few and far between, and how cramped are the places where they live, and that between those blisters and spots where there is habitation, vast unpeopled tracts intervene.[7]

From here, Africanus goes on to measure out for his grandson just how small Rome is in comparison to the globe and how small the globe is in comparison to the universe. In keeping with the goals of a traditional paideia, Africanus seeks to instill in Scipio a sense of man's glory and futility, thus provoking both awe and humility, wonder and gratitude. Just so, the best fairy tales teach us to love *and fear* the power and magic of nature.

---

[6]Cicero, *Nine Orations and The Dream of Scipio*, trans. Palmer Bovie (New York: Mentor, 1967), 299.
[7]Cicero, *Nine Orations and The Dream of Scipio*, 301.

Virtues Versus Values 121

Unlike values, which train us to see prejudice and pettiness in others and tolerance and seriousness in ourselves, virtues, rightly taught and instilled, open our eyes to our strengths and weaknesses, insights and blind spots, abilities and limits.

The paideia of Cicero is a pre-Christian one, and yet it exists in direct continuity with the paideia advocated by England's best-known Christian poet: John Milton. In his prose essay "On Education" (1644), Milton lays out a challenging, interdisciplinary program for reading through the Great Books that combines the Greco-Roman with the Judeo-Christian and includes rigorous training in languages, math, science, music, and physical education. Milton's goal is to produce students who are strong in body and mind but who are equally strong in spirit. Indeed, for Milton, the central telos of education is the acquisition of virtue: "The end, then, of learning, is to repair the ruins of our first parents by regaining to know God aright, and out of that knowledge to love him, to imitate him, to be like him, as we may the nearest by possessing our souls of true virtue, which, being united to the heavenly grace of faith, makes up the highest perfection." Although Milton references the biblical fall of Adam and Eve and the Christian understanding of grace and faith, references to which Cicero did not have access, his vision of virtue nevertheless lines up with that of the great pagan statesman.

For Milton and Cicero alike, virtue is attained by imitating and shaping ourselves against a standard that transcends us, whether that standard be God himself (Milton), the wisdom of the ancestors (Cicero), or the Forms (Plato). Education is less about progress than it is about reclamation, about restoring what has been lost, either by sin or moral degradation or ignorance. Education on its own cannot save our souls, but it can help to realign and reorder them.

As he begins to lay out the early (grammar) stages of his paideia, Milton pauses to explain what he hopes to instill in students beyond the actual content of the lessons:

> But here the main skill and groundwork will be to temper them such lectures and explanations upon every opportunity as may lead and draw them in willing obedience, inflamed with the study of learning and the admiration of virtue, stirred up with high hopes of living to be brave men and worthy patriots, dear to God and famous to all ages: that they may despise and scorn all their childish and ill-taught qualities, to delight in manly and liberal exercises; which he who hath the art and proper eloquence to catch them with, what with mild ineffectual persuasions, and what with the intimation of some fear, if need be, but chiefly by his own example, might in a short space gain them to an incredible diligence and courage, infusing into the young breasts such an ingenious and noble ardor as would not fail to make many of them renowned and matchless men.

How wonderful it would be if schools today made it their goal to shape virtuous students who are brave and noble, diligent and obedient, mature and manly, ardent and eloquent, faithful to God and loyal to country.

This does not mean that all students so taught will be "renowned and matchless men." As in the Newman passage I quoted in chapter six, the goal of a liberal arts education is to form a body of citizens who can serve with honor and dignity in any capacity or profession. "A complete and generous education," Milton explains, is one "which fits a man to perform justly, skillfully, and magnanimously all the offices, both private and public, of peace and war."

The goal of classical Christian education (paideia) is to produce such citizens, for only they can keep a democracy alive and pass down its legacy from one generation to the next.

PART 2

THE NATURE OF THE DEBATE

EIGHT

PLATO'S *REPUBLIC*

The Educational Journey of
the Philosopher-King

HAVING SURVEYED THE NATURE OF MAN in the introduction and the nature of education in part one, I will now put myself in dialogue with ten representative critics who have initiated or advanced the general debate over the proper goals and methods for educating the next generation. Although I will zero in on these ten movers and shakers, I will in my dialogues borrow more widely from other thinkers in the field. By so doing, I hope to sketch out areas of both agreement and controversy.

Any discussion of education in the West must begin with Plato, who preserved and developed the teachings and pedagogical stye of his master, Socrates. It is true that the concept of paideia predates Socrates and that the Sophists had already begun plying their teacher-for-hire trade when Socrates set up his table in the agora of Athens. Nevertheless, a full and integrated philosophy of education did not emerge until Socrates and Plato united metaphysics and ethics and, guided by that synthesis, sought out absolute standards against which to measure human knowledge and virtue.

The Socratic enterprise rises out of a quest for universal definitions of abstract ideas, usually virtues the Sophists defined, if at all, in

126 PART 2—THE NATURE OF THE DEBATE

relativistic terms. In Plato's early dialogues, we get to eavesdrop as a vigorous, indefatigable Socrates tries his best to hammer out definitions for such virtues as courage (*Laches*), friendship (*Lysis*), self-control (*Charmides*), and goodness-beauty (*Hippias Major*). None of these dialogues ever arrives at the sought-for definition, but they do prepare the ground by clearing away the weeds of false (or partial) definitions that had sprung up around the Sophists.

What Socrates begins Plato completes, nowhere more so than in his *Republic*, a lengthy and complex dialogue centered on a single, seemingly simple question: What is justice? By the end of the dialogue, Plato not only succeeds in defining justice, along with the other three classical virtues of wisdom, courage, and self-control, but develops a theory for grounding all definitions in transcendent, metaphysical realities.

According to Plato's theory of the Forms (or Ideas), everything in our transient, earthly, shifting World of Becoming is a shadow, a lesser imitation of something that exists perpetually in the heavenly, unchanging World of Being. In daily life, we encounter chairs, trees, and cats that differ in shape and size, texture and color; yet, we recognize them all *as* chairs, trees, and cats because each individual chair or tree or cat points back to the perfect Form (or Idea) of Chair, Tree, and Cat. The same goes for concepts such as goodness, truth, beauty, justice, and love. They are what they are because they reflect and participate in the Form of Goodness, Truth, Beauty, Justice, and Love.

Although one need not believe literally in Plato's Forms, I would argue that a belief in something *like* the Forms is necessary to support the kind of liberal arts, classical Christian education that I have been describing and defending in this book. If teachers and their students cannot be assured that there is something real and lasting behind the words and concepts being taught, there can be no real growth in wisdom. If Jacques Derrida and his fellow deconstructionists—whose ideas represent, in many ways, a return to the Sophists of old—are

Plato's Republic 127

correct, then Meaning, even if it exists, is perpetually deferred. Language simply cannot carry us back to any kind of original, transcendent source of Truth.

I do not mean to imply that students should accept passively all they are taught. They *must* be encouraged to wrestle with received wisdom in order to make sure that the definitions that have been passed down to them are accurate markers of the truth. I also do not mean to imply that there is a simple, one-to-one correspondence between words and what those words signify. Just as man and nature were cursed at the fall, so language itself was cursed at the Tower of Babel. It is possible that the language of Adam, by which he named the animals, was a divine linguistic vehicle, one in which there was an incarnational relationship between word and Meaning. In fact, I believe as an English professor that poetry at its purest affords us a glimpse back to that original relationship between linguistic signifier and metaphysical signified. After the babbling of human language, however, the vehicle was muddied, and we were left—to borrow a phrase from Milton that I quoted in the previous chapter—to repair the ruins, both of our disobedient first parents and of the rebellious builders of Babel.[1]

Still, this condition of our fallen world should not lead philosophers, linguists, or educators to despair and adopt an attitude of cynicism and skepticism toward the possibility of Meaning. Just as our inability as fallen creatures to possess and to understand fully absolute Goodness, Truth, and Beauty should not dissuade us from seeking after the transcendentals, so our inability to perfectly connect words, ideas, and definitions to their ultimate, God-given Source should not dissuade us from seeking to make as firm a connection as we can. If we give up that dual search, then education becomes a losing battle. If everything is truly relative, if the words we use are

---

[1] The annual conference of the Association of Classical Christian Schools is called, after Milton, "Repairing the Ruins."

128   PART 2—THE NATURE OF THE DEBATE

incapable of pointing back to an original Meaning, a fixed and transcendent Signified, then education is reduced to mere training, the acquisition of skills rather than the instilling of wisdom, the perfecting of technique rather than the cultivation of virtue.

But now let me return to Plato and trace how his goal of finding a universal, transcendent definition for Justice led him to lay out an educational program that has had a profound impact on the nature and goals of classical Christian education. In book 2, Socrates tries to define for his interlocutors the nature of a just man, but he finds the attempt only partially successful. Then he hits on a solution. "We sometimes speak, do we not," Socrates asks Adeimantus "of a just man and also of a just city? . . . And the city is larger than the man?" To both questions, Adeimantus answers yes, prompting Socrates to suggest the following method of inquiry: "Perhaps, then, there would be more of justice in the city; it might also be easier to observe it there. So if it is agreeable to you, let us first inquire into the nature of justice and injustice in the city, and only after that in the individual. In this way we could begin with the larger and then return to the smaller, making comparisons between the two."[2]

In order to properly identify and define justice (Justice) in an individual man, a quality of the soul that can be neither seen nor heard nor touched, Plato compares the small, invisible soul to a large, visible city. If he can shape that city into a fully just one, then he should have little difficulty locating justice within the workings of that city. Once that has been observed and understood, he can work his way back from the macrocosm to the microcosm, the external city to the internal soul.

To be perfectly just, the city will need to be ruled by a perfectly just king—what Plato famously dubbed a Philosopher-King—together with a wider group of Guardians who know good from evil, virtue

---

[2]Plato, *The Republic*, trans. Richard W. Sterling and William C. Scott (New York: Norton, 1985), 64 (Stephanus numbers: 368e-369a).

Plato's Republic 129

from vice, justice from injustice.[3] But how can a city produce such wise Guardians and Philosopher-Kings? That is where education comes in. For a city to achieve justice, a system of education needs to be developed that leads future rulers toward the Forms of Goodness, Truth, Beauty, and Justice. Apart from a knowledge of those divine or at least transcendent standards, neither the Philosopher-King nor the Guardians will be able to rule justly, because they will have no fixed measure against which to test and measure their rulings.

Thus does Plato's attempt to define justice give way to a manual for educating wise and virtuous rulers, one that includes curricular advice on gymnastics, music, and reading and that guides students along a course of study that climaxes with philosophy. The advice that Plato gives on these matters has proven to be quite influential, but that advice pales in comparison to the visionary metaphor he constructs to illustrate the *process* of education by which the Philosopher-King ascends the rising path to wisdom.

In *Republic* 7, Plato spins an allegory (or myth) that captures the vigorous, often painful process by which a young student-philosopher can free his mind from the shifting shadows of our world and catch a glimpse of the eternal and absolute Forms. That myth is known as the Allegory of the Cave, and it should be required reading for all high school students in America. For Plato's allegory reveals a great and central truth about education: much more than a mere accumulation of facts and figures, the paideia that helped give birth to Western democracy and culture marks a movement out of the darkness of error into the light of truth.

In Plato's allegory, we, in our natural, uneducated state, are like people imprisoned in the bowels of a deep, dark cave. All our lives, we

---

[3]Plato, *Republic*, 165 (473d): "Unless philosophers become kings in our cities, or unless those who now are kings and rulers become true philosophers, so that political power and philosophic intelligence converge, and unless those lesser natures who run after one without the other are excluded from governing, I believe there can be no end to troubles . . . in our cities or for all mankind."

have been chained to chairs that have allowed us only to look forward at the back wall of the cave. Behind us a fire rages, while between us and the fire, puppeteers parade puppets of all the things that exist in the real world outside the cave. The fire casts the shadows of the puppets on the wall, and we, the deluded prisoners, think the shadows are reality.

Because we mistake the shadows for reality, our systems of education are based on a study of the shadows. Many of the prisoners become quite adept at guessing which figures will appear next on the cave wall. They often compete to see who best can predict coming sequences, even awarding prizes—dare I say academic degrees!—to those who do. Still, the shadows are nothing but that: shadows.

Then, one day, one of the prisoners is released from his chains and turns his head and body around to face the fire. At first, he is blinded by the light and experiences sharp pain. When he turns his face back to the wall, he finds himself unable to see the shadows clearly or predict their sequence. After a while, he can see the puppets, but he finds them confusing and less substantial than the familiar, comforting shadows he has stared at all his life. He would prefer to remain in his chair, but he is pushed upward through a narrow passage and out into the open air, where the sun blinds him even more cruelly and painfully than the fire had done.

In the end, however, as his eyes adjust to the light, he comes to understand the actual nature of his situation and is thankful that he has been freed from the shadows and allowed to see that which is truly true and really real. Although he wishes now to remain outside the cave and commune with the Good, True, and Beautiful, he must be forced to return and do what he can to awaken his once fellow prisoners to their true condition and lead them out of the darkness of error into the light of truth. He who does so is Plato's Philosopher-King: someone who would prefer to spend his life contemplating truth but who is compelled to return to the world and guide others

Plato's Republic

by the transcendent standards he has come to know both intellectually and intimately.

In the allegory, the cave where the prisoners are chained is a representation of our physical World of Becoming, with the fire being our sun, which shines down on our world of shadows. The world outside the cave represents the World of Being where dwell the Forms, the real originals of which the things of our world are but shadows. The sun in the allegory represents the Form of the Forms, which Plato often referred to as the Good. As our sun illuminates the earth, so the Good illuminates the other Forms.

In his own interpretation of the allegory, Socrates/Plato makes a clear connection between the journey of the philosopher out of the cave and the proper telos of education:

> If this is true, it follows that education is not what some professors say it is. They claim they can transplant the power of knowledge into a soul that has none, as if they were engrafting vision into blind eyes. . . . But our reasoning goes quite to the contrary. We assert that this power is already in the soul of everyone. The way each of us learns compares with what happens to the eye: it cannot be turned away from darkness to face the light without turning the whole body. So it is with our capacity to know; together with the entire soul one must turn away from the world of transient things toward the world of perpetual being, until finally one learns to endure the sight of its most radiant manifestation.[4]

Though good teaching is founded in part on the memorizing of essential names, dates, events, and terms, cramming information into students' heads is not the ultimate goal of education. Rather, it is one of the means to achieve the proper end of turning students away from false idols that deceive and toward the Forms of the Good, True, and Beautiful.

For Plato, the climax of the educative process was philosophy; for the builders of the medieval universities, it was theology. But the

---

[4]Plato, *Republic*, 212 (518c).

difference is not as wide as it might seem. Philosophy for Plato is as much ethical as it is metaphysical; it is inextricably tied to standards and realities that transcend our physical, natural, material world. Plato did not consider theology the queen of the sciences because he lacked the special revelation of the prophets, Christ, and the Bible on which Christian theology rests. Instead, he relied on reason, conscience, and a careful study of the nature of reality.

And something else. What does Plato mean by saying that "the power of knowledge . . . is already in the soul of everyone"? Although Plato the philosopher (and educator) puts most of his focus on reason, he also assigns a central role to intuition. For Plato, our soul does not enter the world, as John Locke would argue, as a blank slate. It carries with it a memory of the World of Being that provides it with an innate form of knowledge that the good teacher can draw out of the student. In fact, in *Meno*, Socrates uses a dialectical method of question-and-answer to draw out of rather than put into the mind of a slave boy a rudimentary understanding of the laws of geometry (see 81c-86b).

I am not suggesting, nor is Plato, that teachers should spend all their time in the classroom trying to ferret out wisdom hidden in the souls of their students. But I would suggest, following Plato's lead, that education is a synergistic process that calls on participation from teachers and students alike. Teachers are those who teach, but they should also be those who guide. As for students, whatever their age or classification, their response must be, to refer back again to the quoted passage, a full-bodied one.

Education is quite literally a process of conversion—a turning away of the entire body and soul from the ephemeral to the lasting, the transient to the perpetual. That process is a rigorous one that often carries with it pain and disorientation. In Plato's allegory the initiate who escapes from the dark cave must push his way through a narrow passage that is clearly meant to suggest the birth canal. Education is

Plato's Republic

not a passive process but a series of deaths and rebirths into greater, more radiant light.

For the last century, educators have debated, often fiercely, whether classrooms should be teacher centered or student centered. Plato's allegory and the pedagogical vision it illustrates offer something of a compromise position. The teacher, of course, must be in charge, for, if he is a true teacher, he has himself already made or at least begun in earnest the journey from shifting shadows to transcendent truths.

It is the teacher's responsibility to make sure that neither he nor his students surrender to the current zeitgeist, the reigning spirit of the age. His job is both to turn them on to the right path and to strip away that which is false and fashionable to reveal to them that which is true and eternal. For this the teacher must possess knowledge, but he must also possess a passion for wisdom and virtue that will rouse in his students a desire to search and to grow. Indeed, his passion and his example should be such that students will willingly model themselves on his teachings and his actions.

As for the students, they must be willing to perform the labor and bear the pain and discomfort that devotion to wisdom and virtue calls for—partly because they sense that some of that wisdom and virtue lies dormant within them. In the end, they will be willing to make the sharp turn, the arduous change, because they trust their teacher when he assures them that such a sacrifice will lead to greater light and goodness. They participate in their own education by trusting, as Milton promises in "Of Education," that "the right path of a virtuous and noble education [is] laborious indeed at the first ascent, but else so smooth, so green, so full of goodly prospect, and melodious sounds in every side, that the harp of Orpheus was not more charming."

Plato's vision is a noble one, one that could invigorate our sagging public schools and universities if educators would only recommit themselves and their students to it. But there is one troubling element of the *Republic* that gives modern educators pause: Plato's seeming advocacy of censorship and his concomitant decision to kick the poets out of his perfect state. For nearly two and a half millennia, Platonic-minded educators committed to the liberal arts have struggled with this part of the *Republic*. How can we base a liberal arts education, they wonder, on a philosopher who distrusted the arts?

This dilemma may best be understood by analogy. Education in the West was born out of a fusion of the Greco-Roman (Plato, Aristotle, Isocrates, Cicero, Quintilian) and the Judeo-Christian (Basil, John Chrysostom, Boethius, Alcuin, Petrarch, Desiderius Erasmus). Yet, nearly all the major Christian educators of the Middle Ages and Renaissance struggled with the writings of two of the greatest fathers of the church: Augustine and Jerome. Despite being prodigious classicists, both men shared testimonies that suggested the need for Christians to distance themselves from the pagan classics. Thus, in *Confessions* 1.13, Augustine repents for weeping more at the death of Dido (in *Aeneid* 4) than over his lack of love for God. Jerome, meanwhile, in a letter to his female follower Eustochium, tells of a dream he had in which the Lord accused him of being a follower of Cicero rather than of Christ.

The way that Christian educators committed to a Great Books education grounded in Greco-Roman literature, history, and philosophy handled this conundrum was to emphasize how much the wisdom and eloquence of Augustine and Jerome was enhanced by their study of the pagan classics. Their rhetorical command of Latin was strengthened manyfold by their knowledge and love of Virgil and Cicero, and those oratorical skills allowed them to be more effective messengers of the gospel and champions of the Christian life of virtue. The rigor associated with a classical education was also salutary for both fathers, honing their skills and making them better interpreters of the Scriptures. All things being equal, educated believers bear more fruit than ignorant and slothful ones.

Plato's Republic 135

Indeed, a close reading of the *Republic* will reveal that Plato himself owed a similar debt to the very literature he claimed to find harmful. In the *Republic* as well as in his other dialogues, Plato never stops quoting Homer, usually, if not always, from memory. Furthermore, the most memorable parts of his dialogues are, like the Allegory of the Cave, products of a distinctly poetic imagination. Plato's wisdom and eloquence owe a great debt to Homer and the poets. It is no exaggeration to say that his works would not be as influential and lasting as they are had he not learned at the feet of Homer. It should also be noted that Plato, who was critical, even dismissive, of the rhetoric of the Sophists, wrote himself with great rhetorical polish and flair.

However, to understand Plato's dismissal of the arts and its connection with a liberal arts education meant to free the mind from manmade idols and direct it toward permanent truths, one must pay closer attention to what it is in Homer and the poets that Plato objects to. In Homer and Plato's day, the gods who made up the Greek pantheon were anything but holy and righteous. They carried on in a quite sinful manner, providing at best an anti-role model for human beings seeking to live a life of virtue.

Worse yet, the depiction of the afterlife in Homer was as miserable as it was hopeless, with everyone, despite the good or evil of their deeds, condemned to the same gloomy eternity in Hades. Aside from a few vague glimpses of heavenly Elysian Fields for dead heroes (see the fate prophesied for Menelaus in *Odyssey* 4), Homer's vision of the afterlife was hardly one to inspire virtuous behavior or warn against vicious behavior in view of postmortem reward or punishment. That is why so many of the myths or allegories that Plato invents for his best dialogues (*Republic, Gorgias, Meno, Phaedo, Phaedrus, Symposium, Timaeus*) describe the fate of the deceased in terms of proper reward and punishment. Those myths that do not do so directly speak of the education of the philosopher (or lover) as a movement from darkness to light, shadow to substance.

Plato's myths, that is to say, represent an alternate poetry that is better equipped to raise up students in the knowledge of transcendent goodness, truth, and beauty and in the path of virtue. In the same way, his theory of Forms represents an alternate metaphysics that grounds that noble trinity—T. S. Eliot's permanent things—in absolute truths rather than relativistic gods. By providing both those aesthetic myths and those philosophical benchmarks, Plato freed succeeding generations of pagan philosophers and orators from Aristotle and Isocrates to Cicero and Quintilian to Seneca and Plutarch to reclaim Homer as a fountain of wisdom and eloquence under the auspices of fixed standards. Needless to say, the Christian educators who followed in Plato's wake could also restore Homer to the curriculum because they possessed a divine touchstone (Christ and the Bible) against which they could measure pagan poetry and mitigate its corrupting power.

Censorship in the *Republic* is not about banning books that pose a threat to political leaders; it is about ensuring the proper moral formation of the young by protecting them from internalizing a false view of the gods and of virtue.[5] Unless we want our own experimental republic to come crashing down around our ears, we had best pay heed to Plato and recommit ourselves to the necessary task of directing the eyes of our children away from the immoral, the false, and the ugly and toward the Good, the True, and the Beautiful.

---

[5]I discuss this matter at greater length in my *From Plato to Christ: How Platonic Thought Shaped the Christian Faith* (Downers Grove, IL: IVP Academic, 2021), 31-39.

NINE

AUGUSTINE'S
DE DOCTRINA CHRISTIANA

Learning to Think Rightly

IN CHAPTER EIGHT, I mentioned how Christian educators in the Middle Ages and Renaissance often struggled with Augustine's seeming rejection of Greek and Roman literature. As it turns out, in Augustine's influential study of education, *On Christian Education* (*De Doctrina Christiana*), he makes two arguments for the inclusion of pagan classics that provided and continue to provide justification for a curriculum that blends Greco-Roman reason with Judeo-Christian revelation. More generally, Augustine lays out a pedagogical program to train students to think rightly so that they will be able to discern *on their own* the false from the true.

Augustine borrows his first argument in favor of reading pagan literature from Origen, basing it on an important historical event from the exodus of the Jews out of Egypt. "If those who are called philosophers, especially the Platonists, have said things which are indeed true and are well accommodated to our faith," writes Augustine in *De Doctrina Christiana* 2.40,

> they should not be feared; rather, what they have said should be taken from them as from unjust possessors and converted to our use. Just as the

138   PART 2—THE NATURE OF THE DEBATE

Egyptians had not only idols and grave burdens which the people of Israel detested and avoided, so also they had vases and ornaments of gold and silver and clothing which the Israelites took with them secretly when they fled, as if to put them to a better use.[1]

The biblical event Augustine alludes to here is known as the spoiling (or plundering) of the Egyptians. As the Jews were preparing to flee from bondage, they, in keeping with God's command and assistance, secured from their Egyptian neighbors gifts of silver and gold (Exodus 3:21-22; 12:35-36), which gifts, Augustine makes clear, they put to better and more godly use.

Allegorically speaking, Augustine goes on to explain, the pagan gold and silver represent Egyptian teachings that contained much superstition and error "but also liberal disciplines more suited to the uses of truth, and some most useful precepts concerning morals." Much that was conducive to instruction in the liberal arts and morality lurked behind that gold and silver, which, though the Egyptians did not know it, was "dug up from certain mines of divine Providence." The role of the good teacher is not to throw out all pagan literature but to purify it by identifying what in it is good, true, and beautiful and then baptizing it as a fit source of godly wisdom and virtue.

Earlier in book 2, Augustine offers a second argument that complements the first. "We should not think," he writes, "that we ought not to learn literature because Mercury is said to be its inventor, nor that because the pagans dedicated temples to Justice and Virtue and adored in stones what should be performed in the heart, we should therefore avoid justice and virtue. Rather, every good and true Christian should understand that wherever he may find truth, it is his Lord's" (2.18). All truth, Augustine insists, is God's truth, no matter its source. When a pagan writer says something correct about justice or virtue, it should be read, studied, and embraced.

---

[1]Saint Augustine, *On Christian Doctrine*, trans. D. W. Robertson Jr. (Upper Saddle River, NJ: Prentice Hall, 1958), 75. Future references will be by book and chapter number.

Augustine's De Doctrina Christiana 139

Although Augustine's advice may seem relevant only to fundamentalist Christians who look with suspicion on pagan mythology, it is equally relevant to some progressive educators who are too quick to cancel any ancient author who harbors a worldview they consider to be less scientific, less egalitarian, or less tolerant than their own. Without a higher standard against which to measure the Great Books of the past, whether written by pre-Christians, Christians, or post-Christians, schools cannot properly sift the good from the bad, the true from the false, the beautiful from the ugly. Christian schools founded on the special revelation of Christ and the Bible are particularly well equipped to do this, but secular schools can do it as well by relying on the general revelation accessible to all people through reason, conscience, the study of nature, and the innate knowledge stored in the soul and capable of being drawn out.

Just as Augustine's musings on the relationship between pagan and Christian literature and philosophy can be given a wider application to public and private secular schools, so his advice on the interpretation of the Scriptures has repercussions beyond Christian schools and seminaries. In his prologue, Augustine explains that he wrote *De Doctrina* not only to help students learn from the great expositors of the Bible but to help them learn to read it themselves and explain it to others. By teaching the basic rules of exegesis, Augustine hoped to empower his readers to interpret the Bible on their own.

Some, he admits, who read his book will find it too difficult and quickly put it down. Others will decide that because Augustine's advice does not "work" for them, it will not work for anyone else. To such critics, Augustine responds boldly: stop being lazy, work harder, pray for wisdom. It is true that God sometimes inspires people directly, as he did the authors of the Bible, but in the normal course of events, God teaches us through other people.

140   PART 2—THE NATURE OF THE DEBATE

> We should not tempt Him in whom we have believed, lest, deceived by the
> wiles and perversity of the Enemy, we should be unwilling to go to church to
> hear and learn the Gospels, or to read a book, or to hear a man reading or
> teaching, but expect to be "caught up to the third heaven," as the Apostle says,
> "whether in the body or out of the body," and there hear "secret words that
> man may not repeat" [see 2 Corinthians 12:2-4], or there see Our Lord Jesus
> Christ and hear the gospel from Him rather than from men.

The understanding of Scripture does not come to us in a flash of inspiration; it demands concentrated labor on the part of the student as well as clear instruction from the teacher.

Paul received visions from God, but that did not excuse him from studying the Scriptures. Even when Paul was struck down blind on the road to Damascus and heard the voice of Jesus speaking to him, he was sent by God to a man named Ananias to receive further instructions (see Acts 9). In the same way, the centurion Cornelius, after receiving direct communication from an angel, was instructed in the faith by Peter (see Acts 10). To these examples, Augustine adds the Ethiopian eunuch learning from Philip (see Acts 8:27-35) and Moses learning from his father-in-law, Jethro (see Exodus 18:14-27).

It need hardly be said that this advice is not only apt for slothful Christians who think they can understand the mysteries of the Bible by skimming through it passively while waiting for the Holy Spirit to fall. All students of all ages naturally take the path of least resistance; that is why they must be kept on track by teachers who will hold them accountable and exercise their mental muscles. Christian and secular students alike must heed the admonition of the author of Hebrews: "For the moment all discipline [*paideia*] seems painful rather than pleasant, but later it yields the peaceful fruit of righteousness to those who have been trained by it" (Hebrews 12:11 ESV).

Discipline rightly administered by a wise and virtuous teacher will free rather than chain the mind of the willing student. It will also form that mind in such a way that it can eventually understand and interpret on its

Augustine's De Doctrina Christiana 141

own. Many teachers today consider it their job to teach students to think for themselves. That is a fine sentiment, but it is one that should come at the *end* of the educational process, not at the beginning. Students must be taught to think rightly before they can think for themselves.

Learning is an active process; to earn the right to think for themselves, students must first, to refer back to the quoted passage, hear, learn, and read with rigor and focus.

A proper paideia, then, can teach students to think rightly and thus think for themselves. But what use shall they make of that ability? How shall they communicate what they have learned with others, and to what end? To answer that, Augustine takes up in book 4 a subject that exerted considerable pedagogical influence on the Middle Ages and Renaissance but which will likely seem strange to modern educators: eloquence. Even though Americans continue to rank the fear of speaking in front of a group as an even greater fear than death, American educators seem increasingly less committed to teaching rhetoric and oratory. That is a sad thing since most of the great premodern thinkers on education placed wisdom and eloquence side by side as twin markers of a truly educated person.

A moment ago, I pointed out how Augustine argues in book 2 that Christians can learn true wisdom from pagan writers. That Augustine was willing to take his own advice is made clear in book 4, where he borrows directly from a number of pagan writers, including the fourth-century BC Greek Isocrates, the first-century BC Roman Cicero, and the first-century AD Spanish-Roman Quintilian. These men may not have had access to the theological truths that Augustine so eloquently propounds, but they understood well the centrality of rhetorical skills to the formation of character. For them, wisdom and eloquence, together with virtue, were essential and inseparable elements of education.

Isocrates, who knew Socrates and Plato and who founded a school of rhetoric in Athens in 393 BC, was horrified by the topsy-turvy morality that increasingly corrupted the city's youth in the years following Athens's defeat by Sparta. His remedy was a renewed effort by teachers to instill wisdom, eloquence, and virtue in their students. Indeed, he firmly believed that what made Athens great was not her wealth or power but her paideia and her liberal arts education. You Athenians, he writes in *Antidosis*,

> are pre-eminent and superior to the rest of the world, not in your application to the business of war, nor because you govern yourselves more excellently or preserve the laws handed down to you by your ancestors more faithfully than others, but in those qualities by which the nature of man rises above the other animals, and the race of the Hellenes above the barbarians, namely, in the fact that you have been educated as have been no other people in wisdom and in speech. . . . For you must not lose sight of the fact that Athens is looked upon as having become a school for the education of all able orators and teachers of oratory.[2]

Thinking, writing, and speaking cannot be separated from one another; together they bear witness to that which is most noble in man. The heroes who expelled the tyrants, defeated the barbarians, and established the democratic institutions of Athens possessed all three skills. They did not scorn oratory but used it to sharpen their minds and persuade their fellow Athenians of what they must do to become great.

Three centuries later, Cicero, taking Socrates as his role model, championed Isocrates's insistence that wisdom, eloquence, and virtue must be combined. If rhetoric (good speech) is not accompanied by ethics (right conduct), it poses great danger to individuals and their societies alike: "If we bestow fluency of speech on persons devoid of those virtues [integrity and supreme wisdom], we shall not have made orators of them but shall have put weapons into the hands of madmen."[3]

Cicero, like Isocrates before him, was well aware that Plato, on account of his negative interactions with the sophists, was distrustful of rhetoric. That is why both Cicero and Isocrates caution against a

---

[2]Isocrates, *Antidosis*, in *The Great Tradition: Classic Readings on What It Means to Be an Educated Human Being*, ed. Richard M. Gamble (Wilmington, DE: ISI Books, 2007), 52.
[3]Cicero, *De Oratore* 1.16, in Gamble, *Great Tradition*, 73.

Augustine's De Doctrina Christiana   143

rhetoric detached from the wisdom and virtue that come with a true study of philosophy. Those who would teach their students the art of persuasive speech must teach them also to make a proper use of that art. The same oratorical eloquence that makes the funeral oration of Pericles one of the classic statements of true democratic virtues was used by demagogues such as Alcibiades and Cleon to draw Athens deeper and deeper into the disastrous Peloponnesian War that brought on the collapse of her once-noble democracy.

Education is not a game; it is a serious enterprise that can be used both to shape virtuous, morally self-regulating citizens and to empower opportunistic politicians and hucksters. In a passage that could have been written today, Cicero shows how sophistical oratory divorced from truth can make the weaker argument (or person) seem the stronger:

> For cunning masquerades as prudence, boorish contempt for pleasure as temperance, pride in over-valuing honours and superciliousness in looking down on them as high-mindedness, profusion as liberality, audacity as bravery, savage hardness as endurance, harshness as justice, superstition as religion, softness as gentleness, timidity as modesty, verbal controversy and logic-chopping on the one hand as skilfulness in argument, and an empty flux of talk on the other as oratorical power.[4]

Socrates and Plato, I argued in the previous chapter, initiated true education (paideia) by insisting that words are not arbitrary names but point back to real things. When rhetoric is divorced from philosophical truth and transcendent meaning, it inevitably leads to the deconstruction and weaponization of language.

Writing a century and a half later, Quintilian agreed with Isocrates and Cicero that the true orator must be both a good speaker and a good man. Indeed, he makes it clear that "if the powers of eloquence serve only to lend arms to crime, there can be nothing more pernicious than eloquence to public and private welfare alike."[5] If education confines

---

[4]Cicero, *De Partitione Oratoria*, in Gamble, *Great Tradition*, 82-83.
[5]Quintilian, *Institutes* 12, in Gamble, *Great Tradition*, 120.

itself to the vocational, teaching rhetoric as a mere skill and end in itself rather than as a tool to serve wisdom and virtue, then it is just as likely to bring about the ruin of a culture as to make it stronger.

Taught, however, within the context of a proper paideia, the oratorical arts can become an expression of goodness, truth, and beauty. "The orator," Quintilian explains, "must above all things devote his attention to the formation of moral character and must acquire a complete knowledge of all that is just and honourable. For without this knowledge no one can be either a good man or skilled in speaking, unless indeed we agree with those who regard morality as intuitive and as owing nothing to instruction."[6]

Neither the mathematical tables nor basic morality is manmade; both are written into the fabric of the universe without and the conscience within. Nevertheless, both must be taught, and both must be learned. Behind the virtue, wisdom, and eloquence that the true teacher seeks to instill in the true student lurk Plato's Forms of Goodness, Truth, and Beauty. Augustine understood this well, though he moved the Forms from Plato's World of Being to the Mind of God (see *Eighty-Three Different Questions* 46).

As he embraced the essence of Plato's theory of the Forms, so Augustine embraced Isocrates, Cicero, and Quintilian's views on rhetoric. Eloquence, he explains in book 4 of *De Doctrina*, is neutral; it can be used either for good or for evil. It is a far better thing to have wisdom without eloquence than to have eloquence with folly or error. Eloquence divorced from wisdom is dangerous and can lead many astray. Conversely, many who lack eloquence in their speech can express eloquence more powerfully through living virtuous lives.

In imitation of Isocrates, Cicero, and Quintilian, Augustine commends the use of oratory for teaching, pleasing, and persuading. In good Aristotelian fashion, he even takes time to distinguish carefully

---

[6]Quintilian, *Institutes* 12, in Gamble, *Great Tradition*, 122.

Augustine's De Doctrina Christiana

between the subdued style of rhetoric, which seeks after truth and understanding; the moderate style, which brings beauty and delight; and the grand style, which persuades to action and obedience. He sprinkles his analysis with examples of rhetoric from the Old and New Testament, always emphasizing that the best rhetorical style is organic rather than ornamental and that the best orator will practice what he preaches. That is to say, Augustine promotes both aesthetic and moral decorum.

There is one part of book 4, however, where Augustine transcends the rules-oriented, technique-obsessed focus of his pagan predecessors to offer a suggestion that our modern schools would do well to heed. "Those with acute and eager minds," Augustine argues, "more readily learned eloquence by reading and hearing the eloquent than by following the rules of eloquence" (4.5). At the end of the day, memorizing rules and techniques of rhetoric is far less helpful than reading good books and imitating good writing. Since the late nineteenth century, American educators have increasingly emphasized methods over knowledge, teaching styles over teaching content.

Augustine understood better how humans actually learn: "Therefore, since infants are not taught to speak except by learning the expressions of speakers, why can men not be made eloquent, not by teaching them the rules of eloquence, but by having them read and hear the expressions of the eloquent and imitate them in so far as they are able to follow them?" Rather than fixating on the latest pedagogical trends and technical innovations, we would serve our students best if we exposed them daily to authors and books where eloquence goes hand in hand with truth, with piety, and with love.

Such a paideia, I believe, is best able to teach students to think rightly and for themselves (wisdom), to express what they have learned effectively (eloquence), and to use their hard-won powers of wisdom and eloquence for the sake of good (virtue).

TEN

JEAN-JACQUES ROUSSEAU'S *EMILE*

The Pedagogical Implications of Denying Original Sin

IN A MOMENT, I will turn my attention to one of the most influential thinkers, for good and for ill, in the history of Western ideas. In addition to the profound impact he had on religious, political, social, psychological, and aesthetic thought, Jean-Jacques Rousseau is the hinge figure in the slow, incremental shift from classical, traditional models of pedagogy to modern, progressive ones. It was he, more than anyone else, who set pedagogy on its modern trajectory toward an authority-distrusting, child-centered, experience-privileging classroom. Before doing so, however, I would like to set the stage by surveying briefly some of the key players between Augustine and Rousseau. Only thus can we see how radical the revolution was that Rousseau set in motion.

Augustinian monk Hugh of St. Victor (1096–1141) played a vital role in keeping alive the classical and Christian emphasis on the seven liberal arts: grammar, logic, and rhetoric (known as the trivium or "three ways") and arithmetic, geometry, astronomy, and music (the quadrivium). "These seven," Hugh explains, "[the ancients]

Jean-Jacques Rousseau's Emile 147

considered so to excel all the rest in usefulness that anyone who had been thoroughly schooled in them might afterward come to a knowledge of the others by his own inquiry and effort rather than by listening to a teacher." Indeed, the trivium and quadrivium are precisely the way by which "a quick mind enters into the secret places of wisdom."[1]

The seven liberal arts are both the foundation stones and philosophical tools for preparing the minds of students to engage with the fullness of wisdom, eloquence, and virtue. Subjects in their own right, they are also and more importantly ways of treating all other subjects, providing methods and perspectives for unlocking goodness, truth, and beauty. Once a student has gained proficiency in them, he can continue to learn on his own without the need of a teacher: he can, as I discussed in the previous chapter, think for himself.

Writing in the middle of the fourteenth century, as the light of the Florentine Renaissance was just about to dawn, poet and man of letters Petrarch (1304–1374) added to Hugh's focus on the classical and Christian liberal arts a unified, lifelong commitment to the pagan classics and the church fathers. Though he read the former more for style and the latter more for substance, he defended both as necessary to the formation of wisdom, eloquence, and virtue.

In a letter he wrote to Bocaccio, whose *Decameron* embodies the same intensity of life and diversity of character as Chaucer's *Canterbury Tales*, Petrarch highlights the importance of great literature: "Neither exhortations to virtue nor the argument of approaching death should divert us from literature; for in a good mind it excites the love of virtue, and dissipates, or at least diminishes, the fear of death. To desert our study shows want of self-confidence rather than wisdom, for letters do not hinder but aid the properly constituted

---

[1]Hugh of St. Victor, *Didascalion* 1.3, in *The Great Tradition: Classic Readings on What It Means to Be an Educated Human Being*, ed. Richard M. Gamble (Wilmington, DE: ISI Books, 2007), 257.

148   PART 2—THE NATURE OF THE DEBATE

mind which possesses them."[2] If we are virtuous of mind, literature can no more hurt us than food can hurt a healthy body. We must simply have the stamina to press on and the discernment to choose wisely.

A century and a half later, as the Renaissance spread across Europe, the great humanist scholar Desiderius Erasmus (ca. 1469–1536) seconded Petrarch's call for a vigorous engagement with the history and literature of the past. Like Petrarch before him, he saw through those who disparaged the pagan classics not, as they claimed, because they were anti-Christian but "because they want a cover for their indolence."[3] God used the Greeks and Romans to prepare the historical factors and the aesthetic genres that would allow Christianity to be disseminated, preserved, and passed down. It was the duty of all Christians who had the means to be properly educated in those factors and genres.

Compared to the animals, man is weak, naked, and defenseless. To remedy this, God gave us reason and a mind equipped for knowledge. Whereas bees and ants do all they do by instinct, man must be taught everything by instruction. Yet, Erasmus complains, many a nobleman who will expend great labor and expense to train his dog or horse will deprive his own son of education and moral training. He does all he can to gather up an inheritance to pass down to his son and then neglects the only kind of education that will allow him to make proper use of the wealth given to him.

Man, Erasmus insists,

> is not born, but made man. Primitive man, living a lawless, unschooled, promiscuous life in the woods, was not human, but rather a wild animal. It is reason which defines our humanity. . . . It is beyond argument that a man who has never been instructed in philosophy or in any branch of learning is a creature quite inferior to the brute animals. Animals only follow their natural

---

[2]Petrarch, "To Boccaccio, May 28, 1362," in Gamble, *Great Tradition*, 307.
[3]Desiderius Erasmus, *The Antibarbarians*, in Gamble, *Great Tradition*, 357.

Jean-Jacques Rousseau's Emile

instincts; but man, unless he has experienced the influence of learning and philosophy, is at the mercy of impulses that are worse than those of a wild beast.[4]

Born a half century before Rousseau (1712–1778), Italian humanist, historian, and philosopher Giambattista Vico (1688–1744) drew together many of the strands of Hugh, Petrarch, and Erasmus to champion a liberal arts education grounded in the classics and directed toward the instilling of wisdom, eloquence, and virtue. As I do in this book, Vico argues that to understand the proper nature of education, one must understand the proper nature of man. Though we bear the *imago Dei*, the fall has brought with it the triple corruption of language, mind, and soul. That is why, as Erasmus insists, man in nature is given to ignorance and lawlessness in his words, thoughts, and deeds.

Still, hope of reining in and civilizing man's fallen nature remains if we will only guide and train our youth through a proper system of education (paideia). To restore the corruption of language and thus bring about eloquence, we must apply the grammar phase of the trivium. To restore the corruption of the mind and thus bring about wisdom, we must follow with the rigorous teaching of logic. To restore the corruption of the soul and thus bring about virtue, we must so foster an understanding of theology and of things that cannot be seen as to provide the discernment necessary for the rhetoric stage.

"Three are the very duties of wisdom," Vico concludes, "with eloquence to tame the impetuousness of the fools, with prudence to lead them out of error, with virtue toward them to earn their goodwill, and in these ways, each according to his ability, to foster with zeal the society of men."[5] Writing half a century after Milton argued that the end of education was to repair the ruins of the fall, Vico makes clear

---

[4]Desiderius Erasmus, *On Education for Children*, in Gamble, *Great Tradition*, 363.
[5]Giambattista Vico, "On the Proper Order of Studies: Oration VI," in Gamble, *Great Tradition*, 479.

that a proper liberal arts education will strengthen not only the individual student but the human community of which he is a member.

To illustrate this noble hope and vision, Vico makes an allusion to the pagan myths of Orpheus, who tamed animals with his lyre, and Amphion, whose song caused inanimate stones to move through the air and form themselves into the walls of Thebes:

> Orpheus and Amphion are the wise who have brought together by means of their eloquence the knowledge of things divine and human and have led isolated man into union, that is, from love of self to the fostering of human community, from sluggishness to purposeful activity, from unrestrained license to compliance with law and by conferring equal rights united those unbridled in their strength with the weak.[6]

Such is the power of a liberal arts education founded in the seven liberal arts and the Great Books that is willing to learn from and heed the wisdom, virtue, and eloquence of the ancients.

A transitional figure between the Enlightenment and the Romantic Age, Rousseau conjures in his *Emile* (1762) an educational vision that glances backward to a traditional, even pastoral past while simultaneously setting in motion wide-ranging changes in the West's perception of the proper way to raise the young. Rousseau's well-conceived and creatively told manual for educating boys and girls in nature is on its surface highly conservative. Though Rousseau did, in later books, advocate state-based educational initiatives to socialize citizens in the "general will," here he holds up an ideal that looks surprisingly like a conservative Christian homeschooling family that wants to raise their children away from the sexualized mores and hypocritical values of high society.

His view of the sexes and the family is complementarian rather than egalitarian, and he affirms, both socially and psychologically, an

---

[6]Vico, "On the Proper Order," in Gamble, *Great Tradition*, 480.

essentialist view of masculinity and femininity. It is true that he refers to God only as Maker, Author, and Creator, never as Lord or Savior or King, and that he grounds morality in human reason and the laws of nature rather than the revealed moral codes of the Old and New Testament. Still, despite his decidedly deistic and undogmatic religious views, he treats reverence for God and virtuous living as central aspects of education. His goal is for his male and female students to be free of mind and soul, morally self-regulating citizens who are at peace with all men and who do their duty to God, family, and country.

Nevertheless, *Emile* set in motion, for good or ill, three paradigm-shifting theories/models that continue to influence education to this day: (1) a denial of original sin and a general distrust of authority, (2) a child-centered approach to learning based on an understanding of childhood as a distinct and separate stage, and (3) a pedagogical privileging of experience over books and nature over habit. In what follows I will weave all three together as I dialogue with Rousseau on the nature of man and of education.

<hr>

Perhaps because he grew up in John Calvin's Geneva with its pessimistic view of man as not just fallen but totally depraved, Rousseau reacted strongly against any notion that man was sinful by nature. The phrase that most people today associate with Rousseau is "noble savage," and he does indeed, both here and in other books (especially *The Social Contract*), present man as being inherently free and good in nature but corrupted by society and institutions, including the church. Indeed, he treats nature as equally unfallen, thus holding out the promise, one picked up on by two generations of Romantic poets, that we can return to an Eden of innocence, freedom, and brotherhood.

The opening line of *Emile* sums up Rousseau's optimism succinctly: "Everything is good as it comes from the hands of the Maker of the

152 PART 2—THE NATURE OF THE DEBATE

world but degenerates once it gets into the hands of man."[7] Such is Rousseau's trust of "unspoiled" nature that he, rather comically, criticizes parents for swaddling their children tightly. Children, he insists, should be left free to move their limbs as they would in nature. In all things, Rousseau would have parents and educators cleave to one simple maxim: "Observe nature and follow the path she marks out."[8] In fact, Rousseau makes the somewhat convincing argument that peasants do not suffer from arachnophobia because when they are young their parents, rather than protect them from spiders, allow and encourage them to interact fully with nature.

Although it would be an exaggeration to say the Romantics *invented* childhood, Rousseau and his heirs did push their contemporaries to appreciate childhood as its own stage of development, with play as a kind of childish work. "Your first duty," Rousseau exhorts his readers, "is to be humane. Love childhood. Look with friendly eyes on its games, its pleasures, its amiable dispositions. Which of you does not sometimes look back regretfully on the age when laughter was ever on the lips and the heart free of care? Why steal from the little innocents the enjoyment of a time that passes all too quickly?"[9]

Surely the hardest hearted of critics could not scorn such a tender and nostalgic sentiment. Surely it is an absolute good to allow children to learn in a natural atmosphere of complete freedom? Or is it? Rousseau's faith in the innocence of nature and childhood carries with it pedagogical implications. Consider how Rousseau contrasts the education of the peasant with that of the savage (or primitive) who grows up fully reliant on nature:

> There are two sets of men, peasants and savages, whose bodies are in constant activity, neither of whom gives any thought to the cultivation of their minds. The peasants are coarse and clumsy; the savages are known for their keen

---

[7]Jean-Jacques Rousseau, *The Emile of Jean Jacques Rousseau*, ed. and trans. William Boyd (New York: Teachers College Press, 1962), 11.

[8]Rousseau, *Emile of Jean Jacques Rousseau*, 17.

[9]Rousseau, *Emile of Jean Jacques Rousseau*, 33.

Jean-Jacques Rousseau's Emile   153

senses and even more for the subtlety of their minds. Why the difference? The
peasant is a creature of routine: he always does what he is told, or what he has
seen his father do, or what he himself has done from childhood. Habit and
obedience take the place of reason. It is a different matter with the savage. He
is not attached to any one place, has no prescribed task, obeys no one, has no
law but his own will, and is compelled to reason about every action in his life.
The more his body is exercised the better his mind becomes. Strength and
reason develop together and help each other.[10]

The contrast here may seem trivial, but it marks a departure from a
pedagogical truism that goes back to Aristotle: habit, along with obedience, is the key to instilling morality and gaining knowledge. For
Rousseau, habit and obedience, far from being a mainstay of virtue and
wisdom, impose the artificial, often corrupt laws of society on the child.

But Rousseau does not stop here. In addition to dethroning habit
and obedience as essential (and positive) tools for forming character,
he begins the slow deconstruction of the two main vehicles for ac-
complishing this task. "Our first masters of philosophy," writes
Rousseau with continued reference to the primitive described in the
passage just quoted, "are our feet, our hands and our eyes. To put
books in place of this experience does not teach us to reason: only to
be credulous and to borrow the reason of others."[11] Books, which had
been hailed for over two millennia as the transmitters of knowledge
and culture (paideia), become here agents of conformity that stifle
and crush, rather than develop and exercise, our reason.

Experience is to take the place of both habits and books, ensuring
that the child learn to think for himself. It is also to replace the classical reliance on memorization, particularly at the grammar school
level, to reinforce that tradition.

Habit, routine and custom mean nothing to [the twelve-year-old child who
learns in nature]. What he did yesterday has no effect on what he does today.
He never follows a fixed rule and never accepts authority or example. He only

---

[10]Rousseau, *Emile of Jean Jacques Rousseau*, 53.
[11]Rousseau, *Emile of Jean Jacques Rousseau*, 54.

154 PART 2—THE NATURE OF THE DEBATE

does or says what seems good to himself. For this reason you must not expect stock speeches or studied manners from him but just the faithful expression of his ideas and the conduct that comes from his inclinations.[12]

"Stock speeches," as Rousseau uses it here, is meant to be spoken with scorn and condescension—exactly the same way that progressive educators for the last century have spoken the phrase "rote memorization." It is only since the late nineteenth century that teachers have doubted the value of memorization and recitation ("stock speeches"). Children, especially at the grammar school level, love to memorize. Not only are they equipped mentally to memorize large chunks of information; they take pride and joy in their ability to do so. To waste those early years when memorization is easy and natural is nothing less than criminal.

It is significant that Rousseau pairs "stock speeches" with "studied manners," since children learn best not only by memorizing stories, poems, dates, places, facts, and figures but by imitating the words and actions of adults they trust. Rousseau, like many after him, harbored a deep distrust of authority, forgetting that students thrive the most when they are taught by a tutor or teacher they respect and love. Rousseau forgets, as well, that the passing down of fixed and ready-made truths is one of the responsibilities of any true paideia—a responsibility that is essential for the maintenance of a civilization.

Rousseau's antipathy to ready-made truths extends even into the field of science. "Do not teach him science: let him discover it. If ever you substitute authority for reason in his mind, he will stop reasoning, and become the victim of other people's opinions."[13] Here Rousseau anticipates by two centuries the rallying cry of American college students in the 1960s: question authority! The battle between experience and authority is an old one that goes back to the Middle Ages—it surfaces, for example, in the prologue to the Wife of Bath's tale in

---

[12]Rousseau, *Emile of Jean Jacques Rousseau*, 57.
[13]Rousseau, *Emile of Jean Jacques Rousseau*, 73.

Jean-Jacques Rousseau's Emile

Chaucer's *Canterbury Tales*—but with Rousseau it begins to take on a knee-jerk quality. Of course authority must be questioned! Of course students should trust to experience and be true to themselves! Such statements are too often taken for granted in our day and age: asserted without being proved.

Especially when coupled with Rousseau's insistence on child-centered learning, the continued privileging of experience over authority whittles away at the traditional pedagogical focus on books. Thus, Rousseau advises his readers, "If instead of keeping a child at his books I keep him busy in a workshop, his hands labour to the benefit of his mind. He becomes a man of science, but thinks himself only a workman."[14] Though there is nothing wrong per se with teaching arts and crafts or with assigning complex projects that call for hands-on creativity, when such pursuits take the place of the reading of and wrestling with challenging, time-tested books, education is compromised, and students fails to develop the reasoning skills necessary to truly think for themselves.

Rousseau's denial of original sin had the effect of placing too much trust in children and experience and too little in authority and the tradition. Until they are taught, by habit and the trivium, to think rightly, children cannot be trusted to think solely for themselves; as long as they learn primarily from immediate experiences, with little attention paid to the time-tested wisdom stored up in the Great Books, they will have no fixed measure against which to shape their growth in wisdom, eloquence, and virtue.

---

[14]Rousseau, *Emile of Jean Jacques Rousseau*, 79.

ELEVEN

JOHN DEWEY'S *DEMOCRACY AND EDUCATION*

The Birth of Progressive-Pragmatic Education

THE LONG LIFE OF AMERICAN PHILOSOPHER, psychologist, and social reformer John Dewey (1859–1952) spans nearly a century, from two years before the start of the Civil War to seven years after the end of the Second World War. He lived during a time of great change and progress in American society, and he embodied the values of the later nineteenth and early twentieth centuries—progressivism, positivism, meliorism, and utopianism—in his still-influential theories of education.

By progressivism I mean both an ideology and a desire to move forward by means of aggressive social change, even to the point of using social engineering to bring about the desired outcome. The opposite of progressivism is conservatism, the belief that it is best to conserve, learn from, and rely on the traditions, virtues, and wisdom of the past. Progressivism often goes hand in hand with positivism, a system that looks to reason and science, rather than faith and religion, for the answers to the ills of man and society. All systems are to be measured, verified, and justified by logical, mathematical, objective

John Dewey's Democracy and Education   157

criteria; appeals to ancient authorities, metaphysics, or fixed moral codes are to be dismissed as superstitious, primitive, and atavistic.

Meliorism is the belief that society naturally improves and that man can so direct progress as to accelerate this process of betterment. Utopianism is the belief that man, through advances in science and technology and through social and moral improvement, can construct an ideal commonwealth that will eliminate ignorance and poverty and usher in a state of universal peace and brotherhood. Although this naive faith in progress and technology was disrupted in Europe by the horrors of World War I—causing H. G. Wells, for example, to switch from writing utopian novels to dystopian ones— Americans continued to look to science, including and especially the social sciences, as a near-absolute good that would lead us to a new promised land.

All four of these "isms" are undergirded by an evolutionary paradigm that looks always forward, never backward. New is necessarily better; old is to be questioned and abandoned, if not eliminated, if it holds back the progression of the species. In England, this spirit manifested itself as utilitarianism, a system that does not ask of a thing whether it is moral or prudent or in keeping with the virtues of the past but whether it will bring the greatest good to the greatest number. Social, institutional, and aesthetic utility, not goodness, truth, and beauty, are to be the measures of whether a thing should be done.

While utilitarianism played a role and continues to play a role in the American psyche and ethos, the far more optimistic and energetic system of pragmatism dominated Dewey's years as a student, philosopher, and educational reformer. American pragmatists such as Dewey, William James, and Charles Sanders Peirce tend to be less cynical and doctrinaire than utilitarian Englishmen such as Jeremy Bentham, James Mill, and John Stuart Mill. They are results-oriented problem solvers who live by a simple motto: if it can be done, it should be done. That utopia might morph into dystopia does not strike fear

158   PART 2—THE NATURE OF THE DEBATE

in the heart of the pragmatist; he is too busy trying to convert his theories into realities. Convinced of the possibility of state-led social and moral improvement, American pragmatists did not hesitate to put initiatives into play that, by means of social engineering, would free us from the prejudices of the past. The most effective pedagogical pragmatist was Horace Mann, who fought for universal public education as a way of uniting the country and making better citizens.[1]

Although careful readers of this book should be able to guess that my assessment of Dewey's progressivism and pragmatism is going to be more negative than positive, I want to make it clear that I harbor much respect for Dewey's liberal desire to provide an education for all Americans, rich and poor, native and immigrant. He was at heart a humanist who believed in the dignity of the individual and tried to hold in balance the integrity of the individual and the needs of the collective. He was also a common sense thinker who tried to see the world through the eyes of children and to construct methods of education that would fit with what he perceived to be their needs and abilities.

Still, for all his humanism, he was a disciple of Darwin and as such considered man to be malleable, a work in progress to be managed. He was also, despite his common sense, a disciple of Rousseau who blinded himself to man's fallen, depraved nature. He did see the dangers of any kind of dualism that would divide body from soul, matter from mind, but his solution was monistic rather than incarnational: that is to say, rather than view man as an enfleshed soul, he subsumed the spiritual into the physical, ultimately robbing us of our full metaphysical meaning and moral agency.

In what follows, I will consider closely what is arguably Dewey's masterwork, *Democracy and Education* (1916). This time, however, I

---

[1]See Lawrence A. Cremin, ed., *The Republic and the School: Horace Mann on the Education of Free Men* (New York: Teachers College Press, 1957). For a balanced critique of Mann, see Bob Pepperman Taylor, *Horace Mann's Troubling Legacy: The Education of Democratic Citizens* (Lawrence: University Press of Kansas, 2010).

John Dewey's Democracy and Education   159

will structure my dialogue with Dewey around a series of direct quotes from his book that capture the richness and even genius of his theories while revealing the dangers inherent in his progressivist Darwinian vision. In wrestling with that vision, I will focus less on the religious implications of Dewey's Darwinism than on its anthropological, sociological, and pedagogical repercussions.

In chapter two of *Democracy and Education*, which Dewey titles "Education as a Social Function," he betrays both the hopes and the hazards of his pedagogical vision. It is, he argues,

> the business of the school environment to eliminate, so far as possible, the unworthy features of the existing environment from influence upon mental habitudes. It establishes a purified medium of action. Selection aims not only at simplifying but at weeding out what is undesirable. Every society gets encumbered with what is trivial, with dead wood from the past, and with what is positively perverse. The school has the duty of omitting such things from the environment which it supplies, and thereby doing what it can to counteract their influence in the ordinary social environment.[2]

Far from presenting the function of education as a conserving force meant to preserve and pass down the wisdom and traditions of the ancestors, Dewey holds up public education as a social vehicle for weeding out the undesirable habits and purifying the perverse beliefs of previous generations.

While it is a good and noble thing to seek to overcome the real ignorance, superstition, and prejudice of the past, who are the watchful social guardians who will decide *what* those superstitions are? Who, to quote ancient Roman satirist Juvenal, will watch those watchers? At least the censorship advocated by Plato in the *Republic*

---

[2]John Dewey, *Democracy and Education: An Introduction to the Philosophy of Education* (New York: Free Press, 1966), 20. Dewey's book, which is available in numerous editions, is extremely well organized, in an almost Aristotelian fashion. He offers a series of short chapters, all of which are broken into several sections (usually three), followed by a concise summary. I will therefore give future references by the chapter number followed by the section number (or the word *summary*).

is based on transcendent standards of goodness, truth, and beauty by which the actions of Homer's licentious gods could be judged. For Dewey's progressive pragmatism, the standard, if it exists at all, is an ever-shifting one that can easily fall prey to the current spirit of the age (or zeitgeist). Once education becomes unmoored from fixed standards, the censors in charge can decide for themselves what is medieval, old-fashioned, and out of date and what is modern, open-minded, and scientific.

Throughout history there have arisen tyrants who have set the generations against each other for their own personal aggrandizement. Here, however, we encounter something new: a definition of education that deems it a good thing, if not indeed a virtuous calling, to teach a son that the beliefs and practices of his father are trivial at best and poisonous at worst. Rather than work in tandem with parents to pass the torch of tradition, Dewey's vision implies that public schools should become social crusaders intent on exposing the folly and small-mindedness of the past and overthrowing the yoke of parental authority.

I do not think that is Dewey's intent, but it *is* the logical and inevitable upshot of his vision. In any case, he does make it clear that it is the role and duty of public educators to eliminate all those things from the past that they consider social evils:

The reconstruction of experience may be social as well as personal. For purposes of simplification we have spoken in the earlier chapters somewhat as if the education of the immature which fills them with the spirit of the social group to which they belong, were a sort of catching up of the child with the aptitudes and resources of the adult group. In static societies, societies which make the maintenance of established custom their measure of value, this conception applies in the main. But not in progressive communities. They endeavor to shape the experiences of the young so that instead of reproducing current habits, better habits shall be formed, and thus the future adult society be an improvement on their own. Men have long had some intimation of the extent to which education may be consciously used to

John Dewey's Democracy and Education   161

eliminate obvious social evils through starting the young on paths which shall not produce these ills, and some idea of the extent in which education may be made an instrument of realizing the better hopes of men. But we are doubtless far from realizing the potential efficacy of education as a constructive agency of improving society, from realizing that it represents not only a development of children and youth but also of the future society of which they will be the constituents.[3]

Here we have expressed with unapologetic clarity public education's central task of socializing the young. Though parents are not directly mentioned, the clear implication that underlies the passage is that the public school always knows better than the parents, for it is more enlightened and can see through the "obvious" social evils of the past. The role of education is to improve the youth, but *not* by instilling in them the best that has been known and thought by their ancestors. Improvement means breaking from the past.

With a stroke of his pen, Dewey dismisses what the best pedagogical minds of the classical, medieval, and Renaissance worlds would have hailed as the main function of paideia: the "catching up of the child with the aptitudes and resources of the adult group." That goal, Dewey argues, may be fine and good for "static" societies; it will not do for progressive societies committed to replacing the "reproducing" of "current habits" with a conscious program of forming "better habits." Again, this goal in and of itself can be a noble one, but who is to determine and define what constitutes "better"? Too often the one who decides is an ideologue who resents the past—and his parents.[4]

---

[3]Dewey, *Democracy and Education*, 6.3.
[4]It is a good thing that each of the last four generations of Americans has seen a slow decline in the racial prejudices of the generation before them. I would argue, however, that this shift would have been smoother, less polemical, and less polarizing had each generation been taught in school not to dismiss their parents' generation as racists but to challenge their elders to live up to the high ideals of our founding documents. See my analysis of Martin Luther King Jr.'s "Letter from Birmingham Jail" in chapter two for just such an approach, one that works with and through the tradition rather than against it.

162 PART 2—THE NATURE OF THE DEBATE

Lest I sound too negative and dismissive of Dewey's thought, I will now shift directions and highlight those areas of *Democracy and Education* that demonstrate keen insight into the pedagogical endeavor. Though Dewey was very much a disciple of Rousseau, he does show himself capable of praising Rousseau's focus on the child while criticizing him for his simplistic views on nature and the so-called noble savage. In passionately asserting "the intrinsic goodness of all natural tendencies," Rousseau neglected the glaringly obvious truth "that primitive impulses are of themselves neither good nor evil, but become one or the other according to the objects for which they are employed."[5] Rousseau may have mounted a needed corrective to extreme versions of total depravity that negatively affected educators' views of children, but he went too far in the other direction to idealize nature as an absolute good.

By carefully placing Rousseau within his historical milieu, Dewey uncovers the weaknesses at the core of Rousseau's theories of education:

> The doctrine of following nature was a political dogma. It meant a rebellion against existing social institutions, customs, and ideals. . . . It is upon this conception of the artificial and harmful character of organized social life as it now exists that he rested the notion that nature not merely furnishes prime forces which initiate growth but also its plan and goal. That evil institutions and customs work almost automatically to give a wrong education which the most careful schooling cannot offset is true enough; but the conclusion is not to education apart from the environment, but to provide an environment in which native powers will be put to better uses.[6]

Rousseau's demonization of society naturally produced its opposite, an overreliance on nature to furnish the means and goals for education. Though Dewey the progressivist *does* agree that existing customs and institutions can be evil and prevent true education, he rejects Rousseau's naive faith that nature can fill in the gap, supplying both an educational telos and an environment in which that telos can be achieved.

---

[5]Dewey, *Democracy and Education*, 9.1.
[6]Dewey, *Democracy and Education*, 9.1.

John Dewey's Democracy and Education   163

Whereas many of Dewey's heirs overcorrected Rousseau, privileging the social over the individual, Dewey himself tried to keep the two in balance: "It is the particular task of education at the present time to struggle in behalf of an aim in which social efficiency and personal culture are synonyms instead of antagonists."[7] In classical American fashion, Dewey calls for an educational system that honors both the individual and the group. Unlike many of his progressivist heirs, who have advocated for rigid, uniform curricula driven by classroom-management strategies that treat students in the mass, Dewey sought to retain flexibility and respect for individual differences.

Our own day has seen a "war on boys" that forces all young students to sit still and conform in a way that is natural for most girls but difficult for most boys. When boys act like boys, they are either punished or advised, if not forced, to take Ritalin or Adderall to control what is diagnosed as attention deficit/hyperactivity disorder.[8] Long before this war began, Dewey warned against it:

> The chief source of the "problem of discipline" in schools is that the teacher has often to spend the larger part of the time in suppressing the bodily activities which take the mind away from its material. A premium is put on physical quietude; on silence, on rigid uniformity of posture and movement; upon a machine-like simulation of the attitudes of intelligent interest. The teachers' business is to hold the pupils up to these requirements and to punish the inevitable deviations which occur.[9]

Dewey also foresaw another ill side effect of progressivism: educators who, in good positivist manner, demand standardized testing to enforce efficiency, conformity, and statistical precision.

---

[7]Dewey, *Democracy and Education*, 9.3.

[8]See the introduction and notes 4 and 5 for more on the war on boys. I do not mean to claim that ADHD is not a real diagnosis; however, I believe the expansion of therapy culture in America has led to an overreliance on diagnosis and medication. See, for example, Abigail Shrier, *Bad Therapy: Why the Kids Aren't Growing Up* (New York: Sentinel, 2024) and Jonathan Haidt, *The Anxious Generation: How the Great Rewiring of Childhood Is Causing an Epidemic of Mental Illness* (New York: Penguin, 2024).

[9]Dewey, *Democracy and Education*, 11.1.

164   PART 2—THE NATURE OF THE DEBATE

Exorbitant desire for uniformity of procedure and for prompt external results are the chief foes which the open-minded attitude meets in school. The teacher who does not permit and encourage diversity of operation in dealing with questions is imposing intellectual blinders upon pupils—restricting their vision to the one path that the teacher's mind happens to approve. Probably the chief cause of devotion to rigidity of method is, however, that it seems to promise speedy, accurately measurable, correct results. The zeal for "answers" is the explanation of much of the zeal for rigid and mechanical methods.[10]

There are other laudatory aspects of Dewey's theories. He explains well the Aristotelian distinction between liberal and servile education and then strives to construct a public educational system that will service white- and blue-collar children alike. More than that, he makes it is his goal "to construct a course of studies which makes thought a guide of free practice for all and which makes leisure a reward of accepting responsibility for service, rather than a state of exemption from it."[11] To borrow terminology from Ralph Waldo Emerson's "American Scholar," Dewey's goal is not to produce thinking men and working men but Men thinking and Men working. A liberal education need not be totally divorced from utility. In fact, it can produce the kind of yeoman farmer that Thomas Jefferson desired: someone who can plow his own field and then sit beneath a tree in the heat of the day to read Virgil in Latin.

Still, despite his grand democratic vision, Dewey is hampered by his progressivist refusal to accept any ends or standards that are real, transcendent, and final: "Greek and medieval knowledge accepted the world in its qualitative variety, and regarded nature's processes as having ends, or in technical phrase as teleological. New science was expounded so as to deny the reality of all qualities in real, or objective, existence."[12] Dewey would have done well to read the work of his contemporary

---

[10]Dewey, *Democracy and Education*, 13.3.
[11]Dewey, *Democracy and Education*, 19.summary.
[12]Dewey, *Democracy and Education*, 21.2.

John Dewey's Democracy and Education   165

G. K. Chesterton. In chapter two of *Orthodoxy* (1908), Chesterton exposes the dangers of what he calls "the false theory of progress" by asking a simple question: "If the standard changes, how can there be improvement, which implies a standard?" If we do not accept a fixed destination, then we will never arrive, no matter how far we travel.

"True individualism," Dewey argues, "is a product of the relaxation of the grip of the authority of custom and traditions as standards of belief. Aside from sporadic instances, like the height of Greek thought, it is a comparatively modern manifestation. Not but that there have always been individual diversities, but that a society dominated by conservative custom represses them or at least does not utilize them and promote them."[13] As before, there is the potential here for the righting of some real wrongs, but it quickly descends into the same knee-jerk mantra of "question authority" we saw in Rousseau.

In the end, it yields just the kind of progressive creed for philosophy that Dewey articulates in the third-to-last chapter of *Democracy and Education*:

> If we are willing to conceive education as the process of forming fundamental dispositions, intellectual and emotional, toward nature and fellow men, philosophy may even be defined *as the general theory of education*. Unless the philosophy is to remain symbolic—or verbal—or a sentimental indulgence for a few, or else mere arbitrary dogma, its auditing of past experience and its program of values must take effect in conduct. Public agitation, propaganda, legislative and administrative action are effective in producing the change of disposition which a philosophy indicates as desirable, but only in the degree in which they are educative—that is to say, in the degree in which they modify mental and moral attitudes. And at the best, such methods are compromised by the fact they are used with those whose habits are already largely set, while education of youth has a fairer and freer field of operation.[14]

Dewey was in most ways a fair and generous man, but this creed, and it *is* a creed, betrays a rather haughty condescension toward older forms

---

[13]Dewey, *Democracy and Education*, 22.summary.
[14]Dewey, *Democracy and Education*, 24.2.

of philosophy, which he sees as dogmatic in the negative sense and inert in changing society. It is a good thing that he wants to turn philosophy into action, but the fact that he wants to start with young people because it is easier to mold and shape their minds should raise red flags to anyone aware of the history of twentieth-century totalitarianism.

Dewey does believe that education has an ethical dimension, but in his final chapter he makes it clear that, in calling for the modification of the "mental and moral attitudes" of the young, he does not mean teaching them to act in accordance with moral standards that are fixed, traditional, and transcendent. What he calls for instead is what has come to be known, in the psychological world of cognitive-behavioral therapy, as values clarification.[15] Moral codes are to be mixed with individual experience to arrive at a personal understanding of ethical behavior. Though I applaud Dewey for helping to break down the cold, duty-bound morality of Kant, what he offers in its place is not much better: a morality that is situational and consecutive rather than absolute and ready-made, that moves and grows with experience rather than adhering to set principles.

As he moves toward the closing pages of his book, Dewey drops any pretense to working within the framework of traditional pedagogy and states his position boldly:

> Moral education in school is practically hopeless when we set up the development of character as a supreme end, and at the same time treat the acquiring of knowledge and the development of understanding, which of necessity occupy the chief part of school time, as having nothing to do with character. On such a basis, moral education is inevitably reduced to some kind of catechetical instruction, or lessons about morals. Lessons "about morals" signify as matter of course lessons in what other people think about virtues and duties. It amounts to something only in the degree in which pupils happen to be already animated by a sympathetic and dignified regard for the sentiments of others. . . . As a matter of fact, direct instruction in morals has

---

[15]See chap. 7 and note 4 for more on values clarification.

John Dewey's Democracy and Education

been effective only in social groups where it was a part of the authoritative control of the many by the few.[16]

Contra Plato, Aristotle, and Isocrates; Cicero, Seneca, and Quintilian; Augustine, Hugh, and Aquinas; Petrarch, Erasmus, and Vico; Milton, Burke, and Newman, Dewey discards as relics of the past what others have thought and written on virtue and duty. The hard-won, eagerly preserved lessons of the great philosophers and educators of the past two and a half millennia are scornfully (and ungratefully) reduced to schoolboy catechisms that can have no binding authority on progressive pragmatists committed to reforming the world one student at a time.

No longer are educators to square their teachings with the moral consensus of the ancestors: "The habit of identifying moral charac- teristics with external conformity to authoritative prescriptions . . . tends to reduce morals to a dead and machine-like routine. Conse- quently while such an attitude has moral results, the results are morally undesirable—above all in a democratic society where so much depends upon personal disposition."[17] No longer are schools to train students in the wisdom, eloquence, and virtue of America's Greco-Roman, Judeo-Christian heritage. Even if, by doing so, the student acquires a real foundation of morality, that morality is to be treated as artificial, impersonal, and undemocratic.

"To possess virtue," Dewey concludes, "does not signify to have cul- tivated a few nameable and exclusive traits; it means to be fully and adequately what one is capable of becoming through association with others in all the offices of life."[18] Morality does not inhere in revealed law codes or philosophical Forms or time-tested works of literature and philosophy; it is both personal and social and must be treated as such by teachers whose calling it is to replace the virtues of yesterday with the values of today.

---

[16]Dewey, *Democracy and Education*, 26.3.
[17]Dewey, *Democracy and Education*, 26.3.
[18]Dewey, *Democracy and Education*, 26.4.

TWELVE

C. S. LEWIS'S
THE ABOLITION OF MAN

Building Students' Chests

IN ADDITION TO WRITING Christian apologetics and children's literature, C. S. Lewis wrote one of the most important pedagogical books of the twentieth century. Published in the middle of the Second World War, as Dewey's *Democracy and Education* was published in the middle of the First, C. S. Lewis's *The Abolition of Man* (1943) traces, with razor-sharp precision, what happens when a nation's education system divorces wisdom from virtue, and both from fixed, objective, transcendent standards.

Lewis begins his analysis of the state of education in England by highlighting a passage in an actual textbook meant for high schoolers that he calls *The Green Book*. The passage tells a story of two tourists who look together at a waterfall. The first calls the waterfall "sublime," while the second calls it "pretty." Romantic poet Samuel Taylor Coleridge overhears them and silently gives his assent to the first. Coleridge does so, for he knows the proper meaning of words and the proper response that a waterfall should elicit from a person.

As such, the story could have been used to teach young people what a rightly ordered (or ordinate) response should be to the power and majesty of a waterfall. "He lives in justice and sanctity," Augustine argues in *On Christian Doctrine*, "who is an unprejudiced assessor of the intrinsic value of things. He is a man who has an ordinate love: he neither loves what should not be loved nor fails to love what should be loved; he neither loves more what should be loved less, loves equally what should be loved less or more, nor loves less or more what should be loved equally" (1.27). In the same way that a person must learn to love things in accordance with their intrinsic value, students must be taught to respond to things in accordance with their inherent and objective qualities. Roses are pretty, but not waterfalls. Waterfalls are objectively sublime.

Again, the story could have and should have been used to inculcate proper responses to nature in the hearts, minds, and souls of students: not only because proper responses lay the foundation for proper taste but because proper taste aids in the formation of proper virtue. Virtues, as I explained in chapter seven, are universal principles written into the cosmos as much as they are into the nature of man. They are objective and external, and as such confront us with external measures and rules to which we must conform ourselves. To instill in students the correct (virtuous) response of numinous awe and reverential wonder that they should feel in the presence of a sublime waterfall is to start them on the road to feeling rightly ordered disgust in the face of an act of treachery, ordinate shame when they themselves deceive others, and proper humility and gratitude when they receive an unmerited gift.

Not so for the authors of *The Green Book*. Influenced by the same evolutionary, experience-over-authority, values-clarification paradigm as Dewey, the authors critique the story as falsely teaching that nature can be objectively pretty or sublime and can thus merit, if not demand, a certain emotional response. Coleridge, they teach the young readers of their textbook, was wrong to side with the first tourist. The tourist who called the waterfall sublime was not saying anything objective about the waterfall; he was merely expressing his own subjective feelings about it. The statement tells us nothing about the waterfall; it only reflects the emotional state of the speaker.

"The schoolboy who reads this passage in The Green Book," Lewis explains, "will believe two propositions: firstly, that all sentences containing a predicate of value are statements about the emotional state of the speaker, and secondly, that all such statements are unimportant."[1] Here Lewis traces the invisible but inevitable link between a student thinking that words such as *pretty* and *sublime* have no objective content and that concepts such as good and evil, virtue and vice are nothing but personal opinions. The name for this school of thought is subjectivism, and in its full form it denies any objective ground to words used in the ethical (the good), metaphysical (the true), and aesthetic (the beautiful) realms. Beauty, like goodness and truth, resides only in the eye of the beholder. So the student will be taught, and so he will conclude that all ethical-metaphysical-aesthetic statements are ultimately subjective and trivial.

That does not mean, Lewis hastens to add, that the student

will make any conscious inference from what he reads to a general philosophical theory that all values are subjective and trivial. The very power of [the authors of The Green Book] depends on the fact that they are dealing with a boy: a boy who thinks he is "doing" his "English prep" and has no notion that ethics, theology, and politics are all at stake. It is not a theory they put into his mind, but an assumption, which ten years hence, its origin forgotten and its presence unconscious, will condition him to take one side in a controversy which he has never recognized as a controversy at all.[2]

The subjectivism that undergirds and energizes *The Green Book*, like the progressivism and pragmatism that drive *Democracy and Education*, is not organic to the educational enterprise, at least as it was understood before Rousseau. Divorced from education's traditional

---

[1]C. S. Lewis, *The Abolition of Man* (New York: Macmillan, 1965), 15.
[2]Lewis, *Abolition of Man*, 16-17.

C. S. Lewis's The Abolition of Man

role of passing down the legacy of the past and instilling wisdom and virtue in the young, subjectivism, progressivism, and pragmatism represent antitraditional worldviews imposed *on* that enterprise. Far from empowering education to fulfill its traditional role, these three "isms" use education to bring about the brave new world they envision and desire.[3]

By encouraging students to treat all value statements as subjective, Lewis argues, the authors of *The Green Book* and educators like them ensure that when students grow older, they will naturally, almost unconsciously, support further initiatives to break the grip of traditional understandings of morality, truth, and beauty in favor of a radical kind of tolerance that seeks to shatter all fixed and absolute standards. That does not mean that subjectivism cannot help students to empathize more and so be able to see the world through the eyes of others. In that way, it *can* play a role in a pluralistic society and engender good dialogue.

But subjectivism inevitably cuts the ground out from under the feet of pluralism—for tolerance cannot be maintained apart from a traditional view of man as having intrinsic value and worth (because of the *imago Dei*) but in need of limits and boundaries (because of the fall). Apart from a firm grounding in the dignity-depravity of man, tolerance will eventually morph into intolerance, pluralism into conformity, free speech into Rousseau's general will, thinking for oneself into socialization.

Since the days of ancient Greece and Rome, groups of students have resisted and rebelled against the authority of their teachers,

---

[3] "What we remark especially about the educational thought of the last few years, is the enthusiasm with which education has been taken up as an instrument for the realisation of social ideals. It would be a pity if we overlooked the possibilities of education as a means of acquiring wisdom; if we belittled the acquisition of knowledge for the satisfaction of curiosity, without any further motive than the desire to know; and if we lost our respect for learning." T. S. Eliot, *Notes Toward the Definition of Culture* (1948), chap. 6, quoted in *The Great Tradition: Classic Readings on What It Means to Be an Educated Human Being*, ed. Richard M. Gamble (Wilmington, DE: ISI Books, 2007), 619.

parents, and political leaders. What is different about the situation today is that the schools themselves consciously train their students to indulge in just such resistance and rebellion. Teachers use their pedagogical authority to undermine their own authority and deconstruct the very Great Books that provide the only foundation for real freedom of thought, including the freedom to deconstruct the ideas that make that freedom possible. Great dissenters from Augustine to Luther, the American Founding Fathers to William Wilberforce and Martin Luther King Jr., *did* break from the status quo, but they did so from a position of faith in God and the tradition. They were radicals in the etymological sense; they insisted on returning to the root (*radix* in Latin) of biblical or democratic authority.

Not so Dewey or the authors of *The Green Book*. For most progressive educators, science takes the place of religion, for the former is closely allied to reality, while the latter is a kind of wish fulfillment. Lewis turns this false distinction on its head. Modern science, beginning with Francis Bacon, bears far more resemblance to magic than does religion, for both magic and science seek the power to bend nature, other people, and reality itself to their will. "For the wise men of old," Lewis explains,

> the cardinal problem had been how to conform the soul to reality and the solution had been knowledge, self-discipline, and virtue. For magic and applied science alike the problem is how to subdue reality to the wishes of men: the solution is a technique; and both, in the practice of this technique, are ready to do things hitherto regarded as disgusting and impious—such as digging up and mutilating the dead.[4]

Knowledge, self-discipline, and virtue have, for over two thousand years, been the domain and the telos of Christianity and classical paideia alike. Both seek to instill wisdom and virtue through a rigorous training of body, soul, and mind, but in such a way that

---

[4]Lewis, *Abolition of Man*, 88.

reconciles us to reality rather than setting us against it in rebellion. It is, Lewis argues, Dr. Faustus, who sold his soul for forbidden knowledge, and Bacon, who taught that knowledge was power, whose goal it is to break us free from all limits. It is Faust and Bacon, not Plato and Augustine, who indulge their inordinate desires, who refuse to be bound by the transcendent truths and moral codes that make and keep us human.

In *The Abolition of Man*, Lewis exposes the disordered, ultimately self-consuming aims of progressive educators who are willing to do whatever it takes to subdue reality—both nature *and* man—to their will. In what remains of this chapter, I will discuss some of those aims and show, with Lewis's help, how they inevitably turn against themselves, leaving their students less wise, less virtuous, and less free.

At the core of Lewis's argument is the traditional belief that a good educator will do more than instruct students in specific skills. To be educated means to possess an understanding of right and wrong that is grounded in a universal moral-ethical code that is ultimately binding on all people no matter their ethnicity or creed. In *The Abolition of Man*, Lewis, in order to highlight the crosscultural nature of that code, calls it the Tao, but he admits that he could just as well have called it "Natural Law or Traditional Morality or the First Principles of Practical Reason or the First Platitudes."[5]

Along with the three Rs of reading, writing, and arithmetic, teachers have traditionally been called on to ensure that the young develop into virtuous members of society who can distinguish, even if they do not always heed, the difference between good and evil thoughts, words, and deeds. Each nation has naturally added to the Tao their own cultural distinctives; however, to the extent that they have hoped to survive and thrive as a people group, they have made it their

---

[5]Lewis, *Abolition of Man*, 56.

174   PART 2—THE NATURE OF THE DEBATE

business to instill the natural law, with its essential, self-evident principles of reason and morality, into the next generation.

Both the subjectivism of *The Green Book* and the progressivism of Dewey and his heirs stand in opposition to the Tao, for both seek to free students from its binding nature. In that enterprise, Lewis warns, they are doomed to fail: "The rebellion of new ideologies against the *Tao* is a rebellion of the branches against the tree: if the rebels could succeed they would find that they had destroyed themselves. The human mind has no more power of inventing a new value than of imagining a new primary colour, or, indeed, of creating a new sun and a new sky for it to move in."[6]

True education is founded, or at least should be founded, on virtues and principles that transcend any given time or place. The classical paideia of Greece was distinctive to Athens, but only in the sense that it preserved and passed down the specific ways in which the Athenians had learned to embody the Tao within their culture. That is why the Christian paideia of the Middle Ages was able to borrow so heavily from the pagan paideia of ancient Greece and Rome. Though Augustine knew what the Greeks did not—that the triune God, not Plato's Forms, was the final Logos (Word, Reason, Logic) behind all goodness, truth, and beauty—the makers of the classical paideia did know that a Logos existed and that both the cosmos and man's soul were ordered by and around it. Apart from that Logos, however precisely it is defined and understood, there can only be chaos and a breakdown of standards. Apart from the Logos, there can be no Tao.

That is a problem, for Logos and Tao, both of which play a foundational role in the passing down of wisdom and virtue, are excluded from progressive paideias eager to unmoor students from the fixed, ready-made truths of the past. Inasmuch as that unmooring sets wisdom adrift, it pushes society toward unsustainable philosophies

---

[6]Lewis, *Abolition of Man*, 56-57.

C. S. Lewis's The Abolition of Man   175

that end up cutting themselves off from the very tree that supports them. Inasmuch as it sets virtue adrift, it threatens to produce a generation of students who cannot regulate their behaviors or commit themselves to the kinds of sacrifices a society needs to survive.

Borrowing a metaphor from Plato, Lewis describes how all people, whatever their culture, must navigate between their rational (angelic) side and their appetitive (bestial) side. In a one-on-one fight between reason and appetite, which Lewis, after Plato, locates in the head and belly, respectively, the belly will always win. Only if the chest is strong enough to come to the aid of the head will it be able to hold the belly at bay. It has been the traditional role of education to build up the chest by feeding it on the Tao and exercising it with the proper sentiments that should accompany the Tao. Unfortunately for students and the societies they will someday lead, progressive education fails to nurture and strengthen the chest, leaving the head prey to every attack from the belly.

Yet, Lewis points out, there is a sad and tragic irony in the way modern educators treat the chest.

> You can hardly open a periodical without coming across the statement that what our civilization needs is more "drive," or dynamism, or self-sacrifice, or "creativity." In a sort of ghastly simplicity we remove the organ and demand the function. We make men without chests and expect of them virtue and enterprise. We laugh at honour and are shocked to find traitors in our midst. We castrate and bid the geldings be fruitful.[7]

We cannot have it both ways. If we systematically shrink the chest by ridiculing or trivializing the principles and the sentiments on which it alone can feed and grow, we will leave our children naked and defenseless against the depredations of the belly. There is some truth to the charge that those who seek to instill virtue in students' chests can do so in a manner that is overly emotional, sentimental,

---

[7]Lewis, *Abolition of Man*, 35.

176 PART 2—THE NATURE OF THE DEBATE

and mawkish. But that danger, real as it is, is not a danger today. Quite the reverse:

> For every one pupil who needs to be guarded against a weak excess of sensibility there are three who need to be awakened from the slumber of cold vulgarity. The task of the modern educator is not to cut down jungles but to irrigate deserts. The right defence against false sentiments is to inculcate just sentiments. By starving the sensibility of our pupils we only make them easier prey to the propagandist when he comes. For famished nature will be avenged and a hard heart is no infallible protection against a soft head.[8]

Just as the best defense against weeds is healthy grass, so the best way to guard against manipulative propaganda is to strengthen and purify the emotions. If we starve the chest from the only food on which it can be nourished, we will render it incapable of coming to the defense of the head when it is overwhelmed by the folly and narcissism of the belly.

While I do not object to public educators seeking to free students from *actual* prejudice, superstition, and intolerance, I do object when potentially good moral education is framed by a self-righteous tone that uncritically ridicules, if not vilifies, parents, patriotism, and the past. Such an approach rarely inculcates wisdom or virtue or eloquence; it more often teaches students to be lazy cynics and smug skeptics, assured, falsely, of their moral superiority to all that came before. Cynicism and skepticism tear down without building up. They do not cause the chest to grow and expand; to the contrary, they cause it to wither and atrophy. They are substitutes for rather than supporters of critical thinking.

Too much of education today focuses on the removal of classical virtues and the explaining away of old verities. Yet, here too, there is a central irony that turns education against itself: "You cannot go on 'explaining away' for ever: you will find that you have explained explanation itself away. You cannot go on 'seeing through' things for

---

[8]Lewis, *Abolition of Man*, 24.

ever. The whole point of seeing through something is to see something through it."[9]

One cannot see through first principles, for it is they that allow us to see everything else. That is why traditional educators argue from the Tao rather than for it. That is why they ground education in a reading and wrestling with the Great Books—those noble, time-tested, Tao-filled repositories of the wisdom and virtue of the ages.

---

[9]Lewis, *Abolition of Man*, 91.

THIRTEEN

DOROTHY SAYERS AND CHARLOTTE MASON

How Best to Train the Young

Has it ever struck you as odd, or unfortunate, that today, when the proportion of literacy . . . is higher than it has ever been, people should have become susceptible to the influence of advertisement and mass propaganda to an extent hitherto unheard of and unimagined? Do you put this down to the mere mechanical fact that the press and the radio and so on have made propaganda much easier to distribute over a wide area? Or do you sometimes have an uneasy suspicion that the product of modern educational methods is less good than he or she might be at disentangling fact from opinion and the proven from the plausible?[1]

From where do you think I have plucked this incisive critique? From a politician or pundit exposing the ills of our primary and secondary education systems? From a public watchdog group warning against the dangers of consumerism? From a professor of writing or of logic bemoaning the lack of preparedness of the modern college freshman?

No on all counts. The critique was written seventy-five years ago by a British translator, apologist, dramatist, detective writer, and

---

[1]Dorothy Sayers, "The Lost Tools of Learning," in *The Great Tradition: Classic Readings on What It Means to Be an Educated Human Being*, ed. Richard M. Gamble (Wilmington, DE: ISI Books, 2007), 603. This essay also appears in the appendix to Douglas Wilson, *Recovering the Lost Tools of Learning: An Approach to a Distinctively Christian Education* (Wheaton, IL: Crossway, 1992), and can be accessed for free online. I will provide page numbers from Gamble's anthology.

public intellectual named Dorothy Sayers (1893–1957). It comes from an essay, "The Lost Tools of Learning," that Sayers first read in Oxford in 1947—four years after her friend C. S. Lewis published *The Abolition of Man*, which itself began as a series of speeches—and then published a year later. In her essay she calls for a time-tested liberal arts method of instruction that frees the mind, arming it against faulty logic, emotional appeals, and manipulative propaganda.

Sadly, Sayers's critique is even truer today than when it was written. In America, we applaud ourselves for having a highly educated populace while overlooking a disturbing reality—our increasingly educated populace has become increasingly less able to distinguish evidence from hearsay, logical argument from personal attack, reasoned discourse from political spin. High school, and increasingly college, graduates too often leave their alma maters in possession of much specialized knowledge but without the ability to weigh, analyze, and assess the endless stream of new "knowledge" that comes to them through their television screens and smart phones.

The lost tools of Sayers's title refer to the classical trivium of grammar, logic (Sayer prefers to use the word *dialectic*), and rhetoric, which I discussed briefly in chapter ten. What Sayers brings to the table is a more modern understanding of the psychological stages of child development and how those stages overlap with the trivium:

> The Poll-Parrot stage is the one in which learning by heart is easy and, on the whole, pleasurable; whereas reasoning is difficult and, on the whole, little relished. At this age one readily memorizes the shapes and appearances of things; one likes to recite the number-plates of cars; one rejoices in the chanting of rhymes and the rumble and thunder of unintelligible polysyllables; one enjoys the mere accumulation of things. The Pert Age, which follows upon this (and, naturally, overlaps it to some extent) is only too familiar to all who have to do with children: it is characterized by contradicting, answering back, liking to "catch people out" (especially one's elders); and by the propounding of conundrums. Its nuisance-value is extremely high. It usually sets in about the Fourth Form. The Poetic Age is popularly known as

the "difficult" age. It is self-centered; it yearns to express itself; it rather specializes in being misunderstood; it is restless and tries to achieve independence; and, with good luck and good guidance, it should show the beginnings of creativeness; a reaching out towards a synthesis of what it already knows, and a deliberate eagerness to know and do some one thing in preference to all others. Now it seems to me that the layout of the Trivium adapts itself with a singular appropriateness to these three ages: Grammar to the Poll-Parrot, Dialectic to the Pert, and Rhetoric to the Poetic Age.[2]

Far from a backward, ineffective, punitive method, as Rousseau, Dewey, and most of their heirs continue to believe, rote memorization in the grammar school years aligns perfectly the skills and delights of the young child with the pedagogical need to supply them with a firm foundation of facts, figures, and dates on which to build their education.

Once the foundation has been laid, the student can move into the logic-dialectic phase. The pert middle-schooler, so eager to question everything and everyone, is now at the right age to learn how to put together the things he has memorized into the different packages we call disciplines. Such students can either waste away their pertness in being disagreeable or have their pertness channeled into logical thinking. Let them use their burgeoning critical skills to see through logical fallacies so that when they are older, they will not be taken in by political ideologies and advertising propaganda.

Once they have learned the building blocks (grammar) and how to think properly within each discipline (logic), they are ready to express and defend their thoughts and conclusions in a coherent and poetic way (rhetoric). If the second stage analyzes the raw material memorized in the first, then the third synthesizes it in a way that is creative and independent but maintains continuity with and respect for the tradition.

Although many public school students today receive piecemeal some of the benefits of the grammar stage, most do not receive the

---

[2]Sayers, "Lost Tools of Learning," 608.

Dorothy Sayers and Charlotte Mason 181

benefits of the logic and rhetoric stages. That is to say, they may memorize some of the major dates and events of history, but they are not trained to put those events into a coherent framework, to think logically about the moral and philosophical issues raised by them, or to articulate and defend the lessons those historical events can teach them (and us). When properly administered, the trivium Sayers seeks to resurrect in her essay teaches students how to sift evidence, gauge the reliability of sources, uncover the presuppositions on which arguments rest, and discern the consequences those arguments will have. It emboldens them to insist that politicians, advertisers, and media experts define their terms carefully, back up their claims with objective, nonskewed evidence, and avoid such common logical fallacies as circular reasoning, ad hominem attacks, and syllogisms with undistributed middles.

When Sayers wrote her essay, she knew that her opinions would not sit well with most academics and educators. But that was not her concern. All she was concerned with was "the proper training of the mind to encounter and deal with the formidable mass of undigested problems presented to it by the modern world." She knew that we were living on capital borrowed from our Greco-Roman, Judeo-Christian legacy of wisdom, eloquence, and virtue and feared that that capital was running out: "One cannot live on capital forever. However firmly a tradition is rooted, if it is never watered, though it dies hard, yet in the end it dies."[3]

Sayers makes this statement in the closing paragraph of her essay. That she is not too hopeful that the death of the tradition she would like to revive can be stopped is made clear in the second paragraph of her essay, when she says, perhaps with a wry smile, "It is in the highest degree improbable that the reforms I propose will ever be carried into effect."[4] Yet, as fate would have it, Sayers proved to be wrong.

---

[3]Sayers, "Lost Tools of Learning," 614-15.
[4]Sayers, "Lost Tools of Learning," 602.

182   PART 2—THE NATURE OF THE DEBATE

Three decades later, a pastor, author, and speaker named Douglas Wilson answered Sayers's call for a return of the trivium and, in 1981, founded the Logos School in Moscow, Idaho. Ten years after that, hopeful that his experience with Logos School would inspire a wider movement, he wrote *Recovering the Lost Tools of Learning*. Since then, over three hundred classical Christian schools have sprung up across the country.

Unlike traditional Christian schools that tend to follow the same progressive models used by public schools—albeit with chapel services, Bible classes, and stricter moral codes—classical Christian schools follow the trivium; teach Latin, usually starting in the third grade; and ground themselves in a close, vigorous reading of the Great Books. They also emphasize Socratic dialogue and an interdisciplinary approach in the upper school, climaxing with a thesis that is defended orally. Though the majority of these schools are Reformed Protestant, they rely heavily on the insights of such pagan authors as Plato, Aristotle, Isocrates, Cicero, Quintilian, and Plutarch, and such Catholic authors as Augustine, Alcuin, Hugh of St. Victor, Aquinas, Erasmus, Vico, and Newman.[5]

While classical Christian schools rest firmly on the authority of Scripture and the essential creeds of Christianity, a number of classical charter schools have also sprung up across the country. As these schools are public, they do not rest on a confession of faith. Nevertheless, they retain a direct continuity with the great classical and medieval schools and universities by following the trivium, teaching Latin, and grounding all classes in transcendent standards of goodness, truth, and beauty. Classical Christian and classical charter schools alike emphasize the qualities I discussed in part one, privileging

---

[5]I survey the history of the classical Christian movement among private schools and homeschoolers in the cover article I wrote for *Christianity Today*, September 2019: "The Rise of the Bible-Teaching, Plato-Loving, Homeschool Elitists: How Evangelicals Are Becoming the New Champions of the Pagan Classics," www.christianitytoday.com/ct/2019/september/classical -christian-schools.html.

liberal arts teaching over vocational training, traditional curricula over ideologically driven ones, the Great Books over textbooks, history over social studies, the humanities over the social sciences, absolute standards over relativism, and virtues over values.

Along with classical Christian and classical charter schools, many homeschooling families—most but not all of whom are Christian—have adopted a traditional, classical model of education for their children. Many of those homeschoolers, however, have found a mentor in another female British writer who was born half a century before Sayers. Charlotte Mason (1842–1923), a Victorian educator and reformer whose work, though grounded in the Bible, has exerted a strong influence on secular and Christian parents alike, offers a helpful contrast to Sayers. Though both women honored the traditional Greco-Roman, Judeo-Christian paideia, Mason's theories factor in a more Romantic, Wordsworthian view of children and nature (see introduction).[6]

Mason rests her theories on the foundational principle that children are born persons and that they are equally capable of good and evil. Our job as educators is not to herd or manage or manipulate them for our own narrow purposes but to guide them into a love of learning that will help order their affections, ennoble their conduct, and mold their characters. As such, she would have agreed wholeheartedly with the passage I quoted in the preface from Lewis's *Abolition of Man*:

> Where the old [traditional form of education] initiated, the new merely "conditions." The old dealt with its pupils as grown birds deal with young birds when they teach them to fly: the new deals with them more as the poultry-keeper deals with young birds—making them thus or thus for purposes of which the birds know nothing. In a word, the old was a kind of propagation—men transmitting manhood to men: the new is merely propaganda.

---

[6]Most of what I say in the following six paragraphs first appeared in my essay, "Raising a Child According to Wordsworth and Charlotte Mason," in *Classis: The Quarterly Journal of the Association of Classical & Christian Schools* (September 2016): 4-8.

184 PART 2—THE NATURE OF THE DEBATE

Mason believes that children's minds, like their bodies, possess from birth all the tools they need to absorb and assimilate the nourishment they are given. Because of this belief, she argues that the role of education should not only be to teach children how to learn—nobody wastes time teaching children how to chew or digest—but to expose them to the right books and activities they need to satisfy their mental hunger. Those books and activities must be offered up in their wholeness and totality rather than in fragmented tidbits, as they do in textbooks, that do not nourish or satisfy.

At the core of Mason's educational theories lies the distinction between synthesis and analysis. Whereas our scientific, technological, utilitarian age puts all its focus on analysis, breaking down knowledge so that it can be memorized for standardized exams and measured by accreditation agencies, Mason's classical vision seeks after a more holistic grasp of God, man, and the natural world.[7] Books are the prime vehicle for achieving that synthesis, but only if they are cherished, enjoyed, taken in as close friends. Rather than use the book merely as a tool for teaching the rules of grammar and syntax or for improving vocabulary, the teacher must invite the student to feast on the book, to live through its characters, to participate in its struggles and victories. Rather than read to win prizes or gain approbation or triumph over their classmates, children must be taught to love reading for its own sake.

As with books, so with science. Let young children explore their world, see it in all its beauty and wonder. Do not coop them up all day

---

[7]Several good books have been published exposing the negative pedagogical repercussions of standardized exams: Anya Kamenetz, *The Test: Why Our Schools Are Obsessed with Standardized Testing—But You Don't Have to Be* (New York: Public Affairs, 2015); Peter Sacks, *Standardized Minds: The High Price of America's Testing Culture and What We Can Do to Change It* (New York: Da Capo, 1999); Alfie Kohn, *The Case Against Standardized Testing: Raising the Scores, Ruining the Schools* (Portsmouth, NH: Heinemann, 2000). Ironically, the best book of all comes from a critic who is against vouchers, which would help increase the classical Christian movement, but who nevertheless is opposed to the standardized testing regime: Diane Ravitch, *Reign of Error: The Hoax of the Privatization Movement and the Danger to America's Public Schools* (New York: Vintage, 2014).

memorizing a series of discrete factoids about rocks or trees or animals. Send them out into nature to see those things in their proper habitat. Let them become as intimate with grass and flowers and birds and sheep as with the characters in the books they are reading. Again, let them do so out of love, not to achieve some kind of utilitarian reward.

Rather than devote their early school years exclusively to filling them to the brim with facts and dates and Latin classifications as if they were little vessels, teachers should encourage their students to take in knowledge as a sponge takes in water: or, better, as an organism takes in food. Once they have learned to see and appreciate the larger picture, then they will be better equipped to narrow their focus. Yes, they need discipline and structure—which includes memorization and the mathematical tables—but how much more effective that discipline would be if it were offered within the bounds of an infectious atmosphere of learning and discovery.

Mason did believe that the discipline of memorization was a good and noble one; however, in contrast to Sayers, she felt it could be so overused as to stunt a child's educational growth. When a second-grader is forced to memorize the names and dates of every major European battle for the last two millennia, we risk turning him off history for the rest of his life. Let us instead take that same second-grader and pique his nascent interest by ushering him into a historical narrative, a grand story of the rise and fall of nations. Let him absorb the pageantry, the heroism, the passion. Once that has settled into his bones, it will stay there and supply him with a desire to fill in all the details with names and dates, rivers and mountains, treaties and manifestos.

"Children have a right to the best we possess," insists Mason in the introduction to *The Philosophy of Education* (1922); "therefore their lesson books should be, as far as possible, our best books. . . . They require a great variety of knowledge,—about religion, the humanities, science, art; therefore, they should have a wide curriculum, with a

186   PART 2—THE NATURE OF THE DEBATE

definite amount of reading set for each short period of study."[8] Though Mason and Sayers desired the same educational telos—virtuous, morally self-regulating citizens with a passion for lifelong learning and the skills to assimilate and critique new knowledge—the former favored a less rigid curriculum that achieved the goals of the trivium in a more organic way that trusted to the child's innate ability for self-education. Sayers's method, I would argue, is better adapted to an ordered classroom, while Mason's lends itself more easily to small groups of children taught in the home. Still, both are firmly committed to passing down to the next generation the best that has been known and thought in the Judeo-Christian, Greco-Roman tradition.

The bigger gap that divides the educational theories of Sayers and Mason is that those of the latter are strongly Romantic, placing a heavier trust in the abilities and relative innocence of the child. Though she does not follow Rousseau in denying original sin, Mason is more hopeful of achieving the education "of the race, of the human nature common to every class and country, every individual child." The "recognition of the potentialities in any child," she insists, "should bring about such an educational renaissance as may send our weary old world rejoicing on its way."[9] Like Dewey, Mason's vision for education was strongly democratic, calling for the same education for rich and poor, aristocrat and worker and believing that all children, whatever their background, possessed the same innate skills and the same mental hunger for knowledge.

Where she parts company with Dewey is in her rejection of the progressive "gospel of education," with its belief that "a utilitarian education should be universal and compulsory; child and adolescent should be 'saturated with the spirit of service, provided with the instruments of effective self-direction.' Behold, Utopia at hand! every

---

[8]Charlotte Mason, *The Philosophy of Education*, The Home Education Series (Living Book Press, 2017), 6:19. This edition can be read for free online.
[9]Mason, *Philosophy of Education*, 47.

Dorothy Sayers and Charlotte Mason

young person fitted, body and soul, for the uses of society; as for his own uses, what he should be in and for himself—why, what matter?" Though she concedes that "eminent educationalists" such as Dewey do not desire to "sacrifice the individual youth to society" but to "raise him, give him place and power, give him opportunity," she yet critiques their utilitarian willingness to sacrifice the mind to the body, starving the mind's spiritual, intellectual, and aesthetic hunger for goodness, truth, and beauty.[10]

As for Rousseau, Mason critiques his "primitive man theory, that a child must get all his knowledge through his own senses and by his own wits, as if there were no knowledge waiting to be passed on by the small torch-bearer."[11] Rousseau's celebration of the primitive in nature severed the age-old link between education and the passing of the torch of tradition. This severing influenced utilitarian pragmatists such as Dewey to privilege experience over authority, efficiency over truth, resulting in an impoverished pedagogy that feeds the body while leaving the soul and the imagination to starve. Utilitarian education, Mason warns, forgets "that it is written, Man shall not live by bread alone, but by every word that proceedeth out of the mouth of God shall man live,—whether it be spoken in the way of some truth of religion, poem, picture, scientific discovery, or literary expression; by these things men live and in all such is the life of the spirit. The spiritual life requires the food of ideas for its daily bread."[12]

Most likely speaking with reference to Maria Montessori, Mason complains, "Our latest educational authority, one who knows and loves little children, would away with all tales and histories that appeal to the imagination; let children learn by means of things, is her mandate; and the charm and tenderness with which it is delivered

---

[10]Mason, *Philosophy of Education*, 280.
[11]Mason, *Philosophy of Education*, 325.
[12]Mason, *Philosophy of Education*, 125.

188 PART 2—THE NATURE OF THE DEBATE

may well blind us to its desolating character."[13] She then makes clear the influence Rousseau exerted on Montessori:

> We recognise Rousseau, of course, and his *Emile*, that self-sufficient person who should know nothing of the past, should see no visions, allow no authority. But human nature in children is stronger than the eighteenth century philosopher and the theories which he continues to inform. Whoever has told a fairy tale to a child has been made aware of that natural appetency for letters to which it is our business to minister. Are we not able to believe that words are more than meat, and, so believing, shall we not rise up and insist that children shall have a liberal diet of the spirit?[14]

Mason does not dispute the real concern, and even love, that Dewey, Montessori, and Rousseau feel for children; she even goes on to commend Rousseau for convincing the parents of his day of the awesome responsibility of educating the next generation. Still, she critiques all three for cutting children off both from the riches of the past and from the riches of their own souls.

Children, Mason believed, are born with an innate hunger for the best stories and histories and ideas and discoveries that have passed down to us, and we abdicate our role as teachers if we do not provide them access to that legacy. Indeed, we cannot, nor were we meant to, live on bread alone.

---

[13]Mason, *Philosophy of Education*, 338.
[14]Mason, *Philosophy of Education*, 338-39.

FOURTEEN

MORTIMER ADLER, E. D. HIRSCH, AND NEIL POSTMAN

How to Educate Americans

ALTHOUGH I HAVE DEVOTED much of the last three chapters to critiquing the pragmatic-progressivist pedagogical theories of John Dewey, I want to begin this final chapter by praising him for taking seriously the unique educational challenges that America has faced over the last century and a half. We have always been a nation of immigrants, but it was not until the late nineteenth century that large numbers of poorer, less educated, non-Anglo immigrants from Ireland, Eastern Europe (Russians, Poles, Hungarians, Germans), and the Mediterranean (Italians, Greeks, Jews, Egyptians) began to pour into America through Ellis Island.

How could we assimilate so many people and from such diverse ethnic and cultural backgrounds? How could we invite them to participate in the political, economic, spiritual, and community values of America without robbing them of their own identities and customs? Above all, how could we provide a unified and unifying educational experience for students whose family structures, language skills, economic status, and comprehension levels varied so widely? The twentieth and twenty-first centuries brought with them successive waves

190 PART 2—THE NATURE OF THE DEBATE

of new immigrants from Latin America, Asia, and Africa—and, with them, even more educational challenges.

I applaud Dewey and some of his progressivist heirs for trying to meet those challenges with practical and efficient solutions. But their solutions are not the only ones on the market. During the closing decades of the twentieth century, three passionate public intellectuals who shared Dewey's love for the American dream rose up to suggest different ways of dealing with the challenges unique to America. Rather than abandon public schools for private schools based on traditional, classical models, they thought long and hard about how the public educational system could be renewed and improved. Without rejecting the need for socialization in public schools, they sought to ground that socialization in the rich, Greco-Roman, Judeo-Christian legacy on which America was founded rather than in political causes or fashionable ideologies.

The first of these, a popular Aristotelian/Thomistic philosopher, educator, and author, went so far as to convene a group to draft an educational reform plan that he called, in conscious continuity with ancient Greece, the Paideia Proposal. Best known for compiling a fifty-plus-volume set of the Great Books of the Western world and for chairing the board of the Encyclopedia Britannica, Mortimer Adler (1902–2001), like Dewey and Mason before him, believed passionately in a democratic form of education that would serve all Americans equally. It was precisely because he believed that the public school system of his day was failing to offer such an education that he published, in 1982, *The Paideia Proposal: An Educational Manifesto.*

Although he dedicates the book to Dewey, Horace Mann, and Robert Hutchins, progressive educators all, Adler's proposal mingles American pragmatism with a firm commitment to the classical tradition, liberal political concerns with a conservative pedagogical vision. When it comes to educational opportunities, Adler adopts a populist-egalitarian framework and mindset: "We are politically a classless society. Our citizenry as a whole is our ruling class. We should, therefore, be an educationally classless society."[1] The only way, Adler argues, that a democracy that grants universal suffrage can thrive is if all American children are given an equal education. Such an education will not only prepare them vocationally; it will make them good citizens who can participate fully in the workings of democracy.

So committed is Adler to his egalitarian principles that he insists that all children receive the *same* educational curriculum from kindergarten to twelfth grade. His proposal makes no allowance for a two-track system with honors classes for higher-performing students and remedial classes for lower-performing students. At the same time, in keeping with his classical vision, he stipulates that his one-track system will not be vocational but will be grounded in the liberal arts—though he does maintain, along with Sayers, that liberally educated students will be able to learn new things easily after they graduate and so perform well in a multitude of jobs. "As compared with narrow, specialized training for particular jobs, general schooling is of the greatest practical value . . . because it will provide preparation for earning a living."[2]

As for the curriculum itself, Adler lays down a threefold plan for providing all students with the acquisition of knowledge, practical skills, and character formation. First, they will be provided with the foundational content they need through traditional lectures and textbooks that cover all the main disciplines. Second, via hands-on coaching, they will hone their reading, writing, and mathematical skills. Third, through intense Socratic discussion of the Great Books and other works of art, music, and drama, they will enlarge their understanding of intellectual and spiritual ideas and moral and ethical values. Adler defines Socratic discussion as "teaching by asking

---

[1]Mortimer Adler, on behalf of the members of the Paideia group, *The Paideia Proposal: An Educational Manifesto* (New York: Macmillan, 1982), 5.

[2]Adler, *Paideia Proposal*, 19.

192 PART 2—THE NATURE OF THE DEBATE

questions, by leading discussions, by helping students to raise their minds up from a state of understanding or appreciating less to a state of understanding or appreciating more."[3]

Whereas one-size-fits-all approaches to education tend to yield lowest-common-denominator results, Adler grounds his characteristically American optimism on a romantic view of children that comes quite close to that of Rousseau and Mason: "Their sameness as human beings—as members of the same species—means that every child has all the distinguishing properties common to all members of the species. They all have the same inherent tendencies, the same inherent powers, the same inherent capacities. . . . Individual differences are always only differences in degree, never differences in kind."[4] To this epistemological faith in the equal capacities of children, Adler adds a political faith that all children in America have the right to the pursuit of happiness promised in the Declaration of Independence.

Although Adler knows that many students will end their education when they graduate, while others will seek out vocational schools, he insists that America needs more liberal arts colleges: "We need more college programs in which the major course of study offered is common to all, with but few if any electives permitted. Such colleges would be ideal institutions for the preparation of the teachers to staff our reformed basic schools."[5] For all his American pragmatism and egalitarianism, Adler's vision is one with the pedagogical vision that begins with Plato and rests on the passing down of tradition and the equipping of new generations to continue that transmission.

Still, lest Adler be accused of setting up a self-perpetuating cycle of teachers and students, he insists, like Newman before him, that free republics cannot survive without the kinds of generalists that a liberal arts education produces: "We need specialists for our economic

---

[3] Adler, *Paideia Proposal*, 29.
[4] Adler, *Paideia Proposal*, 43.
[5] Adler, *Paideia Proposal*, 71.

Mortimer Adler, E. D. Hirsch, and Neil Postman 193

prosperity, for our national welfare and security, for continued progress in all the arts and sciences, and in all fields of scholarship. But for the sake of our cultural traditions, our democratic institutions, and our individual well-being, our specialists must also be generalists; that is, generally educated human beings."[6]

As a follow-up to *The Paideia Proposal*, Adler published a second book to clarify the proposal, *Paideia Problems and Possibilities: A Consideration of Questions Raised by the Paideia Proposal* (1983). In chapter four, Adler addresses thirty-one questions, the first two of which are of special concern to this book. First, Adler explains that although the Paideia Proposal is in part a back-to-basics movement, its focus on Socratic questioning and its willingness to try new methods make it unique. Second, although it is not classical in the sense of teaching Greek and Latin or studying antiquity as an end in itself, it is very much classical in its focus on the Great Books. Still, and this is why Adler makes a good bridge between traditional and progressive paideias, the reason that the Great Books form the core of Adler's Socratic seminars is that they possess a lasting value that modern readers can use to help them wrestle with modern problems.

Five years after *The Paideia Proposal* was unveiled, professor and education theorist E. D. Hirsch (b. 1928) took the publishing world by storm with a surprise bestseller, *Cultural Literacy* (1987), which, though it never references Adler, seconds Adler's commitment to a democratic public education that will equip all Americans with the knowledge and skills to succeed. Like Adler, Hirsch balances political liberalism with educational conservativism, insisting that all students in the public schools be given the same curriculum but that that curriculum lift all students up to the same high standard. Neither Adler nor Hirsch condescends to poor, minority, or immigrant

---

[6]Adler, *Paideia Proposal*, 72.

194 PART 2—THE NATURE OF THE DEBATE

students; they firmly believe that all students deserve and can achieve academic excellence.

Though both Adler and Hirsch express a progressive faith that schools can be improved with a resulting rise in equality, neither treats public schools as sites of social engineering. Indeed, in order to make room for the challenging curricula they propose, they both stipulate that schools must stop offering classes in driver's ed, sex ed, hygiene, and so on, subjects that are best left to parents or churches. The role of education is to teach, not to socialize; and yet, both make clear, when all students are given the same quality education, the natural result will be more effective communication across the racial, ethnic, and class barriers that separate one group from another. The goal is not conformity but the possession of a common cultural language that will allow effective intercourse and collaboration between the diverse groups that make up America.

For Hirsch, American elementary schools in particular have departed from their proper purpose because they have long been "dominated by the content-neutral ideas of Rousseau and Dewey."[7] Though skills are important, if children are not taught community-shared information, they will not be able to dialogue with people outside their group or participate fully in the democratic institutions that define our nation and make possible the American dream. That all-important community-shared information Hirsch calls cultural literacy, a linguistic shorthand that fills in the context of what we read daily. Apart from this collective reservoir of symbols and meanings, we cannot communicate effectively through the written and even spoken word.

The cultural literacy Hirsch expects public schools to teach their diverse student bodies includes classical literature, philosophy, and art, European and American history, and the Bible—that is, the Great

---

[7]E. D. Hirsch Jr., *Cultural Literacy: What Every American Needs to Know* (New York: Vintage, 1988), 19.

Books—but it also includes pop references from movies, sports, television, and music. That Americans have lost touch with cultural literacy only became apparent in the decades following the 1960s, Hirsch demonstrates, since before that time, it was taken for granted that Americans would have a knowledge of their own tradition.

Without wishing to erase or denigrate the unique cultures of America's many immigrant groups, Hirsch insists that the only way for those immigrant groups to succeed in America is to become conversant in the shared culture of America:

> As the universal second culture, literate culture has become the common currency for social and economic exchange in our democracy, and the only available ticket to full citizenship. Getting one's membership card is not tied to class or race. Membership is automatic if one learns the background information and the linguistic conventions that are needed to read, write, and speak effectively. Although everyone is literate in some local, regional, or ethnic culture the connection between mainstream culture and the national written language justifies calling mainstream culture *the* basic culture of the nation.[8]

Those who attack cultural literacy as elitist, racist, or ethnocentric because of its White European roots, Hirsch argues, do not understand how national cultures are formed or the role that cultural literacy plays in bringing unity and allowing marginal groups to succeed within the native or dominant culture. Indeed, one of the first lists of cultural literacy was put together by a Scotsman named Hugh Blair; his *Rhetoric* (1762) was not written to benefit English aristocrats but provincial Scots and colonial Americans who wanted to learn the language of power that would allow them to rise in the world of the British Empire.

If public schools fail their conservative task of preserving and passing down cultural literacy, they will also fail their liberal task of promoting unity and crosscultural dialogue. But how are they to pass

---

[8]Hirsch, *Cultural Literacy*, 22.

down such precious information? On that point, Hirsch comes down firmly on the side of Sayers rather than Mason: "Our current distaste for memorization is more pious than realistic. At an early age when their memories are most retentive, children have an almost instinctive urge to learn specific tribal traditions. At that age they seem to be fascinated by catalogues of information and are eager to master the materials that authenticate their membership in adult society."[9] As I argued in chapter ten, it is nothing less than criminal to waste the natural skills of children in the grammar phase because of a prejudice against fixed curricula, teacher-centered classrooms, and rote memorization, which dates back only to Rousseau, and which would have been thought ridiculous by almost any thinker before him.

To make clear what he means by cultural literacy, Hirsch includes in the lengthy appendix to his book a list of five thousand key names, dates, battles, themes, and quotes that represent "what literate Americans know."[10] However, he also offers in capsule form the American civil ethos that provides the matrix for our cultural literacy:

> Our civil ethos treasures patriotism and loyalty as high, though perhaps not ultimate, ideals and fosters the belief that the conduct of the nation is guided by a vaguely defined God. Our tradition places importance on carrying out the rights and ceremonies of our civil ethos and religion through the national flag, the national holidays, and the national anthem (which means "national hymn"), and supports the morality of tolerance and benevolence, of the Golden Rule, and communal cooperation. We believe in altruism and self-help, in equality, freedom, truth telling, and respect for the national law. . . . [Our civil religion] also has its own bible, a knowledge of which is at the heart of cultural literacy. That bible was not decided upon by a synod once and for all. No doubt some of its "books"—the Declaration of Independence, the Gettysburg Address, some parts of the Bible itself—will always belong in it, but our consensual form of civil religion is much like our legal system in that it allows for change and amendment.[11]

---

[9]Hirsch, *Cultural Literacy*, 30.
[10]Hirsch, *Cultural Literacy*, 146.
[11]Hirsch, *Cultural Literacy*, 98, 100.

Although an argument can be made, and has been made powerfully and convincingly, that the civil religion that Hirsch describes was a creation of thinkers such as Dewey, Mann, and Francis Bellamy, with the intent of displacing the traditional Western Christian paideia with a secular creed of progressivism and pragmatism, Hirsch harbors no such nefarious ends.[12] He simply tries to explain *what* Americans have long acknowledged to be the foundational books, events, and ideas of Western civilization and *how* they have conserved and conveyed that information to their children and grandchildren.

Indeed, Hirsch notes that between the 1893 *Report of the Committee of Ten on Secondary School Studies* and the 1918 *Cardinal Principles of Secondary Education*, there was a dramatic shift from a knowledge-based focus on cultural literacy to a sociology-based focus on health, vocation, citizenship, leisure, and ethical character, a shift that he links to the influence of Dewey, Rousseau, and Wordsworth.[13] Needless to say, the new focus on ethical character was driven by values rather than virtues.

In addition to privileging socialization over education, the negative legacy of Rousseau and Dewey is felt in what Hirsch identifies as the faulty educational theory of formalism. Formalism treats reading as a skill no different than learning to play baseball or skating or riding a bike. But skill alone does not make children into good readers if they lack the context necessary for comprehension. That is why when kindergarteners who are reading at the same level move on to second, third, and fourth grade, the students who possess cultural literacy excel, while those who do not are left behind.

Since the publication of *Cultural Literacy*, Hirsch has continued to call on public schools to provide the kind of education needed to maintain our democracy and to foster dialogue across racial, ethnic,

---

[12]See Pete Hegseth with David Goodwin, *Battle for the American Mind: Uprooting a Century of Miseducation* (New York: Broadside Books, 2022). Also see my bibliographical essay below.
[13]Hirsch, *Cultural Literacy*, 118.

198   PART 2—THE NATURE OF THE DEBATE

and class lines. In one of his more recent books, he puts the blame on progressive schools of education that consistently teach the future instructors of America's youth that content-based education is reactionary and right-wing, dedicated to lockstep thinking and rote memorization. They indoctrinate their students, as they were indoctrinated themselves, to see their child-centered, formalist approach as humane and teacher-centered, traditional approaches as inhumane. "Ever since the 1930s, the identification of set academic curriculum with an anti-liberal, reactionary, authoritarian, elitist, right-wing point of view has continued to be the most successful and persistent rhetorical maneuver of the anti-curriculum movement."[14]

For over a century, the progressive educational establishment has used polarizing slogans that reduce complex pedagogical issues to a stark choice between darkness and light, intolerance and tolerance. In this holy war, fixed curricula are always attacked, and any attempt to come up with a common sense list of cultural literacy is rejected as exclusivist and medieval. Meanwhile, students continue to be robbed of their heritage and of the very language they need to survive and thrive in our modern, multiethnic world.

⬤▬▬▬▬▬⬤

Although he is best known as the author of *Amusing Ourselves to Death* (1985) and *Technopoly* (1992), educator, author, and media critic Neil Postman (1931–2003) devoted much of his career to analyzing and critiquing American schools. His thoughts on education were first laid out in *Teaching as a Subversive Activity* (1969), which he cowrote with Charles Weingartner, and *Teaching as a Conservative Idea* (1979); took on a more sociological slant in *The Disappearance of Childhood* (1982); and climaxed with *The End of Education* (1995). By playing on the double meaning of the word *end*, Postman combines a meditation on the true purpose of education with a warning that

---

[14]E. D. Hirsch Jr., *The Making of Americans: Democracy and Our Schools* (New Haven, CT: Yale University Press, 2009), 53.

"without a transcendent and honorable purpose schooling must reach its finish."[15]

What the public school system in America has lost, Postman argues, is a narrative or overarching story, "one that tells of origins and envisions a future, a story that constructs ideals, prescribes rules of conduct, provides a source of authority, and, above all, gives a sense of continuity and purpose." Apart from such "a narrative, life has no meaning. Without meaning, learning has no purpose. Without a purpose, schools are houses of detention, not attention."[16] For Postman, as for Adler and Hirsch, one of the narratives that has driven America and her public schools is that of the melting pot, of an open society that invites in immigrants from around the world to share in her civil ethos without having to abandon their personal and family culture and traditions.

The *why* of education (its purpose), Postman argues, is far more important than the *what* (its methods). That is why the question of whether America's schools will yield students who are "soulless," "directionless," "self-indulgent consumers" or

> a public imbued with confidence, a sense of purpose, a respect for learning, and tolerance . . . has nothing whatever to do with computers, with testing, with teacher accountability, with class size, and with the other details of managing schools. The right answer depends on two things, and two things alone: the existence of shared narratives and the capacity of such narratives to provide an inspired reason for schooling.[17]

Although, like Hirsch, Postman makes no reference to Adler or his Paideia Proposal, he does partly situate himself vis-à-vis Hirsch. Without rejecting Hirsch's call for a shared language of cultural literacy, Postman insists that information alone is not enough. Beyond learning the facts of cultural literacy, students must be taught to

---

[15]Neil Postman, *The End of Education: Redefining the Value of School* (New York: Vintage, 1996), x-xi.

[16]Postman, *End of Education*, 5-7.

[17]Postman, *End of Education*, 18.

question and assess "whose facts they are, how we come to know them, why they are deemed important and by whom." That is why, in his book, Postman "places little emphasis on what facts can be known, much on what narratives can be believed."[18]

In the second half of his book, Postman explores five narratives—spaceship earth, fallen angel, American experiment, law of diversity, and word weavers/world makers—that he believes have the power to give our failing public schools a unifying vision and shared sense of purpose. Rather than survey all five, I will conclude this chapter by taking a brief look at the third and the second.

America, Postman reminds us, "was the first nation to be argued into existence." Our "Constitution is not a catechism, but a hypothesis." For two and a half centuries, we have been asking ourselves the same central questions: "What is freedom? What are its limits? What is a human being? What are the obligations of citizenship? What is meant by democracy?"[19] Since, Postman argues, we are not the first or the only people to have asked these questions, we address them in part by studying and wrestling with the Great Books and thinkers that came before us.

Because he knows that the ability to engage in this all-important wrestling match calls for shared knowledge of the basic texts of democracy, Postman comes to a position that is not far afield from that of Hirsch and Sayers, or, indeed, any of the advocates of the classical paideia I have discussed in this book:

> I am aware that modern educators disapprove of students being asked to memorize anything, classifying such a task under the dreaded rubric of "rote" learning. I stand with those who are against students playing the "guess what answer I have in my head" game with teachers, but I do not think that such a stand rules out asking students to know by heart certain fundamental expressions of American ideals.[20]

---

[18]Postman, *End of Education*, 119, 75.
[19]Postman, *End of Education*, 71-73.
[20]Postman, *End of Education*, 133.

Once students, and *teachers*, have a firm grasp of our foundational documents and ideas, they can engage in the kind of vigorous questioning that Postman rightly believes will bring new life and true unity in diversity to our schools. As long as we can steer clear of the two extremes of "a mindless, xenophobic nationalism" and revisionist history that focuses only on "the uglier aspects of American history and culture," we can invite each generation of publicly educated students to participate in furthering our ongoing American experiment in self-governance by means of free institutions safeguarded by a system of checks and balances.[21]

Of course, the very possibility of carrying on that experiment rests finally on the central confession of this book: that we were made in God's image but fallen. Postman offers a version of this confession (or narrative) that should speak to most people of all religions as well as most people whose religion is science:

> If perfection is to be found anyplace in the universe, it is assumed to exist in God or gods. There may have been a time when human beings were perfect, but at some point, for various reasons, their powers were diminished, so that they must live forever in a state of imperfect understanding. Indeed, for us to believe that we are godlike, or perfect, is among the most serious sins of which we are capable. The Greeks call the sin "hubris." The Christians call it "pride." Scientists call it "dogmatism."[22]

That is the tragic story; however, it offers a ray of hope. If we will "accept our cosmic status as the error-prone species," we just may find redemption. "Knowing [like Socrates] that we do not know and cannot know the whole truth, we may move toward it inch by inch by discarding what we know to be false."[23]

If we accept this story, then life, and education with it, becomes a kind of drama, a search to uncover our own ignorance as well as the

---

[21]Postman, *End of Education*, 130-31.
[22]Postman, *End of Education*, 67.
[23]Postman, *End of Education*, 67.

goodness, truth, and beauty that ever eludes us. Knowledge, then, will stop being "a commodity to be acquired," which it has sadly become, and return to what it was for Socrates, Plato, and their heirs: "a human struggle to understand, to overcome falsity, to stumble toward truth." In that search, Postman boldly argues, textbooks have been one of the greatest obstacles. Rather than be guides in our search for truth in a fallen world, they "are enemies of education, instruments for promoting dogmatism and trivial learning."[24] By *textbooks*, Postman does not mean readers or even books that argue for a thesis but those that reduce the complex history of a discipline to dogmatic talking points.

How, then, are we to recognize and avoid the errors that have plagued our race since the beginning? By studying history and thus joining the great conversation that links antiquity to the Middle Ages and the Renaissance to our post-Enlightenment world:

> "To remain ignorant of things that happened before you were born is to remain a child," Cicero said. He then added, "What is a human life worth unless it is incorporated into the lives of one's ancestors and set in an historical context?" When we incorporate the lives of our ancestors in our education, we discover that some of them were great error-makers, some great error-correctors, some both. And in discovering this, we accomplish three things. First, we help students to see that knowledge is a stage in human development, with a past and a future. Second (this would surely please Professor E. D. Hirsch, Jr.), we acquaint students with the people and ideas that comprise "cultural literacy"— that is to say, give them some understanding of where their ideas come from and how we came by them. And third, we show them that error is no disgrace, that it is the agency through which we increase understanding.[25]

By quoting Cicero on the need to study history as a means of uniting oneself with one's ancestors, Postman unites himself and his vision of education to both the Greco-Roman and Judeo-Christian legacy and tradition of the West. He makes of education both a static thing, for

---

[24]Postman, *End of Education*, 116.

[25]Postman, *End of Education*, 124-25. To read the quote from Cicero in its context, see Cicero, "The Orator," in *The Great Tradition: Classic Readings on What It Means to Be an Educated Human Being*, ed. Richard M. Gamble (Wilmington, DE: ISI Books, 2007), 81.

it preserves the Great Books and ideas of our ancestors, and a dynamic thing, for it continues to wrestle with those books and ideas.

Postman believes strongly in this narrative, as do I and most of the classical thinkers on education with whom I have dialogued in this book. Indeed, he does not hesitate to promise that an embrace of this tragic-but-hopeful, error-making and error-correcting story of humanity will empower rather than shut down real learning: "Far from creating cynics, such a story is likely to foster a healthy and creative skepticism, which is something quite different from cynicism. It refutes the story of the student learner as the dummy in a ventriloquism act. It holds out the hope for students to discover a sense of excitement and purpose in being part of the Great Conversation."[26] Such is Postman's hope for readers of his book, a hope I share for readers of my own. If only we will come to understand again the true nature of man and the true nature of education, we will be able once again to join the great conversation and, by so doing, preserve and pass on to future generations the best that has been known and thought, and foster in them the goodness of virtue, the truth of wisdom, and the beauty of eloquence.

---

[26]Postman, *End of Education*, 128.

CONCLUSION

FROM A PHILOSOPHY OF LIFE TO A THEORY OF EDUCATION

> Education is a subject which cannot be discussed in a void: our questions raise other questions, social, economic, financial, political. And the bearings are on more ultimate problems even than these: to know what we want in education we must know what we want in general, we must derive our theory of education from our philosophy of life. The problem turns out to be a religious problem.[1]

So wrote T. S. Eliot in 1932. Nearly a century later, we must ask the same question again. What is our philosophy of life? What do we believe to be the nature of God, man, and the universe? What do we mean by goodness, truth, and beauty? How shall we define the good man, the good life, the good state? Are the things we create valuable, and should they be preserved?

It is because I agree with Eliot on this point that I began this book with a lengthy introduction on the nature of man before broaching the topic of the nature of education and the nature of the debate. Rather than come up with a theory of education and then force students to fit that theory, I have attempted to derive a theory of classical Christian education out of a philosophy of life that posits students as enfleshed souls made in the image of God but fallen, moral agents with an inbuilt desire to create and build but with dark urges that need to be tamed, resisted, and reined in.

---

[1] T. S. Eliot, "Modern Education and the Classics," in *Selected Essays* (London: Faber & Faber, 1999), 507.

The young people we must educate are neither domestic animals to be herded and manipulated for our use, nor blank slates on which to inscribe social or political programs, nor free, autonomous agents whom we must encourage to think for and be true to themselves apart from external codes of good and evil, truth and error, beauty and ugliness. Absolute goodness must be instilled in their souls, transcendent truth engraved in their minds, and ageless beauty cultivated in their hearts. They must not be molded to fit and serve capitalist factories or socialist bureaus but shaped against fixed standards grounded in reality.

Throughout this book, I have argued that the most effective method for achieving this end is to conduct young people through a liberal arts curriculum grounded in the humanities, built on the Great Books, and geared toward the nurturing of wisdom as opposed to vocational skills, virtue as opposed to values, and eloquence as opposed to polemics. Although this theory of education is strong in Plato and Augustine, Lewis and Sayers, Mason and Adler, Hirsch and Postman, it was weakened by the utopianism of Rousseau and the progressivism of Dewey. That is not to say that Rousseau and Dewey lacked good ideas or a heart for students. But they did question man's essential dignity and inherent depravity and, by so doing, skewed the nature and purpose of education.

Does that mean that all the educational initiatives of the last century and a half should be discarded? By no means. America continues to be an immigrant nation, and it is one of the duties of our public schools to welcome those immigrants into the grand American experiment that has been going on for 250 years. If we are to continue, however, we must revive an understanding of and a respect for the Greco-Roman, Judeo-Christian traditions that gave birth to that experiment and that continue to draw hopeful travelers here from all over the world. If we do not pass the torch to the next generation, then the glorious flame of liberty, which immigrants to Ellis Island saw as they docked in New York Harbor, will slowly, I fear, go out. Let us keep that lamp of political and intellectual freedom lifted high and burning brightly beside the golden door.

BIBLIOGRAPHICAL ESSAY

HERE IS A ROUGHLY CHRONOLOGICAL LIST of some of the key primary writings on education from the classical, medieval, Renaissance, Enlightenment, Romantic, Victorian, and modern eras. I will give only the author's name and work and leave it to the interested reader to choose a particular edition and translation. In the footnotes above I have given full bibliographical information for the editions from which I quoted. Neither this list nor my bibliography is meant to be exhaustive; it surveys books that influenced my own thoughts and that will provide the reader with an overview of the topic from a mostly traditional point of view.

But first, I highly recommend Richard Gamble's *The Great Tradition*, from which I quote often in the text. This is the best anthology of readings on traditional education, though it does *not* include other pedagogical schools, such as the Romantic school of Rousseau and Wordsworth or the progressivist school of Dewey and Mann. With this caveat, however, it provides a quite thorough overview of the central tradition of education from Plato, Aristotle, and Cicero to Dorothy Sayers, C. S. Lewis, and T. S. Eliot. It is particularly helpful to own since it offers generous excerpts from writers such as Isocrates and Quintilian, Hugh of St. Victor and John of Salisbury, Juan Luis Vives and Thomas Elyot, who will seem a bit arcane for modern readers but who exerted a strong influence on educators. Sadly, as of this writing, this book no longer appears to be in print, though there are Kindle versions available.

CLASSICAL

All serious discussion of the nature and purpose of education in the West must begin with a close reading of Plato's *Republic*. To say that no one would want to live in Plato's ideal city is irrelevant to the vital issues raised in the dialogue about the proper way to shape and educate children. For advice on education that is a bit more practical, see his *Laws*. To consider the key question of whether virtue can be taught, see his *Protagoras* and *Meno*; the latter is particularly important, for in it he explains that the reason his dialectical method of question-and-answer is effective is that it spurs the student to remember the knowledge he once knew in his preexistent state, when he communed directly with the Forms. His *Apology* offers insight into the philosophical and educational goals of his teacher, Socrates; for another view of Socrates the teacher, see Xenophon's *Memorabilia*.

To get a sense of how vital rhetoric was to educators of the past, you might want to pick up a collection of speeches by Isocrates and/or Demosthenes. The *Antidosis* of the former is particularly helpful for exposing the dangers of Sophistry, and so is best read alongside Plato's *Apology*, as well as the importance of virtue and eloquence. Aristotle's *Nicomachean Ethics* is a must-read for what it has to teach about virtue. His *Politics* has much to say on the education of citizens; his *Rhetoric* was an important tool for teaching this classically important subject.

Cicero is a crowning figure, but his thoughts on education are scattered across his many essays and speeches. Gamble offers a helpful compilation of excerpts from his *Pro Archia Poeta* (a wonderful defense of the arts and humanities that should be read in full), *De Oratore*, *De Partitione Oratoria*, and *De Officiis*. To this list I would add his *Dream of Scipio*, which has much to say on the passing down of virtue and citizenship to the next generation. Quintilian's *Institutes* was central to education for a millennium and a half, laying down all the rules for a classical education. Modern readers will likely find it a bit tedious; Gamble offers a generous selection.

Bibliographical Essay 209

To understand the virtues that traditional education sought to instill in the young, I would suggest reading the three great Roman Stoics: Seneca (any collection of his letters will do), Epictetus (his *Enchiridion* is short and highly accessible), and Marcus Aurelius (his *Meditations* reads like a blog on the philosophy of unity and virtue). I would also suggest a collection of essays (or *Moralia*) by Plutarch (better known for his *Lives* of the Greek and Roman heroes) as a window into classical virtues; Gamble does well to anthologize his "On Bringing Up a Boy" and "On the Student at Lectures."

MEDIEVAL

Some of the fathers of the late classical age thought deeply on whether Christians could learn from pagan literature. The best and most representative of these is Basil the Great's "To Young Men, on How They Might Derive Profit from Pagan Literature." This can be read free online, though Gamble anthologizes it along with another helpful essay, John Chrysostom's "Address on Vainglory and the Right Way for Parents to Bring Up Their Children," which can also be read for free online. The Middle Ages really begins with Augustine. His *De Doctrina Christiana* is a must-read, but so is his autobiographical *Confessions*, in which he takes the reader on a journey through his own education, both pagan and Christian. I would suggest reading portions of the following, all of which are excerpted in Gamble: Cassiodorus's *Institutions of Divine and Secular Learning*, the *Letters* of Alcuin, Hugh of St. Victor's *Didascalion*, John of Salisbury's *Policraticus*, and, especially, Aquinas's *On the Teacher*. Dante's *Comedy* can be read as a poem of education about a poet who begins by finding himself alone in a Dark Wood and slowly has his eyes opened to goodness, truth, and beauty.

RENAISSANCE AND ENLIGHTENMENT

Petrarch kicks off the Renaissance with his love sonnets, though it is his *Letters* that give us insight into education. Desiderius Erasmus's

The Education of a Prince lays out a full educational program in wisdom and virtue for would-be princes; it contrasts nicely with the more cynical realpolitik education described and championed in Niccolo Machiavelli's *The Prince*. Gamble's excerpts from Thomas Elyot's *The Book Named the Governor*, Philip Melanchthon's "Preface to Homer," and Roger Ascham's *The Schoolmaster* are fascinating reads, but if you only have time to read one piece, the most important one is John Milton's *Of Education*, which sums up the concerns of the age.

The two sides of the Enlightenment can best be assessed by reading Giambattista Vico's *On Humanistic Education: Six Inaugural Orations* and John Locke's *An Essay Concerning Human Understanding*. The former parts company with Descartes to hold fast to Christian humanism; the latter follows in the wake of Descartes to pursue an empirical education grounded in sensation rather than in the kind of innate ideas that Plato relies on for his dialectic.

ROMANTIC AND VICTORIAN

Although Rousseau lived and wrote during the Enlightenment, he laid the groundwork for Romantic ideals of education by advocating for an education in nature in *Emile*. In his poetic autobiography *The Prelude*, written in the same epic form as Milton's *Paradise Lost*, William Wordsworth documents his Rousseau-like education in nature and how his consciousness was shaped by his interactions with the natural world. While advocating, à la Locke, for the centrality of sensation in the growth of the human mind, he rejects Locke's rejection of innate ideas, even toying with Plato's doctrine of the preexistence of the soul in his "Ode: Intimations of Immortality from Recollections of Early Childhood." For a fuller sense of Romantic notions of how the consciousness is shaped, see Samuel Taylor Coleridge's *Biographia Literaria*, John Keats's *Letters*, and volume two of Mary Shelley's *Frankenstein*, where the monster narrates his own slowly

Bibliographical Essay   211

developing consciousness. Charlotte Mason is very much an heir of Wordsworth and Rousseau, though she is also grounded in classical thought. Ralph Waldo Emerson's "The American Scholar" embodies a strongly Romantic view of education.

The Victorian age birthed one of the best explications and defenses of traditional education that is classical *and* Christian in Cardinal Newman's *The Idea of a University*. It can be profitably read over against T. H. Huxley's *Essays on Education*, which favor a utilitarian education grounded in science over a humanistic one grounded in the classics. Matthew Arnold's "The Function of Criticism in the Present Time" offers a powerful defense of the Great Books; "Literature and Science" carves out a middle way between Newman and Huxley. A good way to gauge the opposing educations of the age is to read Newman's *Apologia Pro Vita Sua* alongside John Stuart Mill's *Autobiography*.

MODERN

The rise of progressive education can best be gauged by reading John Dewey's *Democracy and Education* and *Experience and Education* and Horace Mann's *Education of a Free Man* and *On the Crisis in Education*. Resurgent classicism returns in Irving Babbitt's *Literature and the American College*, Dorothy Sayers's "The Lost Tools of Learning," and T. S. Eliot's *The Idea of a Christian Society* and *Notes Towards the Definition of Culture*. To my mind, the most important twentieth-century book on education is C. S. Lewis's *The Abolition of Man*. He effectively critiques modern egalitarian education in "Screwtape Proposes a Toast," "Equality," and "Democratic Education." Although traditional in its rigor, John Milton Gregory's *The Seven Laws of Teaching* is partly pragmatic in its ethos.

Mortimer Adler's *Paideia Proposal*, E. D. Hirsch's *Cultural Literacy* and *The Making of Americans*, and Neil Postman's *The End of Education* offer a progressive vision of democratic education for all Americans and immigrants alike but by means of an ethos that is more traditional and classical. Another book with a similar vision that was published in the same time period but that focuses more on college than grade school is Alan Bloom's *The Closing of the American Mind* (Touchstone, 1988). To witness American utilitarianism and empiricism taken to its extreme, see B. F. Skinner's *Beyond Freedom and Dignity* (Knopf, 1971).

To understand the concept of paideia that undergirds this book, readers should read the first volume of Werner Jaeger's *Paideia: The Ideals of Greek Culture* and at least skim volumes two and three, which unpack Plato's *Republic* and *Laws* and offer insight into Isocrates and Demosthenes. A modern writer who subjected the progressive theories of Dewey and Mann to a Jaeger-like analysis is Lawrence A. Cremin. See his *Transformation of the Schools: Progressivism in American Education, 1876–1957* (Vintage, 1964) and *Public Education* (Basic Books, 1976). For a recent book that seeks to uncover the progressive agenda that has driven American schools for the last century and a half, see Pete Hegseth's *Battle for the American Mind: Uprooting a Century of Miseducation* (Broadside Books, 2022). Despite the polemical nature of this book, its thesis should at least be considered by those who care about education in America.

For a balanced, three-hundred-page encyclopedia of modern educational thinkers that covers the depth and breadth of modern theories, see *Fifty Modern Thinkers on Education: From Piaget to the Present*, edited by Joy A. Palmer (Routledge, 2001). This book is a sequel to the equally helpful *Fifty Thinkers on Education: From Confucius to Dewey*, also edited by Palmer (Routledge, 2001). One of the best histories of education in the West from a traditional perspective is Christopher Dawson's *The Crisis of Western Education* (Catholic University of America Press, 2010).

The modern classical Christian movement, with its attempt to revive the trivium and quadrivium, the teaching of Latin, and a focus on virtue and the Great Books, was spurred on by the recovery of Dorothy Sayers's essay in Douglas Wilson's *Recovering the Lost Tools of Learning: An Approach to Distinctively Christian Education* (Crossway, 1991). Also see Wilson's *The Case for Classical Christian Education* (Crossway, 2003). Three of the best assessments of this movement and the traditional education it advocates are Robert Littlejohn and Charles T. Evans's *Wisdom and Eloquence: A Christian Paradigm for Classical Learning* (Crossway, 2006), Kevin Clark and Ravi Scott Jain's *The Liberal Arts Tradition: A Philosophy of Christian Classical Education*, 3rd edition (Classical Academic Press, 2021), and Stratford Caldecott's *Beauty for Truth's Sake: On the Re-enchantment of Education* (Brazos, 2017).

Steve Turley's *Awakening Wonder: A Classical Guide to Truth, Goodness and Beauty* (Classical Academic Press, 2015) is well worth reading. For a good practical reader on the ins and outs of classical Christian education, see *Repairing the Ruins: The Classical and Christian Challenge to Modern Education*, edited by Douglas Wilson (Canon Press, 1996). For those interested in practicing classical Christian education at home, see Susan Wise Bauer and Jessie Wise's *The Well-Trained Mind: A Guide to Classical Education at Home*, 4th edition (Norton, 2016). For a book that argues that such an education promotes true freedom and equality, see Angel Adams Parham and Anika Prather's *The Black Intellectual Tradition: Reading Freedom in Classical Literature* (Classical Academic Press, 2022).

Christians who worry that a curriculum heavy in pagan writers will compromise the faith of their children are encouraged to read my *From Achilles to Christ: Why Christians Should Read the Pagan Classics* (IVP Academic, 2007), *The Myth Made Fact: Reading Greek and Roman Mythology through Christian Eyes* (Classical Academic Press, 2020), and *From Plato to Christ: How Platonic Thought Shaped the Christian Faith* (IVP Academic, 2021).

APPENDIX

IN THIS APPENDIX I have included my review of a recent book that fleshes out aspects of the classical Christian movement that should prove of interest to readers of this book. A slightly different version of this review appeared in *The Federalist* on September 16, 2022.

The Black Intellectual Tradition: Reading Freedom in Classical Literature
By Angel Adams Parham and Anika Prather
Classical Academic Press, 2022
272 pages, hardcover, $26.95

"It is well known that the power to think, the power to appreciate, and the power to will the right and make it prevail, is the sum total of the faculties of the human soul. Education which is truly 'educative' must strengthen, develop, 'lead out' these faculties in preparation for those special activities which may be called 'occupative,' because they give the one line of training necessary for the occupation or trade of the individual. . . . The old education made him a 'hand,' solely and simply. It deliberately sought to suppress or ignore the soul. . . . [But] for all men—whether for white men, red men, yellow men, or black men, whether for rich men or poor men, high or low, the aim of education for the human soul is to train aright, to give power and right direction to the intellect, the sensibilities, and the will" (209).

These words were written in the 1930s not by a rich White liberal man offering a progressive, John Dewey vision of education but by a poor

Black woman who was born into slavery in 1858 and devoted her life to providing classical Christian education to "Black Americans [who] were two generations out of slavery, but still struggling mightily with the disadvantages of Jim Crow segregation and the sometimes latent, sometimes overt, violence against Black people of all backgrounds" (101).

The name of that woman is Anna Julia Cooper, and she plays a central role in *The Black Intellectual Tradition: Reading Freedom in Classical Literature.* In this well-conceived and timely book, two African American professors, Angel Adams Parham and Anika Prather, argue that a classical Christian education grounded in the Great Books of the Western intellectual tradition, far from being racist, elitist, or oppressive, has the power to liberate the minds of Black Americans from every socioeconomic class.

By telling the stories of a half dozen Black writers whose faith in Christ and whose study of the Great Books equipped them with the rational, rhetorical, and religious power to overcome oppression and fight for internal and external freedom, Parham and Prather demonstrate that the writings of such dead White men as Homer, Sophocles, Plato, Aristotle, Cicero, Virgil, Plutarch, Dante, Shakespeare, Milton, Locke, and Mill comprise a legacy that transcends race, class, and gender even as it unites diverse groups of Americans by providing a common language and vision for human virtue and growth.

In the case of all these writers, their interactions with the Great Books and with Christ did not rob them of their Black identity or negate the suffering they endured because of their race; rather, it opened the doors for them to participate more fully in what America stands for when she is worthy of herself. It allowed them "to grieve injustice while shunning bitterness and working for healing and justice in our land" (71).

Olaudah Equiano (ca. 1745–1797) was born in Africa but was ripped away from his homeland, his culture, and his name and sold as a slave to many masters before buying his freedom, moving to

Appendix

England, and becoming an abolitionist whose bestselling autobiography awakened European hearts to the evils of slavery. Although "his trust was betrayed by White men who professed to be Christians . . . Equiano embraced the Christian faith and called on White Christians to live up to what they professed to believe" (38). His education taught him that the fight against slavery could be waged within the classical Christian tradition, a truth wielded by Frederick Douglass in the nineteenth century and Martin Luther King Jr. in the twentieth as they fought their own battles against racial injustice.

Phillis Wheatley (ca. 1753–1784) was sold as a slave but the family who bought her recognized her intellectual gifts, raised her in the gospel, and saw that she was well educated. Wheatley matured into one of the finest early American poets, composing from within the classical Christian tradition and using it to speak for freedom of body and soul. Like Equiano, "Wheatley was both deeply steeped in her Christian faith *and* highly critical of the slave system and the hypocritical expressions of Christianity exhibited by many of the European and White American Christians she encountered. . . . Both were able to see past the misuses and abuses of the Christian faith to the liberating message at its center. There is, then, in Phillis Wheatley's writings, a consistent call for liberty that speaks powerfully both to freedom from physical chains and from sin" (53).

Frederick Douglass (ca. 1817–1895), like Equiano, wrote a harrowing autobiography of his journey out of slavery that was a bestseller and that greatly bolstered the abolitionist cause. Like Wheatley, he devoured the Greco-Roman and Judeo-Christian classics and became a virtuous person and a strong communicator because of it. Like both, he "looked to the Christian scriptures both to bolster his faith and to critique the injustice around him. His critique is always aimed at pointing toward the good that could and should come of Christian faith were it to be lived out correctly" (65). In his writing and speaking, he urged his audience "to hold on to their hope in a better future" and pointed them "toward the innate desire for freedom and human dignity placed by God in everyone, whatever their color" (67).

Anna Julia Cooper (1858–1964) fought first for a full classical Christian education for herself (including the learning of Latin, Greek, and French) and then for her fellow Black Americans. To achieve her goal, she needed to fight not only Blacks who thought a liberal arts education was elitist and useless for finding a job but White liberals who promoted a tyranny of low expectations, thinking Blacks capable only of manual labor. Resisted, slandered, and shunned, Cooper fought on; her "deep faith in God caused her to see her work as an educator as a missionary work, in that everything she did was to promote bringing a classical Christian education to underserved populations" (200).

Martin Luther King Jr. (1929–1968) needs no introduction, though we need to be reminded of the centrality of the Great Books to his mission of creating a unified and integrated America. "Both Anna Julia Cooper and Martin Luther King, Jr., received an education in classic and canonical writings that profoundly shaped their individual lives as well as their visions of the good society" (104). Even a cursory reading of his seminal essay "Letter from a Birmingham Jail" will make clear the depth and breadth of his learning and how the good dream that he dreamed for America flowed naturally out of his meditation on the dual legacy of Athens and Jerusalem. King's education freed him to imagine "an aspirational world toward which we can strive," and then to take "us with him up to a summit from which we are able to catch a vision for the kind of society toward which we can work if we dedicate ourselves in a spirit of prayer, service, and goodwill" (91-92).

Toni Morrison (1931–2019), who won the Pulitzer Prize for her novel *Beloved*, was as steeped in the history of her own people as she was in the Great Books. In fact, her novel *Song of Solomon* offers a "beautiful and bittersweet work of poetic prose rooted in African American history and culture and intricately interwoven with classical and biblical themes" (109). Her well-trained ear was sensitive to a multitude of

Appendix   219

voices, and she allows her readers, both Black and White, to hear and sympathize with "the deepest desires of the natally dispossessed: the quest for freedom from oppression; the desire to know one's name; and the deep longing for rootedness, home, and family" (134).

While Parham's half of *The Black Intellectual Tradition* focuses on the educations and accomplishments of these six unique writers, Prather's half narrows its focus to the life and work of Cooper, even offering in the appendices three of her most important essays. In order to provide a context for Cooper's vision for classical Christian education, Prather helpfully situates her between Booker T. Washington (1856–1915), founder of the Tuskegee Institute, and W. E. B. Du Bois (1868–1963), editor of the National Association for the Advancement of Colored People's monthly magazine *The Crisis*.

"Washington believed that the best way to secure Black people's progress, well-being, and acclimation into American life would be to focus on developing certain skills and trades and to not pursue political or intellectual progress" (156). Du Bois, in contrast, "supported providing a classical education to Black people, seeing higher education in classical studies as a way of helping them to fight for their place of equality and progress in American society" (158).

Cooper, certain that American Blacks could only become full members of American society if they spoke the language that gave shape to our nation, favored Du Bois's approach. Still, she advocated, like Washington, for vocational training that would secure for African Americans jobs they could perform with dignity and skill. What she ultimately desired was an education that would train the whole person, body, mind, and soul. "Classical education, in combination with learning skills to make a living," she believed, "could be restorative" (161) for souls that had been ground down by a long history of enslavement and racism.

"Anna Julia Cooper," Prather explains, "was an advocate for making sure Black people were no longer educated just to be the 'help'; she wanted to see Black people educated instead to be colaborers and coleaders in the work of making America a more perfect union. . . . After hundreds of years of oppression and enslavement, cultivating a new mind was essential for the progress and integration of Black people into American society, and classical education was the tool to bring that into being" (161).

We live in a time when King's dream of a unified and integrated America where people are judged by the content of their character rather than the color of their skin seems to be coming apart at the seams. Rather than follow the lead of Douglass and Du Bois, Cooper and King and invite African Americans into a classical education that will train them to think critically and empower them to enter fully into the ongoing American experiment, a growing number of voices from academia and the public schools are claiming that Black people are not liberated but oppressed by reading the Great Books.

When Prather told her dissertation adviser at the University of Maryland that she wanted to devote her "doctoral research to uncovering the Black classical tradition and to showing the effects of classical studies on modern K-12 Black students," she was soundly and condescendingly reprimanded: "Why are you researching classical education in the Black community? Don't you realize that those books are not for your people? This research topic is irrelevant to the Black community!" (139). Thankfully, Prather, like Cooper before her, persisted in her God-given calling; thankfully, as well, Prather and Parham have done the yeoman labor to bring this important book to fruition.

It is my hope and my prayer that *The Black Intellectual Tradition* will help all American educators and students, whatever their race, sex, or creed, to reclaim our Greco-Roman, Judeo-Christian heritage and enter again into the great conversation. The future of our civil society just may depend on it.

SCRIPTURE INDEX

OLD TESTAMENT

Genesis
1:28, *21*
3, *14*

Exodus
3:21-22, *138*
12:35-36, *138*
18:14-27, *140*

Psalms
139:13-14, *3*

Jeremiah
17:9, *6*

NEW TESTAMENT

Matthew
2, *85*
5:17, *65*
7:24-27, *119*

John
1:14, *9*

Acts
7, *85*
7:51-53, *85*
8:27-35, *140*
9, *140*
10, *140*

Romans
7:5, *9*
7:18, *9*
7:18-23, *5*
7:25, *9*
8:1-10, *9*

1 Corinthians
13:13, *116*

2 Corinthians
12:2-4, *140*

Galatians
5:22-23, *116*

Ephesians
2:10, *2*
6:4, *34*

2 Timothy
3:16-17, *34*

Hebrews
12:11, *35, 140*
13:8, *57*